The Vermont
Political Tradition:
And Those Who Helped Make It

By William Doyle

"They hewed this state out of the wilderness, they held it
against a foreign foe, they laid deep and stable the foundation
of our state life, because they sought not the life of ease, but
the life of effort for a worthy end."
—*President Theodore Roosevelt, 1902*

"The record of Vermont as a resolute champion of individual
freedom, as a true interpreter of our fundamental law, as a
defender of religious faith, as an unselfish but independent
and uncompromising commonwealth of liberty-loving patriots,
is not only unsurpassed, but unmatched by any other state in
the Union."

—*George Harvey*
Ambassador to Great Britain, 1921

First Printing, 1984
Second Printing, 1985
Revised Edition, 1987
Revised Edition, 1990
Revised Edition, 1992

ISBN 0-9615486-1-4

Published by
William Doyle
Murray Road
Montpelier, Vermont 05602

Printed by Northlight Studio Press, Barre, Vermont

Dedicated to my wife Olene and children, Lee, Keith and Kelly who helped in my campaigns and encouraged me to write this book.

This book is also dedicated to Governor Richard Snelling and Barbara Snelling for their substantial contributions to the preservation of Vermont's heritage.

in the *Sunday Rutland Herald and Times Argus* in 1982. When
Professor Doyle first told me he was to try writing a history
of Vermont political parties for a newspaper I was frankly
skeptical. "Newspaper editors are notoriously addicted to the
simplest prose and intolerant of footnotes and enlightened
digressions." I carried on in this vein for some time. "For a
college professor to venture into print unarmed with scholarly
paraphernalia requires either blind courage of foolhardiness."
Bill, always the good politician, listened quietly, shook his
head as if in agreement at all the right times, and then, I am
glad to say, ignored my advice and took up his pen. Those
who read the series agree it was an outstanding job.

What we have between these covers is an expanded and
revised version. It retains the virtues of brevity and com-
prehensiveness, yet has incorporated the criticisms of readers,
included additional illustrations, and added a section of
documents. It is the best short introduction to Vermont politics
available, and I hope you enjoy reading it as much as I did.

Sam Hand
Professor of History
University of Vermont

Table of Contents

Introduction

IN 1981 I WAS WORKING ON A BOOK, *New England Political Parties*. Co-editor and responsible for a chapter on Vermont political parties, I had to eliminate much of what I had written because each New England State had to have approximately the same number of pages.

That fall, I met with the editors of the Sunday *Rutland Herald* and *Times Argus* about writing a political history of the State of Vermont. The articles appeared in January and February of 1982, and received favorable comment. Encouraged by the comments, I asked Alan Gilbert, who did an outstanding job as a series editor, to see if the material could be disseminated in Vermont schools. The publishers of the *Times Argus* and *Herald*, Robert W. Mitchell and R. John Mitchell, supported the project and three thousand copies were made available to Vermont schools through the Department of Education.

I next thought about putting the material into book form. In order to do this, I felt I had to make substantial revisions. This is the fruit of that effort.

The book does not pretend to be a complete history of the State of Vermont. It does attempt to provide an overview of the major developments in the state's political history and emphasize its most enduring political traditions. They include:

1. Political independence as exemplified by Ethan Allen's struggle against New York and Matthew Lyon's re-election to Congress from a Vergennes' jail to the unorthodoxy of U.S. Senator George Aiken and non-conformity of Congressman James Jeffords.

2. A citizen legislature with substantial turnover every two years.

3. Broad political participation dating from the State Constitution of 1777 which provided for universal manhood suffrage to Vermont's turnout in 1984 which was the largest ever for the state. Professor Frank Smallwood in a recent publication, *Political Life of the American States*, documents that Vermont's political participation is well above the national average.

4. The Vermont town meeting where many local issues are debated and voted. These meetings, schoolhouses of democracy, have from time to time spoken out on state and national issues from protesting President Jefferson's embargo to nuclear freeze resolutions.

5. A sense of political equity from the Mountain Rule which provided for the rotation of governors east and west of the Green Mountains to the election of Madeleine Kunin in a Reagan landslide and John Easton's refusal to ask for a recount which would have delayed the formation of Governor Madeleine Kunin's administration.

6. A commitment toward equality. Vermont's very first constitution prohibited slavery and granted universal male suffrage. Vermont ranks high in the percentage of women legislators in the nation. In 1954 Vermont elected the first woman lieutenant governor in the nation and in 1984 elected a woman as chief executive.

7. Individuals prominent in national affairs. Any such list would include Matthew Lyon, Justin Morrill, George Edmunds, Redfield Proctor, George Aiken, Ralph Flanders and Warren Austin. Those who moved from Vermont to other states include Calvin Coolidge, Stephen Douglas, Chester Arthur, Levi Morton and Thaddeus Stevens.

8. Support for public education from Horace Eaton who was concurrently a governor and Vermont's first superintendent of instruction and Justin Morrill's land grant legislation through Vermont's most recent governors.

9. Leadership in the environmental movement from George Perkins Marsh to Act 250, a statewide land use program.

Many people have been very helpful in the preparation of this volume. Professor Sam Hand of the History Department of the

University of Vermont contributed countless hours. Professor Hand and Nicholas Muller III gave me permission to include several charts from their book *State of Nature*. Cyndy Brady of Northlight Studio Press deserves thanks for her patience, suggestions and professional talent. Others very helpful include Professor Gary Lord of Norwich University, Professor Frank Smallwood, Professor Selma Guttman of Johnson State College, Robert W. Mitchell and R. John Mitchell of the *Times Argus* and *Rutland Herald*, Weston A. Cate, Director of the Vermont Historical Society, Paul Gillies, Deputy Secretary of State, Gregory Sanford, State Archivist, Professor Eric Davis of Middlebury College, James Hunt, former Commissioner of Banking and Insurance, Steve Farrow, University of Vermont, Marilyn S. Blackwell, co-author of East Montpelier's history, Thomas Segale, Lyndon State College, Robert Jackman, Montpelier Public Schools, my neighbor Alden Guild, Vice President and General Counsel of the Law Department National Life Insurance Company, Marshall True, Professor of History, University of Vermont, and J. Kevin Graffagnino, Curator, Wilbur Collection, University of Vermont, Bethany Greeley, Director of Green Mountain Editors, Lorraine Lachs, Adjunct Professor of English, Johnson State College, Charles Morrissey, former Director of the Vermont Historical Society, Jean Carpenter, Republican State Headquarters.

Librarians very helpful in the preparation of this book include Vivian Bryan of the Vermont State Library, Reidun Nuquist and Mary Pat Brigham of the Vermont Historical Society, Nadia S. Halpern and John L. Buechler of the Special Collections Department of the University of Vermonts' Bailey-Howe Library, Anna Dermody of the Dewey Library of Johnson State College. Special thanks should go to Barney Bloom for indexing this volume.

Many of the illustrations have come from the Wilbur Collection of Vermontiana of the University of Vermont, the Vermont State Library, and the Vermont Historical Society. Capital letter abbreviations appear on next page to give credit for the illustrations.

VHS   Vermont Historical Society
UVM   University of Vermont
VDD   Vermont Development Department
NL   National Life Insurance Company
DCA   Department of Community Affairs
NS   National Survey
VSL   Vermont State Library
SS   Secretary of State
EWG III   Ernest W. Gibson III
PH   Philip Hoff and Joan Hoff
DCD   Deane C. Davis
AP   Associated Press (Toby Talbot)
TA   Times Argus (Betty Pirie)
APL   Aldrich Public Library

King George the III of England, appointed Benning Wentworth Governor.

CHAPTER 1

The Crucial Period

NO PERIOD IN VERMONT HISTORY was more crucial than the years from 1775 to 1791. While Americans were engaged in a desperate struggle against England for their independence, Vermont opposed New Yorkers, fought Great Britain, declared its own independence, wrote its constitution, contemplated a reunion with the British Empire, and petitioned the United States Congress for admission to the Union.

Vermont east of the Green Mountains was primarily settled by farmers from eastern and central Connecticut and Massachusetts. The settlers migrated north as families, established Congregational churches and named some of their towns after town place names in Connecticut.[1] For example, the Vermont towns of Hartford, Hartland, Weathersfield and Windsor are linked together on the Connecticut River as are the Connecticut towns of the same name. By 1777 there were fourteen Congregational churches in eastern Vermont, but only three on the western side of the state. Six years later the numbers had increased to thirty-four and eight respectively.[2]

Western Vermont was populated from western Connecticut, Massachusetts and Rhode Island. Many were free spirits and land speculators, "men of action", such as the Allen brothers.[3] The family system was "not as strictly established, nor was the church" and "every popular heresy flourished." The west-siders were later described as "generous, and careless of expense . . . while they are less public spirited than their trans-alpine neighbors."[4]

1

Benning Wentworth, Royal Governor of New Hampshire. Appointed by King George III of England.

While the settlement of Vermont divided naturally along the spine of the Green Mountains that extend from Canada to Massachusetts, there was great controversy over its borders. For a quarter of a century prior to the American Revolution, a bitter land dispute took place between New Hampshire and New York over the territory that is now Vermont. Benning Wentworth, the Royal Governor of New Hampshire, reasoned that because the Connecticut and Massachusetts boundary lines were twenty miles east of the Hudson, New Hampshire's boundary line was twenty miles east of the Hudson. From 1749 to 1764 Wentworth granted one hundred thirty-five townships in the territory that would become Vermont. The first, Bennington, he named after himself. The first Wentworth grant east of the Green Mountains was Westminster in 1752. Most of the early settlers in the land, later to be known as Vermont, held titles based upon these grants. In every township Wentworth reserved five hundred acres for himself. By selling his own land and collecting fees from proprietors, he later amassed a considerable fortune.[5]

NEW YORK'S RESPONSE

New York's colonial government was extremely annoyed with the Wentworth New Hampshire grants. In 1664 the Duke of York had received a grant from his brother King Charles II, a grant that included "all the lands from the west side of the Connecticut River to the east side of the Delaware Bay."[6] A century later both New York and New Hampshire agreed to have the King and his Council resolve the dispute. In July of 1764 these arbitrators ruled that the west bank of the Connecticut River was the boundary between New York and New Hampshire. The proclamation stated that "His Majesty . . . doth accordingly hereby Order and Declare the Western Banks of the River Connecticut, from where it enters the Province of Massachusetts Bay, as far north as the forty-fifth degree of northern latitude, to be the boundary line between the said two Provinces of New Hampshire and New York." At first, the Order of the King's Council in favor of New York did not disturb the settlers in the New Hamp-

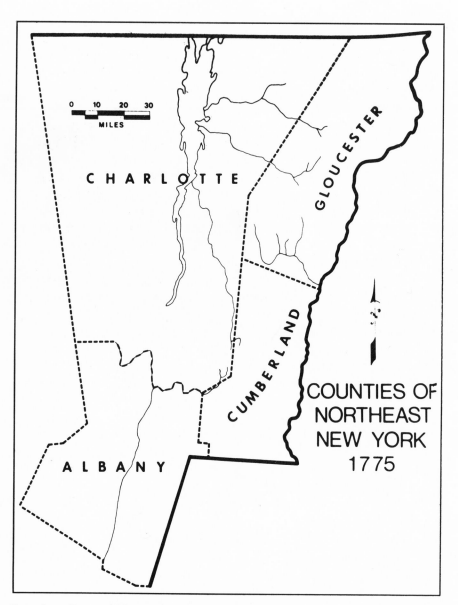

From In a State of Nature *by Muller and Hand*   (VHS)

shire grants because they felt the land titles that they had purchased would not be jeopardized. New York, however, interpreted the Order differently. New York supported by judicial rulings believed that it not only had a right to make future grants, but also that all *previous* grants should have been made by New York; hence it felt that the Wentworth grants were null and void and were subject to ejectment suits.[7]

The grants southwest of the Green Mountains, including Bennington, were annexed to Albany County. The land northwest of the Green Mountains, including parts of New York, became Charlotte County. Two counties were formed on the east side of the Green Mountains. Cumberland County embraced approximately the territory that today would be Windsor and Windham Counties. Gloucester County consisted of the land north of Windsor County extending all the way to Canada.

The New Hampshire grant settlers were expected to exchange their charters and to acquire new grants from New York for small fees. If the New Hampshire grantees accepted new grants from New York, there was no problem. If they did not accept, New York would sell the grants to others. A court system was established in these four counties, and many actions were taken to evict the New Hampshire grantees. These courts generally ruled in favor of the New York claimants; but while it was easy to get a settlement against the New Hampshire settlers, it was more difficult to drive the settlers from their houses and their land.

The "Invitation to Poor Tenants" or Rutland Song by Thomas Rowley, former judge, town clerk and member of the Green Mountain Boys, portrayed conflicting land claims:

> Come all you laboring hands
>   That toil below,
> Among the rocks and sands;
>   That plow and sow
> Upon your hired lands,
> Let out by cruel hands;
> 'Twill make you large amends,
>   To Rutland go.

Your patroons [great landlords] forsake,
　Whose greatest care
Is slaves of you to make
　While you live there:
Come, quit their barren lands,
And leave them in their hands,
'Twill ease you of your bands,
　To Rutland go.

For who would be a slave,
　That may be free:
Here you good land may have,
　But come and see.
The soil is deep and good,
Here in this pleasant wood;
Where you may raise your food
　And happy be.

We value not New York,
　With all their powers;
For here we'll stay and work,
　The land is ours.[8]

ETHAN ALLEN

Ethan Allen became the west-side leader of the settlers of the New Hampshire grants and wrote many pamphlets defending the rights of the New Hampshire settlers. The controversy stimulated the settlers to send agents to England to plead their case and ask for relief from the Crown. As a result of this pleading, the King in 1767 ordered New York to stop making grants of land in the New Hampshire grant territory. "His Majesty . . . doth hereby . . . command that the Governor . . . of his Majesty's Province of New York . . . do not, upon pain of his Majesty's highest displeasure, presume to make any grant . . . until his Majesty's further pleasure shall be known."[9]

New York, however, disregarded the Royal Order by King George and continued to make grants that conflicted with the New Hampshire grants. The granting of land was a very profitable business and England was 3,000 miles away. New Hampshire settlers were evicted from their land by court

Ethan Allen Monument,
Burlington, Vermont.
(UVM)

Ethan Allen Monument,
Statehouse, Montpelier, Vermont
(VDD)

order, and the grants made by the Royal Governor of New Hampshire were not allowed to be admitted as evidence. As a result a military force was created with Ethan Allen as its leader. Organizer of the Green Mountain Boys, he had much to gain by resisting New York claims. With his brothers, Ira and Heman, and cousin Remember Baker, Ethan had formed the Onion River Land Company which sold land titles to potential settlers. Unless the New Yorkers could be driven out, these lands would be lost. The first company sale of 1,200

Ira Allen as an officer in the
Green Mountain Rangers. (UVM)

Daniel P. Thompson, author of
fictional bestseller Green
Mountain Boys.

acres to a group of Salisbury, Connecticut residents had
special significance. One of the purchasers was Thomas Chittenden who would serve as governor of the republic and
state for almost two decades.[10]

In 1772 grantees in the Bennington and Rutland areas met
in convention and decreed "that no person should take
grants, or confirmation of grants, under the government of
New York." Another order forbade all inhabitants in the area
"to hold, take, or accept, any office of honor or profit under
the Colony of New York; and all civil and military officers,
who had acted under the authority of the Governor . . . were
required to suspend their functions."[11] These decrees were
enforced by Ethan Allen and his followers. In one case his
"New England Mob" of over a hundred followers destroyed

the settlement of a New York title holder, Colonel John Reid at Otter Creek. Reid had dispossessed a New Hampshire title holder a few years earlier. It was alleged that the Green Mountain Boys "destroyed six houses", the mill, the millstones and "destroyed most of the wheat, corn and hay." In another case a New York official was beaten "first with a large hickory stick and afterwards with birch rods on his bare back."[12]

The New Hampshire grantees devised unusual punishments for those who were sympathetic to New York. In 1773 Dr. Samuel Adams of Arlington advised his neighbors to purchase land under New York titles. He was arrested and:

> carried to the Green Mountain Tavern, at Bennington, where the Committee heard his defence, and then ordered him to be tried in an arm chair, and hoisted up to the sign (a catamount's skin, stuffed, sitting upon the sign post, twenty-five feet from the ground, with large teeth, grinning towards New-York,) and there to hang two hours, in sight of the people, as a punishment merited by his enmity to the rights and liberties of the inhabitants of the New-Hampshire grants. The judgment was executed to the no small merriment of a large concourse of people. The Doctor was let down, and dismissed by the Committee, with admonition to go and sin no more.[13]

In March of 1774, the New York Assembly responded to the acts of Allen and his followers by passing a law "for preventing tumultuous and riotous assemblies . . . and for the more speedy and effectual punishing the rioters." According to the law, any person who assaulted a civil officer, burned or destroyed grain, corn or hay or destroyed property would "suffer death", as in cases of felony without benefit of clergy.[14] On the same day that this law was enacted, Governor William Tryon of New York offered an award of fifty pounds for the capture of Ethan Allen and other "ringleaders."

This act and Governor Tyron's proclamation only served to unify the New Hampshire grant towns west of the Green Mountains. In April of 1774, some of these representatives met and passed a resolution which said in part, "that for the

Punishing the Yorkers, from Zadock Thompson, "History of Vermont."
Catamount Tavern Bennington.

Eleazar Wheelock, President of Dartmouth College, wanted to form a state consisting of Connecticut River towns.

future, every necessary preparation be made, and that our inhabitants hold themselves in readiness, at a minute's warning, to aid and defend such friends of ours who further merit to the great and general cause, are falsely denominated rioters." In a pamphlet distributed in Albany County, Ethan Allen vowed that anyone who tried to capture him or any of his Green Mountain Boys would be killed.[15] At the same time the New Hampshire grant settlers met in Convention in Manchester and resolved that "we will stand by and defend our friends and neighbors who are indicted at the expense of our lives and fortunes."[16]

"WESTMINSTER MASSACRE"

Despite conflict between the Province of New York and the Green Mountain Boys, the relationship between New York and the New Hampshire grants east of the Green Mountains was relatively peaceful. Most of the residents on the eastern side paid their re-confirmation fees. Although New York was willing to recognize grants on the west side, the cost of converting the Wentworth grants to New York titles was too expensive for large land speculators such as the Allens. There were at least three different groups all with different interests. One faction whose greatest strength was in Windham County was loyal to the government of New York. Further up the Connecticut River another group known as the College party and led by Eleazar Wheelock, founder of Dartmouth College, supported a union of Connecticut Valley towns both east and west of the river with its capital in Hanover, New Hampshire. A third group consisted of debtors mostly farmers who opposed the Cumberland County Court convening because their land could be lost through foreclosure proceedings.

In the spring of 1775 approximately one hundred farmer-debtors armed with wooden clubs occupied the Westminster Courthouse to prevent the court from sitting. The Yorker sheriff and his deputies finally seized the courthouse. In the process two rioters were killed, one being William French who was to become a martyr of the "massacre." Acting New York Governor Cadwallader Colden was disturbed by this

The Bennington Declaration for Freedom

May 1775

PERSUADED that the Salvation of the rights & liberties of America depends, under God, on the firm Union of its inhabitants, in a Vigorous prosecution of the measures necessary for its Safety, and convinced of the necessity of preventing the Anarchy and Confusion which attend a dissolution of the Powers of Government; we, the freeholders and inhabitants of the town of Bennington, on the Newhampshire Grants, in the County of Albany and Province of N. York, being greatly alarmed at the avowed design of the Ministry to Raise a revenue in America, and Shocked by the bloody scene now acting in the Massachusetts bay; do in the most solemn manner resolve never to bee Slaves; and do associate, under all the ties of Religion, honor, & love to our Country, [to] adopt & Endeavor to Carry into execution whatever Measures may be recommended by [the] Continental Congress or resolved upon by our Provincial Convention for [the purpose] of preserving our Constitution and opposing the Execution of Several arbitrary and oppressive acts of the british Parliament until a reconciliation between Great Britain and America on Constitutional principles (which we most ardently desire) can be obtained; and that we Will in all things follow the Advice of our General Committee Respecting the purposes aforesaid, the preservation of Peace and Good Order, and the Safety of individuals and Private Property.

The Bennington Declaration did not call for independence from Great Britain but for reconciliation based upon constitutional principles. (VHS)

Westminster Courthouse

In Memory of William French
Son to Mʳ Nathaniel French Who
Was Shot at Westminster March y̆ 13ᵗʰ
1775 by the hands of Cruel Ministereal
tools of Georg y̆ 3ᵈ in the Corthouse at
a 11 a Clock at Night in the 22ᵈ year of
his Age
Here William French his Body lies
For Murder his blood for Vengance cries
King Georg the third his Tory crew
tha with a bawl his head Shot threw
For Liberty and his Countrys Good
he Lost   his Life his Dearest blood

Cadwallader Colden, Governor of New York. Colden was a scientist, philosopher and friend of Ben Franklin. (UVM)

Epitaph of William French, martyr of the "Westminster Massacre."

Ethan Allen and his followers capture Fort Ticonderoga. May 10, 1775. Courtesy Vermont Historical Society.

event and wrote to London: "I make no doubt they will be joined by the Bennington Rioters who will endeavor to make one common cause of it, tho they have no connection but in their violence to Government."[17] Ethan Allen saw the event as an opportunity to join the east-side and west-side together and sent a company of Green Mountain Boys led by Robert Cochran.

The "Westminster Massacre" had had the effect of drawing together, for the first time, the east and west against a common enemy, New York. Historian Nicholas Muller wrote: "By this dramatic collaboration between men on both sides of the Green Mountains, Allen skillfully began to merge his cause with that of the east side rioters and theirs with his. The Westminster mob and their supporters now had grievances against New York authority that could make them ready allies in the Allen's protracted struggle against New York."[18]

DORSET RESOLUTIONS

Meanwhile the New Hampshire grantees put themselves on record regarding the Revolutionary War. In 1775, Ethan Allen captured Fort Ticonderoga and later that year was taken prisoner at Montreal during the American invasion of Canada. In January 1776, a convention meeting at Dorset drew up a petition to Congress avowing:

> We are entirely willing to do all in our power in the general cause under the continental congress . . . but are not willing to put ourselves under the honourable provincial congress of New York, in such a manner as might, in future, be detrimental to our private property . . . .[19]

In July 1776, the new American nation declared its independence, severing all ties of allegiance to the British Crown. While the declaration made it very clear where the thirteen American Colonies stood, the situation for the people living in the New Hampshire grants was uncertain. One month after the Declaration of Independence, the New York Assembly decreed that all quit-rents formerly due to Great Britain by the New Hampshire grants were now due to New York.

If a poll had been taken in 1776 of the people living in the New Hampshire grants, opinions would have varied widely. Some of the grantees would have preferred to rejoin New Hampshire, some would have expressed loyalty to the British Crown, some would have said that union with New York was the safest course, some would have followed an independent course by setting up their own government and some would have had no opinion. Muller wrote that the land that would become Vermont "exhibited a complex mosaic made up of settlement and landholding patterns, physical features, socio-economic factors, various ideas about government, and the clash of ambition and personality because of the fluid state of the frontier society and momentous events of the period."[20]

In September 1776 delegates from the east and west sides of Vermont again met at Dorset. Twelve delegates from the east and forty-six from the west issued a call for independence from New York authority.[21] Within a year Vermont would declare its independence from New York and Great Britain and write its own constitution.

NOTES

1. Edwin M. Bacon, *The Connecticut River and the Valley of the Connecticut* (New York and London: G.P. Putnam's Sons, 1906), p. 257.
2. John M. Comstock, *The Congregational Churches of Vermont and Their Ministry, 1962-1942, History and Statistics* (St. Johnsbury, Vermont: The Cowles Press, 1942), pp 29-152.
3. Bacon, The Connecticut River, p. 257.
4. David M. Ludlum, *Social Ferment in Vermont 1791-1850* (New York: Columbia University Press 1939), p. 16.
    The differences between eastern and western Vermont are challenged by Donald A. Smith in an unpublished thesis *Legacy of Dissent: Religion and Politics in Revolutionary Vermont 1749-1784* (Montpelier, Vermont: Vermont Historical Society 1982) p. 152. "This superficial political analysis prevalent among earlier students of Vermont migration was the extent of their religious analysis; and it was deficient both for New England and Vermont."
5. Walter H. Crockett, *History of Vermont* (New York: The Century History Company, Inc., 1921) Volume one, pp. 175-200.

6. William Slade, *Vermont State Papers* (Middlebury: J.W. Copeland 1823), p. 17.
7. *Ibid.* pp. 19-20. For a discussion of the validity of the Wentworth land grants, see Allan R. Raymond "Benning Wentworth's Claims in the New Hampshire-New York Border Controversy: A Case of Twenty-Twenty Hindsight?"
   Vermont History, Volume 43, No. 1 (Winter, 1975), pp. 20-32. "New Hampshire appears to have held valid claim to part, if not all, of Vermont, or, at worst, to have been arguing an open point...."
8. Edmund Fuller, *Vermont: A History of the Green Mountain State* (Montpelier: State Board of Education, 1952), p. 126.
9. William Slade, *Vermont State Papers*, p. 21.
10. Charles A. Jellison, *Ethan Allen Frontier Rebel* (Taftsville, Vermont: The Countryman Press, 1969), p. 78.
11. Ira Allen, *History of the State of Vermont* (Rutland: Charles E. Tuttle Company, 1969), p. 30.
12. Walter Crockett, *History of Vermont*, Volume 1, pp. 360-362.
13. William Slade, *Vermont State Papers*, p. 36.
14. *Ibid.* pp. 42-48.
15. *Ibid.* pp. 49-54.
16. Walter H. Crockett, *History of Vermont*, Volume 1, p. 366.
17. Charles A. Jellison, *Ethan Allen Frontier Rebel*, p. 99.
18. H. Nicholas Muller, III, "Myth and Reality: The Politics of Independence in Vermont, 1760-1777," in *Perspectives '76* (Hanover, N.H.: Regional Center for Educational Training, 1976), p. 64.
19. Walter H. Crockett, *History of Vermont*, Volume II, pp. 173-174.
20. Muller, p. 62.
21. Muller, p. 64.

CHAPTER II

Vermont's Declaration of Independence and Constitution

$\mathbf{V}$ERMONT DECLARED ITS INDEPENDENCE about six months after the thirteen original colonies declared their independence from Great Britain. Like the colonies, Vermont declared itself "To be free and independent of the Crown of Great Britain." Vermont joined the thirteen advocates of American independence: "we are at all times ready, in conjunction with our brethern in the United States of America, to do our full proportion in maintaining and supporting the just war against the tyrannical invasions of the ministerial fleets and armies." In the same document Vermont declared her independence from the state of New York and in place of Thomas Jefferson's indictment of George III substituted its own indictment of New York.

The new state was called "New Connecticut" because most of the land was occupied by people from Connecticut. More Vermont town place names came from Connecticut than any other state, and of Vermont's first twelve governors, eight were born in the state of Connecticut.

In April 1777, the new state petitioned Congress to be "ranked among the free and independent states; and delegates therefrom, be admitted to the seat in Congress."[1] New York immediately protested this action and sent letters to Congress stating that the people who lived in the counties of Gloucester, Cumberland and Charlotte were generally loyal to New York. Dr. Thomas Young, an old friend and tutor of Ethan Allen, who suggested that the new state be named Vermont wrote a pamphlet addressed to the people:

Vermont's Declaration of Independence—from New York—was promulgated January 15, 1777 at Westminster. (NL)

Thomas Young, an old friend and tutor of Ethan Allen.

The Battle of Hubbarton, July 7, 1777. (NL)

The Bennington Battle Monument. The battlefield was in Hoosick, New York, near the state line. The battle took place on August 16, 1777. (VTD)

I have taken the minds of several leading members, in the honorable Continental Congress and can assure you that you have nothing to do, but to send attested copies of the recommendations to take up government, to every township in your district, and invite all your freeholders and inhabitants to meet in their respective townships, and choose members for a general convention to meet at an early day, to choose delegates for the general Congress..., and to form a constitution for your state.[2]

In June 1777 Congress took up the New York and Vermont question and rejected Vermont's petition for admission to the Union. A Congressional resolution said Young's statements were "derogatory to the honor of congress, and a gross misrepresentation ... intended to deceive and mislead the people to whom they were addressed."[3]

Shortly thereafter the name of the new state was changed from New Connecticut to Vermont. The change was "engineered through by the Bennington party" because the name New Connecticut may have given greater credence to formation of a Connecticut Valley state by the Dartmouth College party and because a settlement in the Wyoming Valley in Pennsylvania was also called that name.[4]

THE VERMONT CONSTITUTION

Young, having given Vermont leaders a copy of the recently adopted Pennsylvania Constitution, advised them that they must not be content with declaring independence. They must write a constitution and establish a government. On July 2, 1777, a convention of delegates from the east and the west sides met in Windsor to write a constitution. The members of the convention adopted the Pennsylvania Constitution.

Borrowing phrases from the United States Declaration of Independence, Article One stated: "That all men are born equally free and independent, and have certain natural, inherent and unalienable rights, amongst which are the enjoying and defending of life and liberty; acquiring, possessing and protecting property, and pursuing and obtaining happiness and safety." The first article ended with a clause prohibiting slavery, Vermont being the first state to do so.

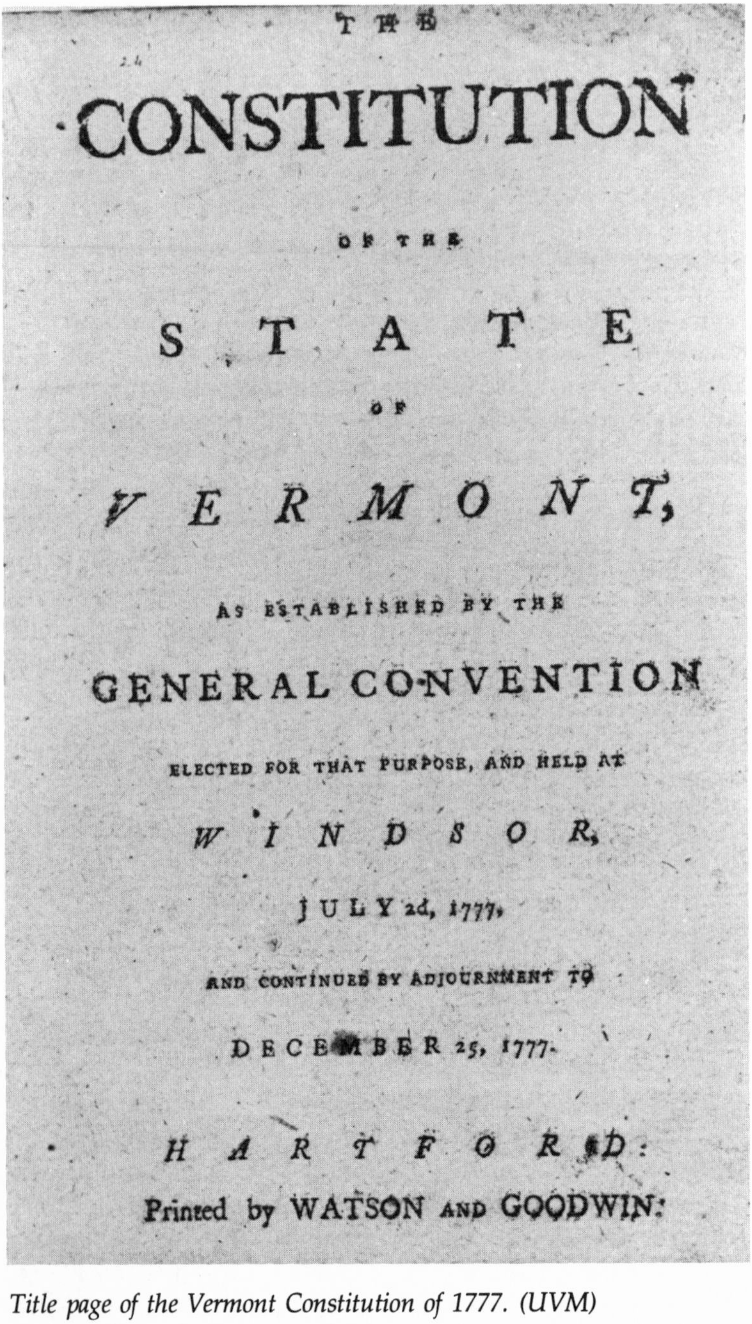

THE

·CONSTITUTION

OF THE

S T A T E

OF

V E R M O N T,

AS ESTABLISHED BY THE

GENERAL CONVENTION

ELECTED FOR THAT PURPOSE, AND HELD AT

W I N D S O R,

J U L Y 2d, 1777,

AND CONTINUED BY ADJOURNMENT TO

DECEMBER 25, 1777.

H A R T F O R D:

Printed by WATSON AND GOODWIN.

Title page of the Vermont Constitution of 1777. (UVM)

Constitution House, Windsor.

Constitution House, Windsor, centuries ago.

Vermont was also the first state to adopt universal male suffrage. Article Eight provided: "That all elections ought to be free; and that all freemen . . . have a right to elect offices, or be elected into office." McMaster in his history of the United States wrote that under most of the early state constitutions "none but property owning, taxpaying men could give that consent from which government derives its just powers. . . . Nowhere, save in Vermont, did manhood suffrage exist. Elsewhere no man voted who did not pay a property tax, or rent a house, or own a specified number of acres, or have a specified yearly income."

Other rights guaranteed by the Vermont Constitution included freedom of speech, press and assembly, protection from search or seizure, and the right to bear arms. Article Sixteen read: "Frequent recurrence to fundamental principles, and a firm adherence to justice, moderation, temperance, industry and frugality, are absolutely necessary to preserve the blessings of liberty, and keep government free."

The constitution provided that the General Assembly would consist of two representatives from larger towns and one representative from the smaller towns. This provision was adopted to maintain a political balance between the east and west sides. After seven years, each town would have one representative "forever thereafter." Each member of the one-house General Assembly would be endowed with "wisdom and virtue" and had to take the following oath: "I do believe in one God, the creator and governor of the universe, the rewarder of the good and punisher of the wicked. I do acknowledge the scriptures of the Old and New Testament to be given by Divine inspiration and own and profess the Protestant Religion."

The Constitution of 1777 contained several open government provisions. The doors of the General Assembly were to remain open to all individuals who behaved "decently." The votes of the General Assembly would be printed weekly. All courts were required to be open and justice "impartially administered." If any court officer collected more fees than the law allowed, the officer would be disqualified "from

Vermont, in 1777, was the first state to adopt manhood suffrage. (NL)

holding any office in this state." A corrupt practices section declared that any voter who accepted any reward for his vote in "meat, drink, moneys or otherwise" would forfeit his voting privileges.

The Vermont Constitution was one of the earliest to provide for a comprehensive system of education from the elementary to the university level. Section forty provided for schools "established in each town, . . . for the convenient instruction of youth. . . . one grammar school in each county, and one university in this State, ought to be established by direction of the General Assembly."

In order to deter the commission of crime, section thirty-five provided that "houses ought to be provided for punishing, by hard labor, those who shall be convicted of crimes not capital."

The Constitutional Convention also provided for a Council of Safety to act as a provisional government until the governor and members of the General Assembly were elected.

Thomas Chittenden was the president of the twelve member Council which was invested with legislative, excecutive and judicial powers. The acts of the Council of Safety had "the force of law; it was itself the executor of them . . .; it exercised judicial power; it served as a board of war; it punished public enemies, or reprieved them; it transacted business, civil and military, with other states and with Congress; it prepared business for the first General Assembly; it was the State."

The preamble to Vermont's constitution, written a few months later, began with the proposition philosopher John Locke enunciated a century earlier that governments are instituted for the protection of the community to enable individuals to "enjoy natural rights." When government does not do this, "the people have a right, by common consent, to change it, and to take such measures as to them may appear necessary to promote their safety and happiness."

While not mentioning Ethan Allen and his followers by name, the preamble indicted New York for offering sums of money, "for the purpose of apprehending those very persons very boldly, and publicly, to appear in defense of their just rights." Declaring that New York State was geographically too large to administer the New Hampshire Grants, the preamble said, "It is absolutely necessary, for the welfare and safety of the inhabitants of this State, that it should be, henceforth, a free and independent state."

PENNSYLVANIA A MODEL?

Although Vermont's constitution was modeled after that of Pennsylvania, there were significant differences. The Pennsylvania Constitution unlike Vermont limited legislative tenure to no more "than four years in seven." Vermont's constitution provided for two representatives from the larger towns and one representative from the smaller towns. Pennsylvania's constitution proclaimed that "representation in proportion to the number of taxable inhabitants is the only principle that at all times secures liberty." Under both constitutions however, elections were held annually and both states had a one-house or unicameral legislature.

Catamount Tavern in Bennington where some meetings of the Governor's Council were held. (UVM)

Fireplace of the Council room in the Catamount Tavern. (UVM)

Under Pennsylvania's constitution no officials were elected statewide. Vermont's constitution called the annual election of fifteen statewide elected officials: the governor, lieutenant governor, treasurer, and a twelve-member Governor's Council elected at large. Pennsylvania also had a Governor's Council which was more decentralized because two councillors were chosen from each county. In both Vermont and Pennsylvania the Governor's Council had the power to review legislative proposals. Vermont's council, however, was stronger because it could introduce bills, amend bills passed by the Assembly and sit on legislative committees.[5]

In addition to possessing significant executive responsibilities, councillors could serve as Vermont Supreme Court Justices. For instance, from 1779-1786 four of the five members of the Vermont Supreme Court were councillors. The at large statewide system of election made it difficult for challengers to defeat incumbents and long tenure was not unusual. In addition, Vermont's early governors had long tenure. With the exception of one year Thomas Chittenden was governor from 1778 to 1797. His successor Issac Tichenor served from 1797 to 1807 and from 1808 to 1809. Vermont historian H. Nicholas Muller III suggests that during the formative years Vermont state government was an oligarchy not a democracy. "Multiple office-holding, long tenure, and the small number of men who served in the office of Governor and on the Council are not statistical accidents and leave the impression of a political oligarchy."[6] In 1786 the Vermont Constitution was amended to provide that the legislative, executive and judicial branches were separate and distinct. Despite this change the Governor's Council still possessed legislative functions and this issue was not finally resolved until 1836 when, by constitutional amendment, the Council was replaced by a state senate.

Both the Pennsylvania and Vermont constitutions provided for a Council of Censors. The purpose of the Council was to see whether the constitution had been preserved, whether legislative and executive branches had performed their duty, whether taxes had been properly levied and whether the laws had been properly executed. The Council of Censors had the power to call a convention in order to make proposals to amend the constitution. Pennsylvania abolished its Council soon after achieving statehood, whereas the Vermont Council was not abolished until 1870.

Not all the towns favored the new government established by the constitution. On Town Meeting Day, the first Tuesday of March, 1778, the town of Brattleboro unanimously resolved to send a protest to the "pretended state" of Vermont. The resolution stated that Vermont by severing its relationship with New York tended "to disunite the friends of America in the present important contest with Great Britain." A survey of some Cumberland County towns (Windsor, Windham) in 1778 [7] revealed that New York had considerable support:

Town	Favoring New York	Favoring Vermont	Neutral
Brattleboro	165	1	0
Springfield	21	19	4
Putney	69	26	41
Weathersfield	11	12	0
Wilmington	12	15	8

Ira Allen in his *History of the State of Vermont* wrote that the constitution itself had little support; "Had the constitution been then submitted to the consideration of the people for their revision, amendment, and ratification, it is very doubtful whether a majority would have confirmed it, considering the resolution of Congress . . . as well as the intrigues and expense of . . . New York, who endeavoured to divide and subdivide the people."[8]

VERMONT GENERAL ASSEMBLY ORGANIZED

The first meeting of the Vermont General Assembly took place on the second Thursday of March in 1778. Reverend Powers gave such an impressive sermon based upon Saint Matthew that the legislators took a collection and paid him $10.[9] The first order of business was the election of three statewide officials: Governor Thomas Chittenden, Lieutenant Governor Joseph Marsh, and Treasurer Ira Allen. Thomas

Ira Allen, Ethan Allen's brother, who was active in state affairs and wrote a history of Vermont. (UVM)

Thomas Chittenden, Vermont's first Governor, who was elected to eighteen one-year terms beginning in 1778. (UVM)

Chittenden, born in 1730 in East Guilford, Connecticut had from 1765 to 1769 been a Justice of the Peace and a member of the Connecticut Colonial Assembly. In 1774 he moved to Williston and speculated in land. In 1777 as a delegate to the Constitutional Convention he helped draft Vermont's Declaration of Independence and became president of the Council of Safety. He was then re-elected governor yearly until 1797, except for one year in 1789 when he lost to Moses Robinson. Ethan Allen claimed that Chittenden was the only person "he had ever known who was sure to be right, even in the most complex cases, without being able to tell the reason why." Since he had lost the sight of one eye, his opponents referred to him as "one eyed Tom."[10]

During the March session, the General Assembly divided the state into two counties. One county on the west side was called Bennington; the eastern county named Unity was soon changed to Cumberland in deference to the east-side settlers. Another act gave the executive branch the power to

Vermont's Great Seal designed by Ira Allen in 1778. (DCA)

dispose of Tories' estates. Connecticut law was used as a model for acts relating to treason and other serious crimes.[11]

It is significant that the Vermont General Assembly enacted Connecticut law while the philosophy of the "radical" Vermont Constitution was influenced by its Pennsylvania counterpart. David Ludlum, in *Social Ferment in Vermont*, wrote that "in supplying substance to this governmental structure the Vermont General Assembly decreed the wholesale enactment of laws 'as they stood on the Connecticut law book' and later established 'the common law, as is generally practiced and understood in the New England States.' On many vital points the liberal aspirations of the constitution and the conservative tenor of the Connecticut common law were in direct opposition."[11]

In June the Assembly met again and voted "to take the incorporated University of Dartmouth located in Dresden, [now Hanover] New Hampshire under the patronage of this state." The president of Dartmouth, the Reverend Eleazar Wheelock, was appointed a Justice of the Peace. Other acts related to the encouragement of manufacture and the assembly voted "to give a bounty for the destruction of wolves." A third session, held in October, was primarily concerned with the annexation of sixteen New Hampshire towns that petitioned to join Vermont.[12]

NOTES

1. William Slade, *Vermont State Papers*, p. 73.
2. *Ibid.* p. 76.
3. *Ibid.* p. 79.
4. Edwin M. Bacon, *The Connecticut River*, p. 268.
5. John N. Schaeffer, "A Comparison of the First Constitutions of Vermont and Pennsylvania" *Vermont History*, Volume 43, No. 1, Winter, 1975, pp. 33-43. Schaeffer argues that Vermont's constitution was much more conservative than Pennsylvania's "radical" constitution. An annotated text of the Vermont constitution of 1777 with comparisons to the Pennsylvania constitution can be found in the *Records of the Council of Safety and Governor and Council of the State of Vermont* (Montpelier, 1783), pp. 81-103. Both the constitutions of 1777 and 1786 provided for the election of representatives to Congress. This is used as evidence that Vermont did not consider itself an independent republic.
6. H. Nicholas Muller, III, "Early Vermont State Government: Oligarchy or Democracy?, 1778-1815" from *Growth and Development of Government in Vermont*, Reginald L. Cook, ed., The Vermont Academy of Arts and Sciences, Occasional Paper #5 (1970), pp. 5-10.
7. Benjamin H. Hall, *History of Eastern New York* (New York: D. Appleton 1885), Volume 1, pp. 324-325.
8. Ira Allen, *History of the State of Vermont* (Rutland, Charles Tuttle, 1973), p. 72.
9. Walter Crockett, *History of Vermont*, Volume 2, pp. 221-222.
10. Crockett, *History of Vermont*, Volume 2, p. 224.
11. Ludlum, *Social Ferment in Vermont 1791-1850*, p. 6.
12. Walter Crockett, *History of Vermont*, Volume 2, pp. 226-227.

CHAPTER III

Policy of Expansion

IN 1778 THE VERMONT GENERAL ASSEMBLY created by the new constitution faced a major challenge when sixteen New Hampshire towns east of the Connecticut River petitioned to be annexed to the state of Vermont. A leader of this movement, Dr. Wheelock, wanted Dartmouth College to become the state university. He hoped that with the addition of the sixteen New Hampshire towns political control would shift to the eastern side of the state so that Dartmouth College would become the cultural center of Vermont. The towns east of the Green Mountains supported annexation because they felt the state had been dominated by westsiders. When the Vermont General Assembly reassembled in Windsor in the fall of 1778, representatives from the east side outvoted representatives from the west side, and the sixteen New Hampshire towns were admitted as part of Vermont.[1]

Enraged by the loss of the New Hampshire towns to Vermont, New Hampshire's chief executive, Mesheck Weare, wrote the sixteen town New Hampshire delegation to protest the action of "the pretended state of Vermont." He also wrote Governor Chittenden saying that the claim of the sixteen New Hampshire towns that they could join any state was "an idle phantom, a mere chimera, without the least shadow of reason for its support."[2] Upon receipt of Weare's letter, Governor Chittenden convened his Council, and

ADDRESS

ON

NEW HAMPSHIRE

AND

VERMONT:

THEIR UNIONS,
SECESSIONS AND DISUNIONS.

DELIVERED BEFORE

The New Hampshire Antiquarian Society,
JULY 15, 1879.

By CLARK JILLSON.

WORCESTER :
PRESS OF CLARK JILLSON.
1882.

*The title page of an address which discussed the unions of New York and
New Hampshire towns with Vermont. (UVM)*

Ethan Allen was asked to travel to Philadelphia to determine the opinion of Congress relating to recent developments in Vermont.[3]

The Allen brothers were upset by the east-side takeover. Ira Allen termed the leaders of the "runaway New Hampshire towns a few restless, uneasy men not having the good of either state at heart, but their own private interests." Ethan Allen called the Dartmouth College people "a petulant, pettyfogging, scribbling sort of gentry."[4] In Philadelphia Allen told the New Hampshire delegation that he would recommend returning the sixteen New Hampshire towns if New Hampshire would support Vermont's admission into the Union.

When Ethan Allen returned, he warned the governor and the Vermont Assembly that Congress was angry about Vermont's "theft" of her neighbor's towns. He asserted that unless Vermont gave back the towns to New Hampshire "the whole power of the United States of America will join to annihilate the state of Vermont to vindicate the right of New Hampshire, and to maintain inviolate the Articles of Confederation which guarantees to each state their privileges and immunities."[5] In a letter to Weare, Allen wrote "I hope that the Government of New Hampshire will excuse the Imbecility of Vermont in the matter of the Union." Allen's argument must have impressed the Vermont Legislature because early in 1779 it declared the first Eastern Union be "made totally void, null and extinct. "

In 1780 New Hampshire, angry over the annexation of the sixteen towns decided to lay claim to the whole state of Vermont and applied to Congress for a favorable decision. New York, still upset over Vermont's Declaration of Independence, asked Congress to uphold its claim to the territory now known as Vermont. Finally, Massachusetts now laid claim to parts of Vermont. Concerned about these actions Vermont legislators thought the leaders of New Hampshire and New York might have made a deal to dismember Vermont so that New Hampshire would acquire all the territory east of the Green Mountains and New York would acquire all of the territory west of the Green Mountains. Congress, too busy fighting the War of Independence, refused to get involved in conflicting land claims by these competing states. Congress was not about to incur the displeasure of New York, one of the most powerful states in the Union.

VERMONT BIDS TO JOIN THE UNION

Meeting in October of 1779 the Vermont General Assembly decided to launch a lobbying effort to convince the new American nation that it should be admitted to the Union. The Assembly appointed a committee to formulate a plan to "defend against the neighboring states" and commissioned Ethan Allen to attend the next session of Congress to vindicate Vermont's right to independence.[7] In December of 1779 Vermont's Governor and Council published a pamphlet entitled "Vermont's Appeal to the Candid and Impartial World." Written by Stephan R. Bradley, who would later become a three-term United States Senator, the pamphlet set forth reasons why Vermont should be admitted to the Union and ended with an appeal to the people of New Hampshire, Massachusetts, and New York:

> We conclude this address to you, in short, to remind you that your liberties are challenged as well as ours; you are now engaged in a bloody war in defense of the same; remember, the measure you meet out to others, heaven will measure back to you again. Can you stand before the throne of God and seek to be protected and defended in your course, while you are ascribing to overthrow and destroy the liberties of the state of Vermont, which stands on as large a scale of reason for independence as any other state on the continent.[8]

Congress turned a deaf ear to Vermont's appeals and in June 1780 resolved that the proceedings of Vermont were "highly unwarrantable and subversive of the peace and welfare of the United States; and that they be strictly required to forbear from any acts of authority civil and military over those of the people who profess allegiance to another state".[9]

Upon receiving this Congressional resolution, Governor Chittenden wrote Congress on July 25, 1780 that if Vermont received no satisfaction from Congress, Vermonters would have no "motive to continue hostilities with Great Britain

VERMONT's
APPEAL
TO THE

CANDID AND IMPARTIAL WORLD.

CONTAINING,

A FAIR STATING OF THE CLAIMS OF MASSACHUSETTS-BAY, NEW-HAMPSHIRE, AND NEW-YORK.

THE RIGHT THE STATE OF VERMONT HAS TO INDEPENDENCE.

WITH AN

ADDRESS TO THE HONORABLE AMERICAN CONGRESS, AND THE INHABITANTS OF THE THIRTEEN UNITED STATES.

BY STEPHEN R. BRADLEY, A.M.

The LORD hath called me from the Womb, from the Bowels of my Mother hath he made mention of my Name. And said unto me, thou art my Servant, O V------ I in whom I will be glorified. And I will feed them that oppress thee with their own Flesh, and they shall be drunken with their own Blood as with sweet Wine, and all Flesh shall know that I the LORD am thy Saviour and thy Redeemer, the Mighty One of Jacob. ISAIAH xlix.

HARTFORD:
Printed by HUDSON & GOODWIN.

A
VINDICATION
OF THE OPPOSITION OF THE INHABITANTS

OF

VERMONT

TO THE GOVERNMENT OF

NEW-YORK,

AND OF THEIR RIGHT TO FORM INTO AN INDEPENDENT

STATE.

Humbly submitted to the Consideration of the impartial WORLD.

By ETHAN ALLEN,

PRINTED BY *ALDEN SPOONER,* 1779
Printer to the State of Vermont.

Title page of Stephen Bradley's Appeal to the Candid and Impartial World. (UVM)

Title page of Ethan Allen's pamphlets vindicating Vermont's position with respect to New York. (UVM)

and maintain an important frontier for the benefit of the United States, and for no other reward than . . . being enslaved by them."[10]

In September 1780 Congress again took up the Vermont question. Stephan Bradley and Ethan Allen were permitted to be in attendance, but not as representatives of Vermont with legislative authority. When Bradley and Allen realized that Congress would not recognize Vermont as a party to the dispute, they withdrew from the hearing and a few days later sent a protest letter to Congress saying that if that body did not change its policy toward Vermont, Vermont was "ready to appeal to God and the world to say who must be accountable for the awful consequences that may ensue."[11]

IN CONGRESS,

JUNE 2d, 1780.

WHEREAS it is reprefented to Congrefs, and by authentic evidence laid before them it appears, that the people inhabiting the diſtrict of country commonly known by the name of the New-Hampſhire Grants, and claiming to be an independant ſtate, have, notwithſtanding the reſolutions of Congreſs of the 24th of September and 2d of October, proceeded, as a ſeparate government, to make grants of lands and ſales of eſtates by them declared forfeited and confiſcated; and have alſo, in divers inſtances, exerciſed civil and military authority over the perſons and effects of ſundry inhabitants within the ſaid diſtrict who profeſs themſelves to be citizens of and to owe allegiance to the ſtate of New-York:

RESOLVED, That the acts and proceedings of the people inhabiting the ſaid diſtrict, and claiming to be an independant ſtate as aforeſaid, in contravening the good intentions of the ſaid reſolutions of the 24th of September and 2d of October laſt, are highly unwarrantable and ſubverſive of the peace and welfare of the United States:

That the people inhabiting the ſaid diſtrict and claiming to be an independant ſtate as aforeſaid be and they hereby are ſtrictly required to forbear and abſtain from all acts of authority, civil or military, over the inhabitants of any town or diſtrict who hold themſelves to be ſubjects of, and to owe allegiance to, any of the ſtates claiming the juriſdiction of the ſaid territory, in whole or in part, until the deciſions and determinations in the reſolutions afore mentioned ſhall be made.

And whereas the ſtates of New-Hampſhire and New-York have complied with the ſaid reſolutions of the 24th of September and 2d of October laſt, and by their Agents and Delegates in Congreſs declared themſelves ready to proceed in ſupporting their reſpective rights to the juriſdiction of the diſtrict aforeſaid, in whole or in part, according to their ſeveral claims, and in the mode preſcribed in the ſaid reſolutions: And whereas Congreſs, by their order of the 21ſt of March laſt, did poſtpone the conſideration of the ſaid reſolutions, nine ſtates, excluſive of thoſe who were parties to the queſtion, not being repreſented; and by their order of the 17th of May laſt have directed that letters be written to the ſtates not repreſented, requeſting them immediately to ſend forward a repreſentation:

RESOLVED, That Congreſs will, as ſoon as nine ſtates, excluſive of thoſe who are parties to the controverſy, ſhall be repreſented, proceed to hear and examine into and finally determine the diſputes and differences relative to juriſdiction between the three ſtates of New-Hampſhire, Maſſachuſetts-Bay and New-York, reſpectively, or ſuch of them as ſhall have paſſed ſuch laws as are mentioned in the ſaid reſolutions of the 24th day of September and 2d of October laſt, on the one part, and the people of the diſtrict aforeſaid, who claim to be a ſeparate juriſdiction, on the other, in the mode preſcribed in and by the ſaid reſolutions.

Extract from the minutes,

Cha Thomſon ſec

Congressional resolution which said that the proceedings of Vermont were "highly unwarrantable and subversive of the peace and welfare of the United States." (UVM)

Greater Vermont, a political invention of the Allens. The shaded area, along the Connecticut, shows the sixteen New Hampshire towns which first joined Vermont. They were: Cornish, Lebanon, Hanover (Dresden), Lyme, Orford, Piermont, Haverhill, Bath, Lyman, Apthorp, Enfield, Canaan, Cardigan (Orange), Gunthwaite (Lisbon), Morristown (Franconia) and Landaff. (NS)

GREATER VERMONT

Keenly disappointed that its bid to join the Union was rejected by Congress, Vermont embarked upon a policy of expansion. If other states made claims upon Vermont, Vermont would make claims upon other states. Although the union between Vermont and the sixteen New Hampshire towns had been dissolved in 1779, many New Hampshire towns still preferred annexation to Vermont. As a result of

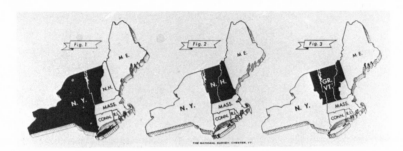

*Fig. 1 shows New England as it would be if New York had had its way;
Fig. 2, if New Hampshire had had its way; Fig. 3, if Greater Vermont
had become permanent. (NS)*

*This press used by Alden Spooner one of Vermont's first and most impor-
tant early printers. (NL)*

this interest, forty-three towns on both sides of the Connecticut River met on January 16 at Charlestown, New Hampshire. Most of the delegates preferred a union with Vermont. In February 1781, the Vermont General Assembly, sitting at Windsor, was informed "that the convention of the New Hamsphire towns was desirous of being united with Vermont in one separate independent government upon such principles as should be mutually thought most equitable and beneficial."[12] Shortly thereafter the General Assembly admitted thirty-five New Hampshire towns and laid "a jurisdictional claim" to a large part of New Hampshire.

PETITION BY NEW YORK TOWNS

While Vermont's General Assembly was admitting New Hampshire towns, it received petitions from several New York towns that desired to join Vermont. Petitioners from Cambridge and Canton complained that "the government of New York have neglected guarding our northern frontier." Petitioners from Granville stated that "ever since the year 1777 we have been left without any provision for defense." In April 1781 the Vermont Assembly voted to accept the New York towns, the affirmative vote consisting of forty-one Vermont towns and seven New Hampshire towns. The negative vote consisted of twenty-seven New Hampshire towns and only twelve Vermont towns.[13] The New Hampshire towns and eastern Vermont towns voted against the annexation of New York towns because they feared the eastern side of the state would lose political influence in the Assembly and statewide offices. Admission of the New York towns meant that towns west of the Green Mountains would not be outvoted by those to the east in the General Assembly.

The Vermont General Assembly referred to the New York townships as the western district. Five New York towns, including Hoosic, Cambridge and Saratoga East, were annexed to Bennington County; nine New York towns including Black Creek, North and South Granville, Fort Edwards, Kingsbury and White Creek became part of Rutland Coun-

ty. On July 18, 1781, Governor Chittenden issued a proclamation recognizing the fourteen New York towns and charged
that New York had been deficient in protecting the citizens
of the New York towns from "the ravages of the common
enemy."[14]

William Slade, editor of *Vermont State Papers* and later two-
term governor, had this to say about Vermont's annexation
of New York and New Hampshire territories: "By this bold
and decisive policy, she had augmented her resources — compelled the respect of her enemies — gained upon the confidence of her friends — quieted disaffection at home — invited emigration, and thus laid the foundation for a large
and powerful state."[15]

NEGOTIATIONS WITH CANADA

Meanwhile new developments were taking place in the
Revolutionary War. France, convinced that the Americans
could win after the Battle of Saratoga in 1777, formed an
alliance with the new nation. This changed British policy,
and commissioners were appointed to make concessions with
the colonies, individually or collectively.

The British, aware of the difficulties that Vermont was having with its neighboring states, particularly New Hampshire
and New York, and also aware of the Congressional indif-
ference to Vermont's joining the Union, recognized a golden
opportunity to make a separate peace with the new independent state. The British chose as their chief negotiator Sir
Frederick Haldimand, the Governor of the Province of
Quebec. Representing Vermont in the secret negotiations
were the Allen brothers, Governor Chittenden, two members
of the Governor's Council and a few other individuals from
the west side of the state.

Historians are divided over the motivations of Vermont
in the Canadian negotiations. Early Vermont historians felt
that the secret negotiations "neutralized the military threat
to Vermont's unprotected frontiers and . . . attempted to
pressure the Congress for recognition of independence and
a grant of statehood." A more recent interpretation holds
that Governor Chittenden and the Allen brothers "desperate-

Frederick Haldimard, Governor of the Province of Quebec, wanted Vermont to rejoin the British empire.

ly worked behind the scenes to bring the tiny republic back into the [British] Empire despite decided public hostility to the scheme." Finally, there are those who take a middle ground arguing that the Chittenden-Allen faction were "deeply involved in preparing the way for Vermont's return to the British Empire" but were motivated by "a genuine concern for the future of Vermont."[16]

In 1779, Sir Henry Clinton, Commander-in-Chief of the British forces in America, wrote to General Haldimand, asking him to negotiate with Vermont. Clinton's letter said in part, "That drawing over the inhabitants of the country they call Vermont to the British Crown appears a matter of such vast importance for the safety of Canada, . . . that I think it is right to repeat to you the King's wishes that you may be able to effect it, though it should be attended with considerable expense."[17] In September of the same year Haldimand wrote that he would try "to reclaim the Vermont people," whom he called "a profligate banditti."[18] A few months later, Haldimand wrote to Clinton: "No dependence can be placed on the word of Allen or of those associated with him in Vermont, who cannot be bound by laws or ties. If Allen could arm 4,000 men, it would not be safe to trust him in this province, for, under pretense of joining the King's troops, he may watch for an opportunity to seize the province."[19]

Ethan Allen stated his position thus: "I am confident that Congress will not dispute my sincere attachment to the cause of my country, though I do not hesitate to say I am fully grounded in the opinion that Vermont has an indubitable right to agree on terms of cessation of hostilities with Great Britain, provided the United States persists in rejecting her obligation for a union with them: for Vermont, of all people, would be the most miserable, were she obliged to defend the independence of the united claiming states, and they at the same time at full liberty to overturn and ruin the independence of Vermont."[20]

The British government's confidence that Vermont would defect and join the British cause was expressed in a letter written by Lord George Germaine, Secretary of State for colonial affairs, to Sir Henry Clinton, the British Commander, in February 1781. Unfortunately for the British, the letter was intercepted and published in an American newspaper. The letter said in part: "The return of the people of Vermont to their allegiance is an event of the utmost importance to the King's affairs; . . . General Haldimand, who has the instructions with you to draw over those people, and give them support, will, I doubt not, push up a body of troops, to act in conjunction with him, to secure all the avenues, through their country into Canada; and when the season admits, take possession of the upper parts of the Hudson and Connecticut Rivers, and cut off the communication between Albany and the Mohawk country."[21]

When the contents of the letter became known, public opinion swung sharply toward the admission of Vermont into the Union. Congress, responding to that opinion, gave Vermont much more encouragement than it had received before and in August 1781, passed a resolution that "preliminary to the recognition of the independence of the people, inhabiting the territory called Vermont, and their admission to the federal union that they give up their claims of land in New York and New Hampshire."[22]

On November 14, 1781, Chittenden wrote Washington: "Vermont, being thus driven to desperation, by the injustice of those who should have been her friends, was obliged to adopt policy, in the room of power." Chittenden said the Congressional change of heart with respect to the admission of Vermont was not due to the influence of Vermont's friends but the power of its enemies: — "Lord George Germaine's letter wrought on Congress, and procured from them, which the public virtue of this people could not."[23] Chittenden was too optimistic. Shortly thereafter Congress again denied Vermont admission.

NOTES

1. William Slade, *Vermont State Papers*, p. 90.
2. *Ibid.* p. 91.
3. *Ibid.* p. 92.
4. Edmund Fuller, *Vermont: A History of the Green Mountain State* (Montpelier: State Board of Education, 1952), p. 112.

5. Slade, *Vermont State Papers*, p. 93.
6. E.P. Walton, *Governor and Council*, Volume II (Montpelier: Steam Press of J. and J.M. Poland 1873), p. 426.
7. Slade, *Vermont State Papers*, p. 113.
8. *Governor and Council*, Volume II, p. 222.
9. Slade, *Vermont State Papers*, p. 117.
10. *Ibid.* p. 120.
11. *Ibid.* pp. 125-126.
12. *Ibid.* p. 130.
13. *Governor and Council*, Volume II, p. 299.
14. *Ibid.* p. 308.
15. Slade, *Vermont State Papers*, p. 141.
16. Frederick F. Van DeWater, *The Reluctant Republic: Vermont 1724-1791* (Taftsville, Vermont: The Countryman Press, 1974), Introduction, pp. VII-X.
17. Walter Crockett, *History of Vermont*, Volume II, p. 315.
18. *Ibid.* p. 315.
19. *Ibid.* pp. 316-317.
20. *Governor and Council*, Volume II, p. 407.
21. *Ibid.* p. 406.
22. Slade, *Vermont State Papers*, p. 159.
23. *Collections of the Vermont Historical Society*, Volume II (Montpelier: Vermont Historical Society 1871), pp. 203-204.

CHAPTER IV

Admission to the Union

IN NOVEMBER OF 1781 Governor Chittenden wrote General George Washington that the neighboring states of New Hampshire, New York and Massachusetts "have severally laid claims, in part or in whole, to the State, and . . . have used every art which they could devise to divide her citizens, to set Congress against her, and finally to overturn the government and share its territory among them. The repeated applications of this State to the Congress of the United States, to be admitted into the Federal Union with them upon the liberal principles of paying a just proportion of the expenses of the war with Great Britain have been rejected."[1]

General Washington replied to Chittenden, in January of 1782, "It appears, therefore, to me, that the dispute of the boundary, is the only one that exists, and that being removed, all other difficulties would be removed also, . . . You have nothing to do but withdraw your jurisdiction to the confines of your own limits, and obtain an acknowledgment of independence and sovereignty, . . . for so much territory as does not interfere with the ancient established bounds of New York, New Hampshire and Massachusetts."[2]

In January of 1782 New Hampshire's chief executive, Weare, gave "Vermonters forty days to leave the East Union or acknowledge the jurisdiction of New Hampshire." To protect the west side of the state, the New Hampshire Legislature

George Washington, Vermont's Best   Samuel Williams, Vermont
Advisor.   *historian and founder of the*
                                   Rutland Herald. *He was also a*
                                   minister, scientist and philosopher.

authorized a force of one thousand men.[3] At the same time
fighting almost approaching a civil war broke out in the
western district between New Yorkers and Vermonters.

On February 22, 1782, the Vermont General Assembly for-
mally gave up its claims to territory in New Hampshire and
New York.[4] Samuel Williams described the breakup of the
Eastern Union with New Hampshire towns and the Western
Union with the New York towns this way: "Thus was dissolved a union which had been constantly acquiring
numbers, extent, popularity, and power, from its first formation: which, it was generally believed had prevented the
division of Vermont, by New Hampshire and New York;
and which if it had been continued, would probably have
extended much further into those states. It was not without
a struggle, that the measure could be effected; and it was
not without resentment, that the members from the towns
in New Hampshire and New York, found themselves ex-
cluded from a seat or a vote in the assembly."[5]

Having taken General Washington's advice by comply-
ing with the conditions, Vermont in April of 1782 applied

James Madison, gave reasons why Vermont was rejected from the Union.

Governor Clinton of New York opposed Vermont's admission into the union.

for admission as a state in the federal union. Once again Congress turned down Vermont's request. This rejection was not well received in Vermont. Governor Chittenden, in a long letter to the president of Congress, said in part: "How inconsistent then, is it in Congress, to assume the same arbitrary stretch of prerogative over Vermont, for which they waged war against Great Britain? Is the liberty and natural rights of mankind a mere bubble, and the sport of state politicians?"[6]

James Madison gave the following analysis for Vermont's rejection:

> The independence of Vermont and its admission into the union are opposed by New York for reasons obvious and well known.
>
> The like opposition is made by Virginia, North Carolina, South Carolina and Georgia. The grounds of this opposition are, first, habitual jealousy of a predominance of eastern interests; secondly, the opposition expected from Vermont to western claims; thirdly, the inexpediency of admitting so important a state, to an equal vote, in deciding on peace, and all the other grand interests of the union . . . ; fourthly, the influence of the example on the premature dismemberment of the other states.[7]

General Washington thought there might have to be a military showdown between Congress and Vermont. In a letter to a member of Congress in February 1783 Washington wrote: "The country is very mountainous, . . . and extremely strong. The inhabitants, for the most part, are a hardy race, composed of that kind of people who are best calculated for soldiers; in truth, who are soldiers;"[8] On several occasions the State of New York had asked Congress to send troops into Vermont to regain New York territory. In April of 1784, Governor Chittenden warned Congress "that Vermont does not wish to enter into a war with the State of New York, but that she will act on the defensive and expects that Congress and the twelve states will observe a strict neutrality, and let the contending states settle their own controversy."[9]

In May of 1784, Congress made one last attempt with its first Constitution, known as the Articles of Confederation, to admit Vermont into the Union, an act favored by a majority of states. The necessary votes were not obtained. Admission was opposed by New York along with the southern states.[10]

During the revolution, the major effort of Congress was to win the war, and any attempt to take sides with respect to boundary disputes between New York, New Hampshire and Vermont could have weakened the effort. After the Treaty of Paris was signed in 1783, however, there was much more reason for Congress to act favorably upon Vermont's request, particularly when Vermont had accepted Congress' conditional offer.

However, Congress, under the Articles of Confederation, had very little power. There was no central government, no executive branch, no supreme court. Thirteen states were bound together by a loose confederation, "a league of friendship." Continental Congress was a unicameral body, and regardless of size, each state had one vote. Any major legislation had to win the approval of nine states, and to amend the Articles of Confederation all thirteen states had to approve. Congress had no power to impose taxes, only request them. And Congress could not regulate interstate commerce. Under such circumstances, it is little wonder that Congress could not deal with the Vermont question.

THE REPUBLIC GROWS IN STRENGTH

With the coming of peace and the threat of invasion from Canada much lessened, Vermont found itself in a rather enviable position. Vermont had no debt, taxes were low, land was plentiful, and settlers were moving into Vermont in large numbers. The United States had lost the unifying power of fighting a common enemy, had a dissatisfied and unpaid army, a depreciated currency, no stable form of revenue and

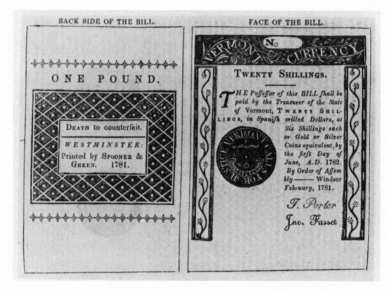

Vermont's paper currency in 1781. (UVM)

Vermont coins, 1786. (UVM)

Vermont's first post office was located in Bennington in 1783. The postal rate from Bennington to Albany, New York was 3 pence. (NL)

was in great debt. Under these circumstances, thoughtful American leaders began to consider scrapping the Articles of Confederation and writing a new constitution.

While the United States was experiencing its difficulty, Vermont was slowly gaining strength. Vermont began to coin its own money, establish post offices and post roads, negotiate with foreign powers and sell public land. A policy of free trade was developed with the Province of Quebec. From 1779 to 1791 the Vermont General Assembly chartered over one hundred new towns and incorporated 7 counties. During this period there was a significant migration to Vermont and by 1791 the population totaled over 85,000.[11]

While Vermont had little debt compared to the thirteen original states after the Revolutionary War, it was not immune to currency inflation. As before the war many old and new settlers used credit to buy land and build homes. Many

INCORPORATION DATES OF
VERMONT'S FOURTEEN COUNTIES

Bennington	February 11, 1779
Windham	February 11, 1781
Orange	February 22, 1781
Rutland	February 22, 1781
Windsor	February 22, 1781
Addison	October 17, 1785
Chittenden	October 22, 1787
Caledonia	November 5, 1792
Essex	November 5, 1792
Franklin	November 5, 1792
Orleans	November 5, 1792
Grand Isle	November 9, 1802
Washington	Jefferson County November 1, 1810 name changed November 8, 1814
Lamoille	October 26, 1835

settlers became financially overextended, and when they could not pay their creditors, foreclosure proceedings were instituted in the courts.

In 1784 people from Wells and other towns nearby met in convention and adopted resolutions "for a redress of grievances." While the grievances were not printed, the following poem in the *Vermont Gazette* illustrates the concern about debt and courts:

> Then lawyers from the courts expel,
> Cancel our debt
> and all is well —
> But they should finally neglect
> To take the measures we direct
> Still fond of their own power and wisdom,
> Will find effectual means to twist 'em.[12]

Governor Chittenden, responding to these concerns, made a public address to Vermonters that was printed in Vermont newspapers. In discussing the reasons for the discontent, he said, "law suits are become so numerous that there's hard-

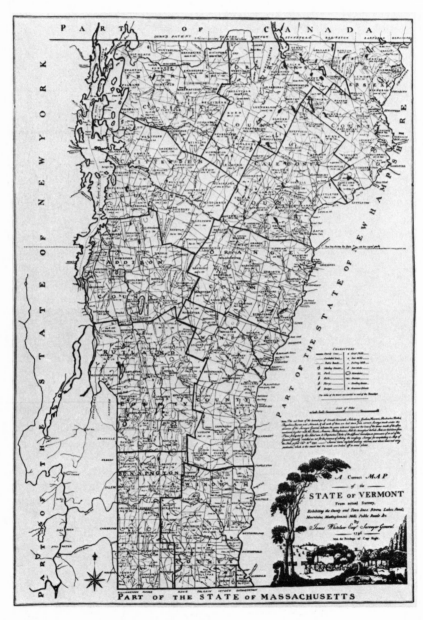

Vermont counties formed by 1796.

Windham County Courthouse, Newfane.

ly money sufficient to pay for entering the actions, not to mention the debts or lawyers' and officers' fees, I have reason to believe that the expense of law suits for two years past, has been nearly equal to that of any two years of the war."[13]

In 1787 the Vermont General Assembly passed an act making livestock and grain "legal tender." This act made it much easier for debtors to pay off their creditors and avoid foreclosure.

In 1786, the Council of Censors made its first report to the people of Vermont, criticizing the executive, the legislative and judicial branches of government and suggesting that the constitution be amended so the number of representatives in the General Assembly would be set at fifty. Changes to the constitution were recommended in order that Vermont government might be "less expensive and more wise and energetic." The General Assembly was criticized for passing so many laws: "Few acts of general concern but have undergone alterations at the next session after passing of them, and some of them at many different sessions; the revised laws have been altered, realtered, made better, made worse, and kept in such a fluctuating position that persons

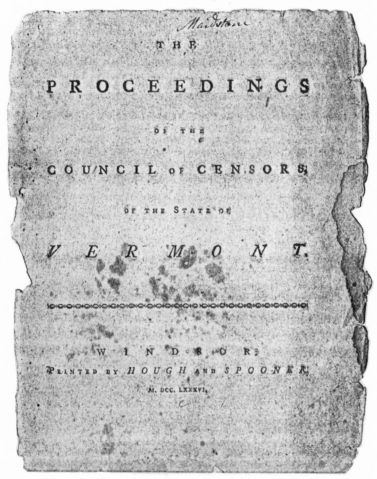

First Report of the Council of Censors 1786. (VSL)

in civil commissions scarcely know what is law or how to regulate their conduct in the determination of causes."[14]

THE VERMONT-KENTUCKY COMPROMISE

While Vermont was busy with internal affairs, New York began to reexamine its Vermont policy. In 1787, Alexander Hamilton, a member of the New York Assembly, introduced a bill that called for the recognition of the in-

Alexander Hamilton, led the fight for Vermont's admission to the Union.

John Jay. Jay Peak and Jay were named after him.

Governor Moses Robinson 1789-1790. Gave Thomas Chittenden his only defeat.

By his Excellency

Thomas Chittenden, Esq;

Governor, Captain General and Commander in Chief in and over the State of Vermont,

A Proclamation.

The supreme Disposer of Events having been graciously pleased to to order the Providential Occurrences of the Year past, as to call loudly for the Praise and Adoration of individuals, and of Community at large. And as a Public Acknowledgement of the inestimable and unceasing Bounties of a gracious and merciful G O D, is at all Times an incumbent, and ought to be a delightful Duty of every rational Mind :

I HAVE thought fit by and with the Advice of my Council, and at the Request of the General Assembly, to appoint, and I do hereby appoint, THURSDAY the 27th Day of November next, to be observed as a Day of PUBLIC THANKSGIVING AND PRAISE, throughout this State.

And I do hereby earnestly recommend to all Persons residing within the same, strictly to observe said Day, that we may with united Hearts render unfeigned Praises to the munificent Bestower of every desirable gift, for the manifold Mercies of the Year past, both of a public and private nature : That it has pleased him to order the Seasons in infinite Mercy, abundantly to replenish the Earth, and to crown the Labour of the Husbandman with plentiful Harvests : That he has caused a Spirit of Unanimity to pervade all Ranks of People among us ; and preserved us from internal Feuds and from foreign Invasion : And humbly to implore that he would direct to and bless such Means as may be necessary to put into Execution the FEDERAL GOVERNMENT of the UNITED STATES, and establish it on a permanent Basis, so that it may contribute to the best good of that extensive Empire ; That it may graciously please his adoreable Majesty to order, in the course of Events, that the United States offer their Friendship and the Protection of their Government, on equitable Terms, to this State, so that we may be enabled to join with them in PERFECT UNION: That under the divine Auspices we may become a Band of Brothers, a People zealous of Good Works, whose highest Ambition shall be to honor and adore his Name, and under the Banner of the divine Redeemer, to erect an Empire that shall prove an Assylum for the persecuted and distressed from every Quarter of the Globe.

At the same Time under a deep Sense of our Unworthiness, to implore his Forgiveness of our manifold Sins, and a continuance of his Favor towards us, our Allies, and the whole World of mankind.

GIVEN under my Hand in the Council Chamber, in Manchester, this 20th Day of October, 1788, in the twelfth Year of our Independence.

Thomas Chittenden.

By his Excellency's Command,

Joseph Fay, Sec.

God save the People.

Proclamation by Governor Thomas Chittenden hoping Vermont would join the federal union.

dependence of Vermont. Speaking on behalf of his bill before the New York Assembly, Hamilton expressed concern that "without any relative importance in the union, irritated by neglect or stimulated by revenge," Vermont might form a Canadian connection.[15]

At the time there was a debate as to whether the capital of the new nation would be located in New York or Philadelphia, and Hamilton realized that if Vermont were admitted to the Union, her vote would be most important. He also realized it was important that a northern free state be admitted to offset two southern slave states, Kentucky and Tennessee, which would soon join the Union. To Nathaniel Chipman, Alexander Hamilton wrote, "one of the first subjects of deliberation with the new Congress will be the independence of Kentucky, for which the southern states will be anxious. The northern will be glad to send a counterpoise in Vermont."[16] Of the first thirteen original states seven were northern and six southern. The one-state northern edge was maintained when Vermont was admitted in 1791 and Kentucky in 1792. The admission of Tennessee in 1796 created a balance of northern and southern states which was maintained until 1848 when each section could claim fifteen states.

New York and Vermont agreed to negotiate the differences between conflicting land claims. In the summer of 1789, as a result of negotiations, Vermont agreed to pay New York $30,000 compensation while New York gave up her Vermont land claims. Vermont's next step in the process of admission to the Union was to ratify the new United States Constitution.[17] In January 1791, a convention authorized by the Vermont General Assembly met in Bennington to consider ratification. One of the delegates to the convention, Supreme Court Judge Nathaniel Chipman, said Vermont was too small in relation to a new powerful union to remain independent. "Whenever our interests clash with those of the union, it requires very little political sagacity to foretell that every sacrifice must be made on our part. . . . United we become great, from the reflected greatness of the empire with which we unite."[18] The United States Constitution was ratified one hundred and five to four by Vermont. The adoption was favorably received throughout the nation. In Albany, New York, the event was celebrated by a parade and a fourteen-gun salute.[19]

By Act of Congress on March 4, 1791, Vermont was admitted to the Union as the fourteenth state, the first state to join the union. The Congressional Act declared "that on the 4th day of March 1791, the said State, by the name and style of the State of Vermont, shall be received into this Union as a new and entire member of the United States of America."[20] A few days later, a large gathering of citizens in Rutland celebrated this event. Sixteen toasts were drunk, including some of the following: "The union of Vermont with the United States, - may it flourish like our pines and continue unshaken as our mountains." "May we never experience a less happy moment than the present under the federal government." "May the Vermonters become as eminent in the acts of peace as they have been glorious in those of war." The following stanzas were sung to the then popular tune of "Washington's Birthday":

> Come every federal son,
>   Let each Vermonter come,
>   And take his glass,
> Long live great Washington,
> Glory's immortal son;
> Bright as the rolling sun
>   O'er us doth pass.
>
> Hail hail this happy day,
> When we allegiance pay,
>   T' our federal head,
> Bright in these western skies,
> Shall our new star arise,
> Striking our enemies
>   With fear and dread.
>
> Come each Greenmountain boy,
> Swell every breast with joy,
>   Hail our good land,
> As our pines climb the air,
> Firm as our mountains are,
> Federal beyond compare,
>   Proudly we stand.[21]

Vermont's evolution from the New Hampshire grants to independence and then admission to the Union was difficult. The great controversy with New York might never have taken place if that province had been content to accept the territory west of the Connecticut. Congress did procrastinate in acting upon Vermont's application for admission into the Union, but to have admitted Vermont during the war would have alienated New York, one of the most powerful states in the Confederation. New York's attitude changed when it perceived that Vermont's admission would help balance the admission of the new State of Kentucky and improve New York City's chances of becoming a permanent capital. In 1791 the State of Vermont was ready to begin anew as a member of the Union.

NOTES

1. *Collections of the Vermont Historical Society,* p. 200.
2. William Slade, *Vermont State Papers,* p. 167.
3. Walter Crockett, *History of Vermont,* Volume II, p. 308.
4. Slade, *Vermont State Papers,* pp. 168-169.
5. Samuel Williams, *Natural and Civil History of Vermont* (Burlington, Vermont: Samuel Mills, 1809), p. 229.
6. *Collections of the Vermont Historical Society,* pp. 318-319.
7. *Ibid.,* p. 268-269.
8. Walter Crockett, *History of Vermont,* Volume II, p. 38.
9. *Ibid.,* p. 384.
10. *Ibid.*.
11. Jay M. Holbrook, *Vermont 1771 Census* (Oxford, Massachusetts: Holbrook Research Institute 1982), p. XII.
12. *Governor and Council,* pp. 358-359.
13. *Ibid.,* p. 410.
14. Slade, *Vermont State Papers,* Volume III, p. 540.
15. *Governor and Council Volume III,* p. 423. See also Chilton Williamson, *Vermont in Quandary 1763-1825* (Montpelier, Vermont: Vermont Historical Society 1949), pp. 293-294. "Chief among the supporters of the Constitution who saw clearly that Vermont looked to the north rather than to the south was Alexander Hamilton .... He believed that, if Vermont were not eventually to join the British, New York must abandon its claims at once."
16. *Governor and Council,* p. 442.

17. *Ibid.*, pp. 461-462. According to James Duane, a New Yorker who had large land holdings in Vermont, "The bargain was made by our [New York] politicians to obtain a new state to overbalance Southern influence, and in this paramount object with them compensation to the comparatively few landholders among her citizens was almost entirely overlooked."
18. *Governor and Council Volume III*, pp. 468-472.
19. *Ibid.*, p. 482.
20. *Ibid.*, p. 488.
21. *Ibid.*, pp. 483-484.

Old Vergennes City Jail where Vermont Congressman Matthew Lyon was imprisoned in 1798. Courtesy of Ralph Ryan, Vergennes.

CHAPTER V

The Roots of Party Politics

in Vermont

IN THE MILD SPRING OF 1791, Thomas Jefferson and James Madison rode from Philadelphia to New York and then on to New England on what they called a "botanizing excursion." From Bennington Jefferson wrote home about speckled trout and black striped red squirrels, and observed silver fir, white pine, "spruce pine" juniper, "paperbirch," wild cherry and "sugar maple in vast abundance."[1]

When they arrived in Bennington on June 4, the *Vermont Gazette* was enthusiastic about their visit: "Examples like these bespeak the gentleman of good breeding . . . and are worthy of imitation by all ranks and descriptions of men in our republic." Jefferson wrote that their stay in Bennington was extended because of Vermont's Blue Laws "not permitting us to travel on Sunday."[2]

The real purpose of the expedition, however, had very little to do with plants or animals. The expedition was to identify political "specimens" and cultivate support for Jefferson, who was emerging as the leader of an opposition to the policies of President George Washington.

Political parties were not a part of the first years of the United States. Indeed, Washington and other founding fathers warned against them. But dissent is the hallmark of democracy, and soon after the adoption of the Constitution America's early leaders were dividing into two groups. The first was the Federalists who believed in a strong national government as advocated by Alexander Hamilton.

Thomas Jefferson.

But the adoption of the Constitution had not been easy. Many argued the national government would be much too strong, and argued for amendments guaranteeing certain basic rights. Jefferson and Madison came to be identified with this group, and after adoption of the Constitution and Bill of Rights, they found themselves increasingly in the role of the loyal opposition. Their group was called the Jeffersonian-Republicans or Democratic-Republicans.

PARTIES AND POLITICS

The Federalist cartoons of the day portrayed the Jeffersonians as "cannibals, drunkards, and pirates." The Jeffersonians, in turn, accused the Federalists of "working toward a monarchy and an hereditary privileged class."[3] The

Federalists' policies generally enhanced commercial and business interests, while the Jeffersonians identified more with agrarian concerns. A preponderance of the lawyers, merchants and Congregational clergy were Federalists. As late as 1811 a Jeffersonian noted that Federalists in Vermont included "four-fifths of the lawyers, nine-tenths of the merchants, and 19 out of 20 of the clergy."[4] In general, the Federalists were stronger on the eastern side of the Green Mountains, and the Jeffersonians stronger on the western side. For example, in the election of 1800, Jefferson carried every county west of the mountains while Adams carried every eastern county.[5]

The conflict between France and England and the French Revolution also played an important role in the early development of political parties. The Jeffersonians sided with the French, while the Federalists were concerned about the excesses of the French Revolution, which had broken out in 1789, the same year the American republic began. Those who admired the ideas and ideals of the revolution formed Jeffersonian societies in several Vermont counties.

Vermont's first governor, Thomas Chittenden tried to steer a neutral course between Jeffersonians and Federalists. With the death of Chittenden, Federalist Issac Tichenor, born in Newark, New Jersey and known as "Jersey Slick," was elected governor. Party conflict became much more evident during his administration.

A celebrated instance of partisanship, the "Vergennes Slaughter," occurred in 1798, during Tichenor's term. In the absence of a statehouse, the Assembly met in Vergennes. Under the Vermont Constitution, the selection of judges was in the hands of the Legislature, and the Federalist Legislature failed to re-elect many Jeffersonians to judicial posts, including Israel Smith, the Chief Justice of the Vermont Supreme Court. A Federalist Albany newspaper said that the pro-French faction was "being punished in Vermont . . . A measure which should be universally imitated . . .[to] Consign the sons of clamor and sedition to neglect and contempt."[7]

Isaac Tichenor, popular Federalist Governor. (UVM)

Matthew Lyon, hot headed Vermont Congressman.

MATTHEW LYON

The story of Matthew Lyon focused national political attention on the new-born state of Vermont and offers a good illustration of the intensity of political strife in the 1790s.

Lyon came to this country from Ireland as a "redemptioner," meaning the cost of passage was paid by some potential American employer in return for a contracted period of work, usually seven years. He settled in Litchfield, Connecticut, the home of many early Vermont settlers. He eventually married a cousin of Ethan Allen. (Litchfield County would give Vermont four governors, seven congressmen, seven Supreme Court justices and three United States senators.

Like many of his friends, Lyon began to buy land at bargain prices in the north. He chose a tract in Wallingford, which at the time consisted only of "a few rough log huts scattered in the surrounding woods." During the Revolution Lyon joined the Green Mountain Boys. He participated in the capture of Fort Ticonderoga in 1775 and the Battle of Hubbardton in 1777, but was involved in a questionable case of desertion that was to haunt him later.[8]

Lyon's first wife died shortly after the war, and he married one of Governor Chittenden's daughters. Shortly thereafter Lyon founded the town of Fair Haven, establishing the first store, the first hotel, a paper mill, gristmill, sawmill, two forges, an iron furnace and a newspaper. He twice represented Fair Haven in the General Assembly.

Lyon saw himself as a self-made, self-educated leader of Vermont democracy fighting against the well-educated Federalist lawyers who he claimed represented an aristocracy. It was with such a Federalist that Lyon had his first public tussle. Legislator Nathaniel Chipman defended Tory claims to lands seized by the colonists during the American Revolution. Lyon, who had become the clerk of the Board of Confiscation, favored those who had bought and lived on the confiscated land. One day Chipman and Lyon met face to face. Lyon charged that "no man with a spark of honesty" could have supported the Tory position. Chipman replied by calling Lyon "an ignorant Irish puppy." Lyon seized Chipman by the hair, and Chipman responded by picking up a pen and attempting to stab Lyon. Although obviously neither of the men had the longest of tempers, it was the politics of the time that led to the fight.[9]

One year later Lyon issued a call for the formation of Democratic Societies in Vermont. Lyon asked "that the great body of people themselves undertake to watch over the government." In time there were more Democratic Societies in Vermont than in any other state except Pennsylvania. Societies were formed in the counties of Chittenden, Addison and Rutland. Lyon's newspaper reported that from July 8, 1794 to September 30, 1794, many new members were admitted to Rutland Societies from Fair Haven, Poultney, Wells, Orwell and Middletown. In that year the Rutland Society expressed its disapproval "of the evasive conduct of some people in power who have suffered themselves to be cajoled into a state of stupor and inactivity against British abuses."[10]

LYON IN CONGRESS

In May of 1797, after several unsuccessful attempts, Lyon was elected to Congress. He had been in office only three weeks when he objected to the Congressional custom of walking to the Executive Mansion to deliver a reply to the President's inaugural address. Lyon was upset because President Adams had called a special session to place the nation in a state of military preparedness. The French had refused to receive our new United States minister. Lyon moved "that such members as do not choose to attend upon the President to present the Answer to his Speech, shall be excused."[11]

Lyon went on to say that he "trusted our magnanimous President would, with the enlightened yeomanry of America, despise such a boyish piece of business . . . he had spent a great part of his life amongst a people whose plainness of manners forbids all pageantry. . . . Were he acting in his own personal character, he perhaps might conform to the idle usage, but acting as he was for eighty thousand people, every father of family in his district would condemn for such an act."[12]

Lyon was sharply criticized by the Federalists. Nathaniel Chipman who by then became a United States Senator wrote: "You cannot, with all your knowledge of the man easily conceive how incredulous a figure he makes. . . . I think, however, he will be of use, as by choosing to take the seat among the Jacobins [those sympathetic towards France]. He will make many more doubtful men of the party ashamed of their association."[13]

Federalist Congressman John Allen, another Litchfield Law School graduate, said that there was enough American blood in the House to support the President. Lyon, stung by aspersions to his Irish background, angrily retorted, "before yesterday he never heard of a gentleman boasting of their blood in that House."[14]

The whole affair caught the attention of satirists, including St. John Honeywell, who composed a poem, "Speech of a Democratic Lyon:"

As still as mice the members sat
Expecting royal fun Sir

Jeffersonian Congressman Matthew Lyon duels with Federalist Congressman Roger Griswold of Connecticut. (VHS)

The speaker gently moved his hat
And Lion thus begun Sir.

I'm rugged Mat, the Democrat,
  Berate me as you please Sir,
True Paddy whack ne'er turn'd his back
  Or bowed his head to Caesar.

Refrain:
Horum, scorum vendum, roarum
Spittam, spattum, squirto,
Tag, rag, derry, merry, raw head and bloody bone,
Sing, Langolee nobody's hurt O!

The Yankee Crew, long since I knew,
  At home I duel them daily,
There's not a man, of all their Clan
  But knows my old Shelalee.[15]

In January 1798, with congressional feelings running high over a possible war with France, Lyon was talking to several fellow congressmen. Roger Griswold, a Federalist from Connecticut, joined the group. Lyon immediately began baiting

John Adams, second President of the United States, refused to pardon Lyon—"Penitance must precede pardon."

Griswold. Griswold, in turn, accused Lyon of being a deserter during the Revolution. Tempers flared and harsh words were exchanged. Lyon ended up spitting in Griswold's face. The Federalists tried to have Lyon expelled from the House, but the Jeffersonians had enough votes to forestall the action.[16]

Federalists in Congress referred to Lyon as a "nasty, brutish, spitting animal." One Federalist from Massachusetts declared that this "kennel of filth" should be expelled from Congress "as citizens removed impurities and filth from their docks and wharves." A Bostonian said, "I feel grieved that the saliva of an Irishman should be left upon the face of an American and he, a New England man."[17]

Lyon defended his actions, saying: "Perhaps some will say

I did not take the right method with him. We do not always possess the power of judging calmly what is the best mode of resenting an unpardonable insult. Had I borne it patiently, I should have been bandied about in all the newspapers on the continent, which are supported by British money and federal patronage, as a mean poltroon."[18]

Griswold was not satisfied with matters and decided to take them into his own hands. One day in Congress, he walked up to Lyon as he sat at his desk and began to beat him with a heavy cudgel. Griswold himself described the scene this way: "As soon as I saw him (Lyon) in his seat I took my cane and walked across the floor in front of the speaker's chair, which is more than 40 feet in extend. – he saw me before I struck him, and was endeavoring to draw a sword when I gave him the first blow – I call'd him a scoundrel and struck him with my cane, and pursued him with more than 20 blows on his head and back until he got possession of a pair of tongues (tongs), when I threw him down and after giving several blows with my fist, I was taken off by his friends."[19]

Lyon survived the physical attack, perhaps even gaining additional political energy from the incident. He continued expressing his Jeffersonian views in his newly founded Vermont newspaper, and it was this activity that ran him afoul of the Alien and Sedition Acts.

WAR FEVER

In March 1798, the "XYZ Affair" gave the Federalists good reason to have the nation prepare for war with France. French pirateers were seizing United States ships on the high seas. Agents of the French foreign minister, known as X, Y and Z to assure their anonymity, said France would only negotiate with the United States, if a bribe were paid, a loan made to the French government and an apology offered for remarks made by President Adams.

Adams refused to comply, and the nation rallied to the cry of "millions for defense but not 1 cent for tribute." Federalist editors warned the "eyes of the devouring monsters are upon us," that "horrid Frenchmen threaten your houses and farms with fire, plunder and pillage," Congress increased defense spending for the navy and provisional army.[20]

In this war-like atmosphere Congress passed the Alien and Sedition Acts, which were purported to provide for national security in the event of war. But in reality they were a muzzle on political opposition. The Alien laws restricted citizenship and rights of aliens, while the Sedition laws made it a criminal offense to "write, publish or utter anything of a false, scandalous or malicious nature against the government, Congress or the President of the United States." The punishment was a fine up to $2,000 and two years imprisonment.

The Jeffersonians were roundly criticized for their pro-French leanings, and Lyon's notoriety as an outspoken Jeffersonian made him the target of renewed Federalist criticism. He found himself denounced as a "tool" of the French and an enemy of the nation. Statements he had made just prior to passage of the acts that charged Adams with "a continued grasp for power . . . an unbounded thirst for ridiculous pomp, foolish adulations and selfish avarice" attracted particular attention. On a trip home at the end of a legislative session, Lyon was serenaded by a band playing "The Rogue's March." It became clear that Federalists were gunning for him. "A seditious foreigner in our council may endanger us more than a thousand Frenchmen in the field," one Federalist writer observed. He said the opposition had to be suppressed to curb "the pernicious influence" of the Jeffersonians. The Jeffersonians should not only be defeated, they should be "exterminated."[21]

The editor of the *Rutland Herald*, Samuel Williams, was Lyon's key Federalist opponent in 1798. The *Herald* constantly referred to Lyon as a "Vermont beast." When the *Herald* refused to print Lyon's letter of defense, Lyon established his own newspaper, *The Scourge of Aristocracy*. The first editorial on October 1, 1798, proclaimed its creed: "When every aristocratic hireling from the English Porcupine [a reference to William Cobbett, a Federalist editor] . . . down to the dirty hedgehogs and groveling animals of his race . . . are vomiting forth columns of lies, malignant abuse and deception, the *Scourge* will be devoted to politics."[22]

Lyon found himself in trouble almost immediately. Two days after the *Scourge* hit the streets, a grand jury met in Rutland to consider charges against him under the as-yet-untested Sedition laws. The federal circuit court for Vermont, meeting in Rutland under Supreme Court Justice William Paterson, instructed the jury to pay careful attention "to the seditious attempts of disaffected persons to disturb the government." The jurors said, "we solemnly feel what the Honorable Judge has so powerfully expressed, that licentiousness more endangers the liberties and independence of a free government than haste in invading foes." Based upon the assumption that "Lyon was a dangerous domestic enemy of the government," he was indicted for sedition on October 5, 1798.[23]

The other judge sitting on the case was Samuel Hitchcock, Ethan Allen's son-in-law, who had been Lyon's opponent in the congressional runoff election in 1796. The prosecuting attorney was Federalist Charles Marsh, another alumnus of the Litchfield Law School. Lyon was unable to obtain legal counsel and conducted his own defense.

Lyon's trial was brief. In short order he was found guilty of stirring up sedition and bringing "the President and Government of the United States into contempt." He was fined $1,000 and given a four-month prison term.

The Federalist press around the country greeted the conviction with jubilation. Boston's *Columbian Sentinel* proclaimed, "Justice though late is sure." The *Hartford Courant* said that "the beast was now caged and on exhibit in Vergennes (where he was jailed)." He was the same "creature that had been seen in Philadelphia cavorting like a monkey . . . where he was taken for an Ass for his braying, for a Cur by his barking, for a Puppy for his whining, for a Hog for his spitting, and for a Lyon, by nothing but being the greatest of beasts."[24]

Jefferson expressed concern over Lyon's conviction: "I know not which mortifies me most, that I should fear to write what I think or my country is in such a state of things. Yet Lyon's judges . . . are objects of national fear."[25]

State of Vermont, ss.

BY

ISAAC TICHENOR, GOVERNOR

IN AND OVER THE STATE OF VERMONT.

To the first constable of the town of Dorset   *or in his absence, the town-clerk, or in the absence of both, the select-men of said Town*   GREETING.

Whereas it appears, by the return to me made, by the Committee appointed by the General Assembly, to receive and count the votes for a Representative to Congress, from the WESTERN DISTRICT of Vermont, *" That there is no choice of a Representative by the said district,"* and the following is a correct statement of the number of Votes for each candidate, in the former meeting, viz.

Matthew Lyon,	3,482	Roger Enos, jun.	3
Samuel Williams,	1,544	Samuel Miller,	2
Daniel Chipman,	1,370	Joel Linsly,	2
Abel Spencer,	268	John Burnham,	2
Israel Smith,	236	Isaac Clark,	1
Gideon Olin,	22	Martin Chittenden,	1
Samuel Hitchcock,	16	Nathaniel Chipman,	1
Jonas Galusha,	14	James Witherill,	1
Moses Robinson,	8	Thomas D. Rood,	1
Jonathan Robinson,	6	John Strong,	1
Isaac Tichenor,	3	Amos Marsh,	1

These are, *therefore*, by the authority of the State of VERMONT, to direct you, and each of you, whose duty it is made by law, to warn the freemen of the town of *Dorset* in the county of *Bennington* to meet at the usual place of holding freemens' meetings in said town, on the *first* Tuesday of December next, at one of the clock in the afternoon, to elect a person to represent this State in the *Congress* of the *United States;* and that you govern yourself or your-selves, in all things according to the statute in such case made and provided. For which these shall be your sufficient warrant.

Given under my hand at the Council Chamber in Vergennes, this 25 day of October — one thousand seven hundred *and ninety eight.*

Isaac Tichenor

PRINTED AT THE VERGENNES PRESS BY GEORGE AND ROBERT WAITS.

Message from Governor Tichenor calling for a congressional reelection in 1798 since no candidate had received a majority. Matthew Lyon, who lacked a majority by eleven ballots, won the run-off election. Vermont had two Congressmen during this decade. (VHS)

LYON IN PRISON

Upon Lyon's arrival in Vergennes, where the General Assembly was meeting and where he was to serve his prison sentence, he was paraded through the center of town. His cell had a glassless window and no heat, and "afforded a stench about equal to the Philadelphia docks in the month of August." Many of Lyon's followers wanted to free him by destroying the jail, but Lyon wrote that he preferred to "suffer any kind of death here, rather than to be taken out by violence."[26]

During all of the legal proceedings against him, Lyon was a candidate for one of Vermont's two congressional seats (although Vermont now has only one House seat, at one time the state had as many as six seats, owing to the proportionly larger population of the state then). While in jail Lyon learned he was leading his main opponent, Williams. But by eleven ballots he failed to win a majority of the 6,985 votes cast, and according to Vermont law a runoff was held.[27]

In another part of Vergennes the Federalist-dominated Vermont General Assembly wrote a supportive message to President Adams. The Assembly was confident that the President could "distinguish between the voice of your county and the clamor of party; we here offer you the genuine sentiments of our constituents, the freemen of Vermont, as delivered through their constitutional organ, the legislature." The message was drafted by Lyon's opponent, Williams.[28]

President Adams was pleased by the support of the Vermont Legislature and in a reply to the Assembly wrote: "The dishonest and impious . . . commit mischief. [Restraints must be placed upon the wicked] . . . and then the sordid animal becomes too tame under the curb, the lash and the spur." Although the reply by Adams was used as campaign literature against the re-election of Lyon, Lyon won the runoff by almost 600 votes.[29]

Lyon thanked his constituents for their support. In his letter to "the Freemen of the Western District" on January 12, 1799, Lyon gave his address as the Vergennes Jail. Lyon's "crime" was his refusal to bend "to the view of those who wish to see a luxurious court, crowded with shoals of military cour-

HISTORY OF VERMONT'S
CONGRESSIONAL DISTRICTS

Number of Congressmen	The number of representatives is based upon relative population as determined by the U.S. Census
2	1791-1803 Two districts, eastern and western
4	1803-1813 Four districts, northeastern, northwestern, southeastern, southwestern
6	1813-1819 Six Congressmen elected at large
6	1819-1821 Six Congressional districts
5	1821-1831 Five Congressional districts
5	1831-1833 Congressmen elected at large
5	1833-1843 Five Congressional districts
4	1843-1853 Four Congressional districts
3	1853-1883 Three Congressional districts
2	1883-1933 Two Congressional districts
1	1933- One Congressional district

tiers, speculators, and stock-jobbers, fattening on the labours of the farmers and poor mechanics." Lyon ended his letter by stating that while two judges and a jury had declared him guilty, the votes of his constituents made him not guilty.[30]

Before Lyon was re-elected, thousands of Vermonters had petitioned President Adams to pardon him. Lyon himself had not asked for a pardon, and the President refused to receive the petitions, noting that "penitence must precede pardon."

LYON FREED

Fellow Jeffersonians rallied to Lyon's support. Senator Steven Mason of Virginia, with whom Lyon had lodged during congressional sessions, collected $1,000 in gold from Jeffersonian leaders such as Jefferson, Madison and Monroe to pay Lyon's fine. He was released from jail on February 9, 1799.[31]

When he stepped out of the Vergennes jail building, he was greeted by enthusiastic supporters. He was driven to Middlebury in a sled drawn by four horses, and it was said the procession that followed was twelve miles long.[32]

Congressional reaction to Lyon's return was less than enthusiastic, however. Federalists called him "a notorious and seditious person, and of a depraved mind, and wicked and diabolical disposition." They tried to expel him from the House, but failed. They bristled with contempt at Lyon's pivotal role in swinging the 1800 presidential election to Jefferson. Jefferson and Aaron Burr won a majority of electoral votes that year, and the House had to pick a winner. The decisive vote for Jefferson on the thirty-sixth ballot was cast by Lyon. [33]

THE JEFFERSONIANS FIGHT BACK

Jefferson was shocked by the Alien and Sedition Acts, and he tried to undermine them by secretly writing nine resolutions that asserted the right of states to nullify congressional acts. They were first introduced in the Kentucky Legislature and became known as the Kentucky Resolves.

The Vermont Legislature considered the resolutions in 1799, but rejected them as a danger to the Union. The Assembly adopted a Report which said in part:

> Suppose each Legislature possesses the power you contend for, each State Legislature would have the right to cause all the acts of Congress to pass in view before them, and reject or approve at their discretion and the consequences would be that the government of the Union, falsely called general, might operate partially in some States, and cease to operate in others. Would not this defeat the grand design of our Union?[34]

The Federalists had obviously made a major political blunder by passing the Alien and Sedition Acts, and the move probably cost Adams re-election in 1800. The resolutions were used by New Englanders to support secession at the Federalist-dominated Hartford Convention in 1814 and 1815 and later by the South to support nullification and secession. Perhaps more importantly, however, the acts polarized America into two political camps, allowing the formation of distinct parties — something Washington had warned against so forcefully. In Vermont, people such as Lyon acted as catalysts in that polarization.

NOTES

1. H.A. Washington, Jefferson's Complete Works Volume 5 (Washington, D.C.: Taylor and Maury, 1853), pp. 265-266. In the same year, 1791, a Virginian wrote a friend in Bennington also describing Vermont. As cited by *Governor and Council*, Volume 4, pp. 423-424:

   > "Before I left Virginia, I had conceived but a very indifferent opinion of the northern states, and especially of the state of Vermont. I had formed the idea of a rough barren country, inhabited by a fierce, uncivilized, and very unpolished people. I made my tour up Connecticut river, east of the green mountains, near the northern boundary of your state, and returned on the western side, by the lake through Bennington. I must confess I was surprised and astonished beyond measure, to find a fertile luxuriant soil, cultivated by a virtuous, industrious and civilized set of inhabitants; many of whom lived in taste and elegance, and appeared not unacquainted with the polite arts."

2. Roger Butterfield, *The American Past* (New York: Simon and Schuster 1947), pp. 20-21.

3. *Ibid.*.

4. *The Washingtonian*, November 11, 1811 as cited by Chilton Williamson, *Vermont in Quandary 1763-1825*, p. 259.

5. David Ludlum, *Social Ferment in Vermont 1791-1850* (Montpelier, Vermont: Vermont Historical Society 1948), p. 15.

6. Zadock Thompson, *History of Vermont* (Burlington: Chauncey Goodrich 1842), p. 89.

   > "It was during this session, that proscription, on account of political opinion, was first practiced in the distribution of the civil offices in Vermont. Israel Smith, who had held the office of chief justice of the state, and who was a man of uncorrupted integrity and virtue, was dropped on account of his attachment to the republican party, and another person chosen chief justice in his stead."

7. Austin Noble, *The Federalist Party in Vermont*, Unpublished paper Harvard University, April, 1950, p. 62.

8. Alaine Austin, *Matthew Lyon: "New Man" of the Democratic Revolution, 1749-1822* (State College, Pennsylvania: The Pennsylvania State University Press), p. 13.

9. *Ibid.*, p. 46.

10. Judah Adelson, "The Vermont Democratic-Republican Societies and the French Revolution," Volume 32.

11. Walter Crockett, *History of Vermont Volume 2*, pp. 554-555.

12. Aleine Austin, *Matthew Lyon*, p. 91.
13. *Ibid.*, p. 91.
14. *Ibid.*, p. 92.
15. *Ibid.*, pp. 92-93.
16. Walter Crockett, *History of Vermont*, Volume 2, p. 556.
17. John C. Miller, *The Federalist Era 1789-1801* (New York: Harper and Row), pp. 208-209.
18. Austin, *Matthew Lyon*, p. 98.
19. *Ibid.*, p. 100.
20. James Morton Smith, *Freedoms Fetters* (Ithaca, New York: Cornell University Press), p. 222.
21. *Ibid.*, pp. 224-225.
22. *Ibid.*, p. 227.
23. *Ibid.*, p. 229.
24. *Ibid.*, p. 236.
25. *Ibid.*, pp. 235-237.
26. Austin, *Matthew Lyon*, p. 120.
27. *Ibid.*, p. 124.
28. Smith, *Freedoms Fetters*, pp. 239-240.
29. *Ibid.*.
30. *Ibid.*, p. 241.
31. Crockett, *History of Vermont*, p. 560.
32. *Ibid.*, p. 561.
33. Austin, *Matthew Lyon*, pp. 128-130. Austin wrote:

> "That Lyon cast the deciding vote for Jefferson hardly entitled him to this dubious credit for Jefferson's victory. He did, however, earn more valid credit for making a major contribution to the Republican victory of 1800. His imprisonment under the Sedition Act brought to national attention the extent to which the Federalists were stifling the right to dissent. Civil liberties became one of the major campaign issues of the election, and Lyon's resistance to suppression was vindicated when the electorate cast their votes in favor of the founding principles of Republicanism."

> "Lyon's role on the Vermont political scene ended in 1801, when he moved to Kentucky. He remained active in politics there and was elected again to the House from that state. But he apparently experienced a shift in his political thinking, for he drifted away from Jefferson and started voting with his old enemy Griswold and the Federalist Party. At one point he said of Jefferson: 'I made him and can unmake him.'"

34. *Governor and Council*, Volume 4, p. 527.

CHAPTER VI

The Embargo and the War of 1812

The Existing War—the Child of Prostitution. May no American Acknowledge it Legitimate.
A Federalist Toast during the War of 1812.

TRADE EMBARGO

ALTHOUGH THE FEDERALISTS REMAINED POWERFUL IN VERMONT, reaction to the Alien and Sedition Acts enabled the Jeffersonians to make gains in Vermont and the nation in the election of 1800. By 1807 the Jeffersonians had captured the governorship for the first time by electing Israel Smith, as well as a majority of the General Assembly, and had substantial representation in the United States House and Senate.

In his inaugural address Smith stressed the need for a state prison. He argued for confinement rather than corporal punishment and claimed that a prison could be a source of revenue. As a result of Smith's leadership, the first state prison was put in operation in 1809, in Windsor.

The Jeffersonians' success must have been due partly to their superb organization. Spooner's *Vermont Journal*, dated 1809, mentions a letter signed by a Federalist who explained the Jeffersonian plan for the next election. He alleged that instructions were distributed as follows:

There shall be a Grand Inspector on each side of the Green Mountains, who shall appoint a county committee in each coun-

Silhouette of Governor Israel Smith 1807-1808.

ty. Every county committee shall appoint a centre committee in each town in its county; and each centre committee shall divide its town into small districts, and in each district appoint a sub-committee, who shall make a true list of the names of all the freemen in such district, and against each man's name write his political character by noting him to be Federal, Democratic (Jeffersonian diminished), Doubtful, or Wavering, . . . [2]

The Jeffersonians' gains however, were nullified, by Jefferson's Embargo, halting trade with England. The fact the state shared a border with British Canada made Vermont more sensitive to the young nation's foreign policy decisions than many other states. When Jefferson called for an embargo on trade between the United States and Britain (and its colonies), many Vermonters were outraged. The young

Historical marker at Smuggler's Notch noting the significance of the pass through the mountains. (DCA)

state shipped a considerable amount of its products north to Canada, and received goods from the country. To have the trade cut off was an economic hardship. Many defied the ban, skirting marshals patroling the trade routes. Smuggler's Notch received its name in this period because the remote mountain gap was used as a pathway north. It was reported that in 1809, there were as many as 700 sleighs carrying oak and pork on the road from Middlebury to Mon-

Political cartoon from 1811 criticizing the embargo of trade with Great Britain and her colonies. The embargo is symbolized by a snapping turtle led by President Thomas Jefferson. A smuggler curses at the "Ograbme," or "embargo" spelled backwards.

treal.[3] Angry citizens transposed the letters of "embargo" to "o grab me" or "go bar em" as a way of denouncing the "dambargo."

Vermont's violations of the Embargo Act were so numerous that the United States customs collector in Vermont wrote to the Secretary of the Treasury that the law could not be enforced without military assistance. President Jefferson's response was to direct the collector to arm and equip vessels to prevent illegal trade. If this were not successful, the United States Marshal was authorized to raise a group of men "to aid in suppressing the insurrection or combination." Jefferson's orders enraged many Vermonters, "who resented imputations of treason." As a result of a town meeting, St. Albans wrote the president denying the charge of insurrection.[4] Vermont Federalists accused the Jefferson administration of supporting French radicalism.

As a result of the embargo, the Jeffersonians paid a heavy political price in the 1808 elections. The Federalists captured

The first State House at Montpelier, built in 1806-1807. A granite building replaced this wooden structure in 1836. The land was given by Colonel Jabot Davis, Montpelier's first settler. Montpelier citizens pledged $8,000 for the building that cost $10,000. [Montpelier was centrally located and was "neutral ground" between Vermont's towns located on the east and west side of the state for the honor of being the capital.]

three out of the state's four congressional seats, and Isaac Tichenor recaptured the governorship.

Governor Tichenor's Inaugural Address declared that "we sincerely regret that the law [Embargo] was not accompanied with that evidence of national necessity or utility which . . . would have commanded obedience and respect."[5] The Jeffersonians with a majority of sixteen in the General Assembly replied that the Embargo "was the only practicable measure that could have averted the dangers and horrors of war."[6]

The General Assembly remained in Jeffersonian control, however, and that opposition dogged Tichenor's entire administration. When he suggested that compassion be accorded the smugglers, he was charged with "dereliction of duty." The Jeffersonians parlayed this charge into treason and

*Jonas Galusha. Early Jeffersonian
Governor who helped his party
wrest control from the Federalists.*

used it effectively in the election of 1809, which Tichenor
lost to the Jeffersonian candidate, Jonas Galusha. Interestingly, Galusha, like the hot-headed Matthew Lyon, had married a daughter of Thomas Chittenden, the state's first governor. Galusha won four successive one-year terms to the
governorship, and the Jeffersonians retained control over
the one-house General Assembly.

In 1810 Federalists in New England had formed pro-British
organizations called Washington Benevolent Societies, which
favored trading with England. Brookfield, Royalton and
Williamstown were centers of Washingtonian Societies.
Finanical supporters of these societies included Federalists
Nathaniel Chipman and Isaac Tichenor. The Jeffersonians
charged these societies were advocating treason, and one
Jeffersonian newspaper called for a "committee of public safety" to deal with "traitors parading for their Malignancy."[7]

In his Farewell Address in 1797, President Washington had
urged a policy of neutrality for the young nation. The *Montpelier Watchman* in June of 1812 asked its readers to support
all Federalist candidates to show that the "political character
of Vermont is really WASHINGTONIAN."

The pro-French Jeffersonian societies that had been encouraged by Matthew Lyon in the 1790s, continued their pro-
French activity and supported a war against Great Britain.

The competition between the two parties was even

An act altering the name of the county of Jefferson and for other purposes.

SEC. 1. *It is hereby enacted by the General Assembly of the State of Vermont,* That the name of the county of Jefferson be, and hereby is altered to that of Washington, and the said county shall hereafter be called and styled the county of Washington, instead of the county of Jefferson, with all the rights, immunities and powers, given to it by the name of the county of Jefferson, and be and remain under the same liabilities.

SEC. 2. *It is hereby further enacted,* that all records, judgments, processes and proceedings, of whatever name or nature, existing or pending in said county, by the style and in the name of Jefferson county, or which may be had or commenced in and by that name, before the first Monday of December next, shall have the same effect and validity, and all officers of said county, shall exercise their respective offices, in the same manner, as though the name of said county had not been altered ; and all commissions to all officers,

appointed within and for said county, commencing their duties on the first day of December next, shall describe them respectively as officers of the county of Washington, late the county of Jefferson.

SEC. 3. *And it is hereby further enacted,* that the probate district of Jefferson, shall hereafter be called and styled the district of Washington, instead of the district of Jefferson ; and the Judge of probate appointed within and for said district, whose duties will commence on the first Monday of December next, shall be commissioned as Judge of probate for the district of Washington, late the district of Jefferson.

SEC. 4. *And it is hereby further enacted,* that the county grammar school in said county, now called Jefferson county grammar school, shall hereafter be called and styled Washington county grammar school, instead of Jefferson county grammar school.

Passed Nov. 8, 1814.

An act changing Jefferson County to Washington County.

reflected in place names. In 1810, the General Assembly created a new county in central Vermont, and the legislators from the towns comprising the county asked that it be named Washington. But the Assembly was controlled by the Jeffersonians, who voted 101-90 to call the county Jefferson. In 1814, a Federalist-controlled General Assembly renamed the county Washington.[8]

THE WINDS OF WAR

The Jeffersonian and Federalist parties pumped the war issue for all its worth, with the Jeffersonians using an offensive posture to cow the Federalists. Vermont Supreme Court Justice Royall Tyler—jurist, playwright, poet and novelist, and a Federalist-turned-Jeffersonian—wrote to Jeffersonian Congressman James Fisk of Barre that a declaration of war was the only way confidence could be restored in the national government:" it will derange their present plans which are calculated only for political campaigns . . . above all it will place the [Federalist] opposition on slippery ground, and drive them into rebellion."[9]

Tyler's letter illustrates the way the Jeffersonians, or at least a faction of the Jeffersonians, used the war as a political weapon against the Federalists.

Royall Tyler, Vermont jurist and writer. He left the Federalists for the Jeffersonians and saw war as a political weapon.

Scene from the first American play, "The Contrast" by Royall Tyler, a Chief Justice of the Vermont Supreme Court. (NL)

Martin Chittenden, Federalist Governor who tried to recall Vermont militia during War of 1812. (UVM)

ANTI-WAR EFFORTS

In Vermont, Federalist Congressman Martin Chittenden, the son of Vermont's first governor, led the fight against the War of 1812. Of the four member Vermont congressional delegation, he alone voted against the war declaration. Chittenden argued the war had come about because Madison's pro-French party had caused commercial difficulties with the British. He criticized the Jeffersonians for their commitment to territorial expansion and charged the "war hawks" had blackmailed Madison.

Even U.S. Senator Stephen Bradley, a Jeffersonian sympathizer, had doubts about the wisdom of the war. In a speech several weeks before, he had said: "If we are going to war to redress grievances, to revenge injuries received,

A MONSTER.

FRIGHTFUL AS TEN FURIES!!

TERRIBLE AS HELL!

The following is copied from the JOURNAL kept by Mr. Jacob M. Berriman, during his tour to the Westward of Fort Recovery.

May 27, 1794. THIS morning about an hour after sunrise as we proceeded on our rout about a mile west from the place where we had lodged the preceding night, we were alarmed by a terrible barking of our dogs a-head, & all eagerly pushed forward to take possession of the game thus pointed out by our faithful dogs. About a quarter of a mile a-head we discovered the most terrible Monster which human eyes ever beheld, to which our dogs dare not approach ; but only stood barking at a considerable distance. At the sight of so monstrous a creature, every hair on our heads seemed to stand on end with fear : Though we had no reason to apprehend ourselves in danger, for he was busily employed in destroying a large Panter, which seemed as incapable of resistance, as a common squirrel would have been in competition with one our dogs.

We halted, and placed ourselves to the best advantage in order to view his manner of dispatching the Panter, which he did by winding his tail around him and drawing to such a degree as to crush and break his bones, which we could frequently hear sounding like the snapping of a whip, accompanied by the most hideous howls of the agonizing animal. A consultation was next held in order to choose the most effectual method of attacking so formidable an enemy. It was finally determined, that one of the company should go back to the house and procure a horse, on which one of us, being mounted and armed with a musket, should approach within a convenient distance and giving him a well-aimed shot, should retreat precipitately in case he was attacked.— Accordingly the person appointed, proceeded back to the house, and in less than an hour returned mounted on a horse well calculated for the purpose. It was then concluded to suspend our attack till he should have devoured his game ; which he did in the following manner :—After having broken all his bones, he licked him with his mouth till he appeared all over wet and slippery, and then swallowed him without much difficulty. The large animal which he had now gorged appeared to have greatly abated the agility of his motion, which we thought a circumstance much in our favor ;— but on the other hand, we were not without great apprehen-

sions of his scales being so hard that a ball could not penetrate them—However, having mounted the horse myself, I attacked him in the manner above described, and, after giving him three shots, he was so far disabled that we all approached with long gads, and dispatched him without much further difficulty. It was not till about two o'clock in the afternoon, that we accomplished a part of our business so satisfactory, both to our fears and curiosity—. We had now an opportunity to view him leisurely, and such a mixture of horror and beauty, I believe was never before seen blended in one object. After we had drawn him out straight, we proceeded to measure his dimensions, which we did exactly, and found him to be no less than 36 feet 2 inches in length and the largest part of his body to be 5 feet 1 inch in diameter—His eyes were indiscribably large and piercing—His head was of a most beautiful changeable green, towards the top inclining to a yellow, but darker towards his neck and round his jaws—Upon the top of his head was a large oval black spot—His neck was incircled with three rows of spots of the most beautiful crimson—His back, from his neck nearly to the end of his tail was covered with scales of the most beautiful green I ever beheld, on each side was a row of large black scales, between two small red stripes. His belly was perfectly white along the middle, but bearing upon a yellow towards each side. The next part of our business was to determine upon the best manner to dispose of the skin, which we looked upon as a most valuable part of our game.

As the day was so far spent that we could not complete the skinning of it before dark, and as we could not possibly carry it away whole, we concluded to leave it until morning. Accordingly we went back to the abovementioned hut, and in the morning returned with knives, and in about three hours we completed the business to our satisfaction. The skin we carefully washed and stuffed it with hay until it was dry, when we opened and rolled it up for the convenience of carrying.

☞ As many persons, perhaps, will doubt the truth of the above account, they may satisfy themselves by calling at Mr. PEAL's Museum in Philadelphia, where the Skin was presented.

PRINTED AND SOLD AT WINDSOR—(VT.)
1812.

Anti-war, anti-British cartoon. (VHS)

we should choose our own time. It would be a great error to put this country, by a forced vote of Congress into war. You cannot lead this country to war as a butcher leads his flock to the slaughter house. This is a government of opinion; the public sentiment will not be driven, but it must be followed." On the roll call for a war declaration, he did not vote.[10]

In February 1812 Madison's supporters called for a war demonstration at the statehouse in Montpelier. The hall of the General Assembly was nearly filled to capacity. At first, the meeting was controlled by Federalists who voiced opposition to the war. In time, however, enough Madison supporters came and passed war resolutions.[11]

The Anti-War Movement, however, remained vital, the town of Poultney refused to pay soldiers who had enlisted for the war. Rockingham did not assist in the enlistment of soldiers, and anti-war groups in Bennington impeded the assembling of troops.[12]

Although many in his party were pushing for war, President James Madison was perceived by some of the nation's rising young leaders as too timid to deal with the embargo and the violation of American rights at sea. The nation's leadership gradually slipped from the republic's first statesman to another generation of ambitious politicians. Henry Clay was among these younger Jeffersonians, leading a group of "war hawks." Clay preferred "the troubled oceans of war to the putrescent pool of ignominious peace." The Federalists referred to them as "young politicians, half hatched, the shell still on their heads."[13]

It was this group that pressured a reluctant Madison into declaring war. Madison was told that his nomination in 1812 for a second term depended upon "screwing up his courage to a declaration of war." Party interest and national pride drove the young nation into challenging the most powerful country in the world, for the second time in forty years.

But when war was finally declared, it did not go well for the Americans. Within a year enough Vermonters seemed dissatisfied with the Jeffersonians' policies that Martin Chittenden, Thomas Chittenden's son, challenged Galusha.

Galusha received slightly more votes than Chittenden (16,828 to 16,532), but since it wasn't a majority of the votes cast the election was thrown into the General Assembly. The Federalists had regained control of that body and elected Chittenden on a razor-thin 112-111 vote. [14] In his Inaugural Address Chittenden declared:

> The war in which we are engaged, would require the united wisdom and energy of the nation to sustain. It was declared under circumstances which forcibly induced a great proportion of the people to consider it at least doubtful, as to its necessity, expedience, or justice . . . The conquest of the Canadas, of which so much has been said, if desirable under any circumstances, must be considered a poor compensation for the sacrifices which are, and must be made.[15]

Chittenden said that he had always considered the Vermont militia "adapted and exclusively assigned for the service and the protection of the states," and that it was a misinterpretation of the Constitution to suggest that "by any kind of magic" the militia could be transformed into a "regular army for the purpose of foreign conquest."[16]

On November 10, 1813, Chittenden issued a proclamation ordering home the third brigade of the Vermont militia stationed in Plattsburgh, New York. Chittenden claimed that "an extensive section of our own frontier is left unprotected" and that Vermonters were "exposed to the retaliatory incursions and ravages of an exasperated enemy." He vowed, "The military strength and the resources of this State must be reserved for its own defense and protection . . . except in cases provided for by the Constitution of the United States."[17]

The third brigade refused to obey their governor. They answered forcefully that "An invitation or order to desert the standard of our country will never be obeyed by us." The militia regarded the Proclamation "with mingled emotions of pity and contempt for its author, and as a striking monument of his folly."[18]

Vermont's gubernatorial election of 1814 was a rematch between Chittenden and Galusha. This time Chittenden gained a plurality at the polls, by 55 votes, but the lack of a majority again threw the election into the General

BY HIS EXCELLENCY

MARTIN CHITTENDEN, Esquire,

GOVERNOR, CAPTAIN-GENERAL, AND COMMANDER IN CHIEF, IN AND OVER THE STATE OF VERMONT,

A PROCLAMATION:

Whereas, it appears, that the Third Brigade of the Third Division of the Militia of this State, has been ordered from our frontiers to the defence of a neighbouring State :—And, whereas it further appears, to the extreme regret of the Captain General, that a part of the Militia of said Brigade have been placed under the command, and at the disposal, of an Officer of the United States, out of the jurisdiction or control of the Executive of this State, and have been actually marched to the defence of a sister State, fully competent to all the purposes of self defence, whereby an extensive section of our own Frontier is left, in a measure, unprotected, and the peaceable, good citizens thereof are put in great jeopardy, and exposed to the retaliatory incursions and ravages of an exasperated enemy :—And, whereas, disturbances, of a very serious nature, are believed to exist, in consequence of a portion of the Militia having been thus ordered out of the State :—

Therefore....to the end, that these great evils may be provided against, and, as far as may be, prevented for the future :—

Be it Known....that such portion of the Militia of said Third Brigade, in said Third Division, as may now be doing duty, in the State of New york, or else-where, beyond the limits of this State, both Officers and men, are hereby ordered and directed, by the Captain General and Commander in Chief of the Militia of the State of Vermont, forthwith to return to the respective places of their usual residence, within the territorial limits of said Brigade, and there to hold themselves in constant readiness to act, in obedience to the Orders of Brigadier General JACOB DAVIS, who is appointed, by the Legislature of this State, to the command of said Brigade.

And the said Brigadier General DAVIS, is hereby ordered and directed, forthwith, to see, that the Militia of his said Brigade be completely armed and equipped, as the Law directs, and holden in constant readiness to march on the shortest notice, to the defence of the Frontiers; and, in case of actual invasion, without further Orders, to march with his said Brigade, to act, either in co-operation with the Troops of the United States, or separately, as circumstances may require, in repelling the enemy from our territory, and in protecting the good citizens of this State from their ravages or hostile incursions.

And in case of an event, so seriously to be deprecated, it is hoped and expected, that every citizen, without distinction of party, will fly at once to the nearest post of danger, and that the only rallying word will be—" OUR COUNTRY."

Feeling, as the Captain General does, the weight of responsibility, which rests upon him, with regard to the Constitutional duties of the Militia, and the sacred rights of our citizens to protection from this great class of community, so essentially necessary in all free countries; at a moment too, when they are so imminently exposed to the dangers of hostile incursions, and domestic difficulties, he cannot conscientiously discharge the trust reposed in him by the voice of his fellow citizens, and by the Constitution of this and the United States, without an unequivocal declaration, that, in his opinion, the Military strength and resources of this State, must be reserved for its own defence and protection, *exclusively*—excepting in cases provided for, by the Constitution of the United States; and then, under orders derived *only* from the Commander in Chief.

Given under my hand at Montpelier, this 10th day of November, in the year of our Lord One Thousand Eight Hundred and Thirteen; and of the Independence of the United States, the thirty eighth.

MARTIN CHITTENDEN,

BY HIS EXCELLENCY'S COMMAND,

SAMUEL SWIFT, *Secretary.*

Proclamation by Governor Martin Chittenden recalling the Vermont militia from Plattsburgh. (VHS)

Assembly. The Legislature, still Federalist, returned him to the governorship by twenty-nine votes.

In 1812, the Jeffersonians had amended the congressional district law of Vermont to provide for state-wide election of congressmen. They had hoped this would result in the election of more Jeffersonian congressmen. Instead, six Federalist congressmen were elected in 1814, and Isaac Tichenor was elected to the Senate by the Federalist-dominated Assembly. The result was a sharp repudiation of President Madison's war policy. Adding insult to injury, the Assembly removed Chief Justice Tyler and replaced him with his old political enemy, former Senator Nathaniel Chipman.[20]

In 1814, Governor Chittenden transmitted to the Vermont General Assembly an invitation by the Massachusetts Legislature to send delegates to a convention of New England States to be held at Hartford, Connecticut. The purpose of the convention was to:

> deliberate upon the dangers to which the eastern section of the Union is exposed by the course of war, and which there is too much reason to believe will thicken round them in its progress, and to devise, *if practicable,* means of security and defense which may be consistent with the preservation of their resources from total ruin, and adapted to their local situation, mutual relations and habits, and NOT REPUGNANT TO THEIR OBLIGATIONS AS MEMBERS OF THE UNION.[21]

The Massachusetts Federalists wanted to develop a New England regional policy relating to the defense of the region, preserve their power against growing western power and end the war.

Despite the disclaimer of any intent by the New England states to leave the Union, the Hartford Convention was seen as the first step in secession. It was a political move the North would regret, particularly when southern secessionists pointed to it in later years as justification for separating from the Union.

Vermont declined to participate officially in the convention. Nathaniel Chipman strongly opposed the state's participation. He felt that Vermont Federalists should not discuss common problems with "potential separatists." Chipman

THE BATTLE OF PLATTSBURGH.

From an old print.   Reproduced by permission of Col. C. S. Forbes, Editor of " The Vermonter."

(UVM)

REPUBLICAN TICKET

FOR STATE OFFICERS AND MEMBERS OF CONGRI ..

FOR GOVERNOR—HIS EXCELLENCY,

JONAS GALUSHA.

FOR LIEUT. GOVERNOR—HIS HONOR,

PAUL BRIGHAM.

FOR TREASURER,

BENJAMIN SWAN, ESQ.

FOR COUNCILLORS,

HON. DAVID FAY, *Bennington County.*
THEOPHILUS CRAWFOD, *Windsor Co.*
PLINY SMITH,   ⎰ *Rutland Co.*
THOMAS HAMMOD, ⎱
AARON LELAND, *Windsor Co.*
HORATIO SEYMOUR, *Addison Co.*
DANIEL PEASLEE, *Orange Co.*
TRUMAN CHITTENDEN, *Chittenden Co.*
EZRA BUTLER, *Washington Co.*
WILLIAM CAHOON, *Caledonia Co.*
FREDERICK BLISS, *Franklin Co.*
TIMOTHY STANLEY, *Orleans Co.*

FOR MEMBERS OF CONGRESS,

SAMUEL C. CRAFTS,   CHARLES RICH,
EZRA MEECH,   MARK RICHARDS,
WILLIAM STRONG,   ORSAMUS C. MERRILL.

*Jeffersonian Republican Ticket in 1817. Vermont
had six Congressmen at this time.*

was opposed to measures that he thought were "a violation of constitutional principles, or as establishing a precedent which might prove injurious to government." The General Assembly, although Federalist, rejected the invitation to send voting members.[22]

THE FEDERALISTS CRUSHED

Successes in the war proved the salvation of the Jeffersonians and the ruin of the Federalists. Although the War of 1812 is generally seen as a military draw between the United States and Britain, American forces defeated the British at Plattsburgh, New York, and later New Orleans, Louisiana. These victories silenced opposition to the war. The basic policy of the Federalists at the time was opposition to the war, and when the war "turned the corner in favor of the Americans," the Federalists were left with no political platform. The fact the British invaded United States territory and burned Washington, D.C. greatly angered Americans. Many Vermonters volunteered to defend their country, especially during the Plattsburgh battle.

The war ended in 1815 with what Americans felt was a political victory. The British, having defeated the French on the European Continent, no longer felt the need to harass the Americans for being friendly to their former allies. The young nation seemed safe from foreign interference, and the way was paved for the country to move west.

As time went on, Americans began to forget about the opposition of the New England Federalists to the war. As the war became a memory, so did the Federalist party. As for the Jeffersonians, they prospered and ushered in the so-called "Era Of Good Feeling," as the nation returned briefly to consensus rule.

In Vermont, Galusha was returned to the governorship in 1815 and subsequently won four more terms. The General Assembly became Jeffersonian and Vermont cast its vote for James Monroe, the party's candidate for president, in 1816. In 1817 Vermont Federalists breathed their last gasp when they ran former Governor and United States Senator Isaac Tichenor against Galusha. Galusha won easily by a 2-1 margin. It was the death knell for the party.

COMMODORE MACDONOUGH'S VICTORY.

FREEMEN, raise a joyous strain!
  Aloft the Eagle towers,
"We've met the enemy" again—
Again have made them 'ours!'

Champlain the cannon's thundering
  voice,
Proclaims thy waters free;
High arching from the rocket's blaze,
And echo—*Victory!*

The striped flag upon the wave,
  Triumphantly appears,
And its unruffled landsmen, brave,
A flag of poomiie bears.

Now to the world Fame's trumpet sounds
  The deed with new applause,
While from a *Conquer'd Fleet* refounds
Our seamen's loud huzzas.

Britannia, round thy haggard brows
  Bind bitter wormwood still!
For lo! again thy standard bows
To valiant Yankee skill.

But, O! what chaplet can be found
  MACDONOUGH's brows to grace?
'Tis done! the deathless wreath is bound,
Which time can ne'er efface.

And still a just—a rich reward,
  His country has to give,
He shall be first in her regard,
  And with her PERRY live!

Columbia! though thy cannon's roar
  On inland seas prevail,
And there alone—while round each shore
  Outnumbering ships afsail.

Yet deed with deed, and name with name
  Thy gallant fons shall blend,
Till the bright arch of lasting fame,
  O'er the broad ocean bend!

Not a Cent for Tribute."----"*We have met the enemy, and they are ours.*"

CAPT. DOWNIE.

GEN. MACOMB.

GOV. PREVOST.

GENIUS of AMERICA in Combat with OLD JONNY BULL.

[COPY-RIGHT.]

We won't give up the Soil.----Free trade, Sailor's rights, and no impressment.

PEACE!

Treaty of PEACE signed & arrived!

CENTINEL-OFFICE, Feb. 13, 8 *o'cloch in the morning.*

WE have this instant received in Thirty-two hours from N. York, the following

Great and Happy News!

To BENJAMIN RUSSELL, Esq. Centinel-Office, Boston,
New-York, Feb. 11, 1815.—*Saturday Evening,* 10 *o'clock.*

SIR—

I HASTEN to acquaint you, for the information of the Public, of the arrival here this afternoon of H. Br. Majesty's Sloop of War FAVORITE, in which has come passenger Mr. CARROLL, American Messenger, having in his possession a

TREATY OF PEACE

Between this Country and Great-Britain, signed on the 26th December last.

Mr. BAKER also is on board, as Agent for the British Government, the same who was formerly Charge de Affairs here.

Mr. Carroll reached town at eight o'clock this evening. He shewed to a friend of mine who is acquainted with him, the pacquet containing the Treaty, and a London Newspaper of the last date of December, announcing the signing of the *Treaty.*

It depends, however, as my friend observed, upon the act of the President to suspend hostilities on this side.

The gentlemen left London the 2d Jan. The *Transit* had sailed previously from a port on the Continent.

This city is in a perfect uproar of joy, shouts, illuminations, &c. &c.

I have undertaken to send you this by Express—the rider engaging to deliver it by *Eight* o'clock on Monday morning. The expense will be 225 dollars—If you can collect so much to in lemnify me I will thank you so to do

I am with respect, Sir, your obedient servant,

JONATHAN GOODHUE.

Printed at the Portsmouth Oracle-Office.

NOTES

1. *Governor and Council*, Volume 5, p. 394.
2. L. Samuel Miller, *The Vermont Democratic Party and the Development of Intra-Party Responsibility* (unpublished master's thesis, University of Vermont, Burlington), pp. 10-11.
3. Nicholas Muller, "Smuggling into Canada: How the Champlain Valley Defied Jefferson's Embargo," *Vermont History*, Volume 38, No. 1 (Winter, 1970), pp. 5-12.

    Muller wrote: "Throughout February and March 1809 towns on both sides of Lake Champlain – Burlington, Williston, St. Albans, Monkton, Plattsburgh, Bakersfield and Fairfield – held meetings that declared 'the late act to enforce the Embargo 'to be' in its nature odious and oppressive.' The meetings issued many unabashedly treasonable statements, but some of the intemperance was politically inspired, as the embargo policy had become a main issue of contention between Federalists and Republicans. The Enforcement Act of 1890 permitted 'federal officials to seize without warrant any goods thought to be intended for foreign destination.'"
4. *Governor and Council*, Volume 5, p. 474.
5. *Ibid.*, p. 397.
6. *Ibid.*, p. 399.
7. Edward Brynn, "Patterns of Dissent: Vermont's Opposition to the War of 1812", *Vermont History*, Volume 40, No. 1, (Winter, 1972), pp. 1-9.

    Brynn concluded: "... four of ten Vermonters were decidedly opposed to the embargo by 1810, and perhaps five to six of ten to the war by 1814. This represents considerable alienation, and our perspective suggests some reasons why this was so. Probably economic factors were most important; because its economy was young, reserves of capital few, and risky business adventures and a gambling psychology still widespread, the embargo proved particularly devastating. Beyond this, Vermont's orientation was still northward, and only the canal-building era would alter that. Montreal was near; New York City was distant. The nation's honor was important, but heroic sacrifice required a close identification with the national interest, and in two decades of statehood this had not yet been forged. Finally, there was a real fear of France and its revolutionary tendencies. Vermont was rapidly divesting itself of frontier characteristics. Vermont's population explosion was over; an exodus of young people would soon be reflected in the decline of dynamism. Challenging Britain over complex maritime rights was no substitute for economic stability and a peaceful border. Only a question of deeper moral consequence, slavery, would challenge Vermonters' deepest emotions."
8. Crockett, *History of Vermont*, Volume 3, pp. 33-34.
9. Roger H. Brown, "A Vermont Republican Urges War: Royall Tyler, 1812 and the Safety of the Republican Government," *Vermont History*, Volume 36 (1968), pp. 13-18.

10. Crockett, *History of Vermont*, p. 39.
11. *Ibid.*, p. 40.
12. *Ibid.*, p. 54.
13. Butterfield, *The American Past*, pp. 52-53.
14. Crockett, *History of Vermont*, p. 71.
15. *Governor and Council*, Volume 6, p. 421.
16. *Ibid.*, p. 420.
17. *Ibid.*, p. 492.
18. *Ibid.*, p. 493.
19. Crockett, *History of Vermont*, pp. 115-116.
20. *Ibid.*, p. 116.
21. Theodore Dwight, *History of the Hartford Convention* (New York: N. & J. White, 1833), p. 343. See also Harold R. Burroughs, *The Hartford Convention of 1814: The Reasons Behind Vermont's Independent Stand* (Middlebury College, 1980 unpublished thesis), p. 26.
22. *Governor and Council*, Volume 6, p. 462.

"King Andrew Jackson the First" is shown obstructing the will of the people by the use of the presidential veto and trampling on the United States Constitution.

CHAPTER VII

Abolition and the Rise of the Republican Party

T HE FEDERALISTS HAD BEEN TORN APART and eventually destroyed by the politics of the War of 1812. The Jeffersonians capitalized on the British bullying of the young republic and used the war as a political tool against the Federalists. This strategy proved effective, and because the Federalists had few positions other than opposing war with Great Britain, the Federalists collapsed as the United States scored military successes against the British.

The country returned to a one-party system, and for about fifteen years the Democratic-Republicans, the party of Thomas Jefferson, ruled Washington and Vermont. But just as the Federalists had fallen prey to the single issue of the War of 1812, the Jeffersonians—who eventually splintered into the Whigs and Jacksonian Democrats following the 1824 election—fell prey to the slavery issue. The reluctance of the Jeffersonians and their successors, and of several other parties that developed during the era, to oppose unequivocally the extension of slavery in the United States, led to the formation of the Republican party.

The parties that existed before the Civil War attempted to maintain their national coalitions by making concessions to the slave interests. This made them lose credibility in the eyes of a majority of Vermonters who were predominantly anti-slavery. By maintaining an uncompromising stand against the expansion of slavery, the Republicans—who appeared on the political scene in the 1850s, shortly before the

John Quincy Adams   *Andrew Jackson*

Civil War—attracted Vermonters of all previous political per-
suasions. Although the slavery issue was not the sole reason
for Vermont Republican successes, it was an overriding issue.

Vermonters rallied to the anti-slavery cry, and it was no
wonder the Republicans did so well. Vermont's Constitution of 1777 was the first to forbid slavery. In 1786 the Vermont General Assembly had announced that "the idea of
slavery is totally exploded from our free government." The
Vermont judiciary never recognized slavery. In a well-known
case, a plaintiff sought recovery of a fugitive slave from New
York state. A Vermont Supreme Court judge refused to grant
relief without evidence of ownership. Such evidence, he
wrote, would be nothing less than a "bill of sale from God
almighty."[1]

In 1818 the Vermont General Assembly opposed the admission of Missouri as a slave state. A legislative report said
"the right to introduce and establish slavery in a free government does not exist."

Shortly thereafter the Assembly passed the following
resolution which said in part:

> That in the opinion of this Legislature, slavery or involuntary
> servitude, in any of the United States, is a moral and political

evil, . . . That Congress has a right to inhibit any further introduction, or extension of slavery, as one of the conditions upon which any new State shall be admitted into the Union.

That the Senators from this State in the Congress of the United States be instructed, and the Representatives requested, to exert their influence and use all legal measures to prevent the admission of Missouri as a State into the Union of the United States with those anti-republican features and powers in their Constitution.[2]

During the Missouri debate the Vermont Colonization Society was founded in the State House in Montpelier. The basic purpose of the Society was to raise money to send free Blacks to Africa. Many members of the General Assembly were present at the meeting including Governor Galusha. On the next day Galusha issued a proclamation for a fast and prayed that "Almighty God" would put down all tyranny and oppression, and open a way for the emancipation of all that degraded class of human beings, who are held in slavery, especially those in this highly favored country."[3]

ANNUAL MEETING

of the

Vermont
Colonization Society,

At the BRICK CHURCH,

THIS (Thursday) EVENING, at 6 1-2 o'clock.

Oct. 17, 1850.

(UVM)

THE WHIG PARTY

On the national level; the "Era of Good Feeling" came to a close with the election of 1824. Four men ran for president that year—John Quincy Adams, Henry Clay, Andrew Jackson and William Crawford—and none gained a majority. The election was thrown into the House of Representatives, and Adams with Vermont Congressional support won.

Jackson, stung by defeat, started running almost immediately for the 1828 election, which he won. Jackson believed he spoke for the "little man," the man with a farm who was looking west. His followers were known as Jacksonian Democrats. Many historians believe that this was the beginning of the Democratic Party.

While Jackson won the presidency in 1828, he failed to carry a single Vermont county. The supporters of Adams felt that this was a true reflection of Vermont political character: "The results are worthy of the character of the Green Mountain Boys', and the consciousness of having done their duty to themselves and their country . . ."[4] During this period the Vermont General Assembly rejected a Constitutional Amendment which would have limited the presidency to one six year-term.[5]

Adams was supported by the more business-minded interests of the country. His following termed themselves National Republicans. They later became known as Whigs.

The Whigs opposed President Andrew Jackson, whom they tagged "King Andrew the First." The Whigs were an "organized incompatability," including northerners who wanted a high tariff, southerners who wanted a low tariff, small northern farmers and wealthy southern planters. In Vermont the Whigs appeared to include former Federalists, anti-Jacksonians and National Republicans who wanted internal improvements such as canals.

In Vermont, the heirs of the Jeffersonian Republican-Democratic Party won the governorship and legislature during most of the 1820s. In 1828, however, Samuel Crafts, the National Republican candidate, won the gubernatorial race. In 1831 an Anti-Mason, William Palmer from Danville, won.

*Governor Richard Skinner
1820-1823.*

*Governor Cornelius P. Van Ness
1823-1826.*

*Governor Samuel C. Crafts
1828-1831. (UVM)*

*Governor William Palmer,
Vermont's anti-Masonic governor.
Served from 1831-1835. (UVM)*

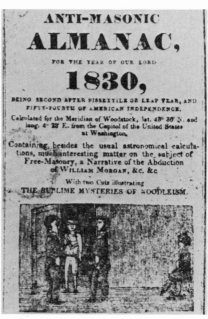

(UVM)   (VSL)

The Anti-Masons were a single-issue party; they worried that the secrecy of the Masonic order was a threat to the democratic process. Their strength in Vermont was great. Palmer won election four times, and in the national election of 1832 Vermont was the only state that voted for the Anti-Masonic candidate for president, William Wirt.[6]

The Anti-Masonic movement was short-lived. By 1836 it had lost its momentum. Most of its adherents, led by William Slade, who would later become governor and congressman, joined the Whigs.

Vermont politics were unstable at this time, and as often as not no candidate for governor was able to gain a statewide majority. The ultimate in political instability was reached in 1835 when no candidate for governor was able to gain a majority. The unicameral General Assembly was incapable after three days of wrangling and thirty-five ballots to choose a governor. As a last resort it was decided that Lieutenant Governor Silas Jenison should be elevated to governor.[7] This debacle was an important factor in the adoption of a con-

For Congress,
JOHN MATTOCKS.

For Governor,
SILAS H. JENISON.

For Lt. Governor,
DAVID M. CAMP.

For Treasurer,
HENRY F. JANES.

For Senator,
JACOB BATES.

Joseph Smith, born in Sharon, was the founder of the Mormon Church.

Ballots in the 1830's and 1840's. (SS)

Vermont's second State House included a Senate Chamber.

Silas Jenison, first native Vermonter elected Governor. (UVM)

SPEECH

OF

HON. DANIEL CHIPMAN,

DELIVERED IN THE

CONVENTION HOLDEN AT MONTPELIER,

ON THE SIXTH OF JANUARY 1836.

WHILE IN COMMITTEE OF THE WHOLE ON THE PROPOSED ARTICLES OF AMENDMENT
TO THE CONSTITUTION, CONSTITUTING A SENATE.

———

VERMONT— *" With all thy faults I love thee still."*—Goldsmith.

MIDDLEBURY:
PRINTED BY E. R. JEWETT,

....

1837.

Title page of Daniel Chipman's speech supporting the creation of a Vermont Senate. (VSL)

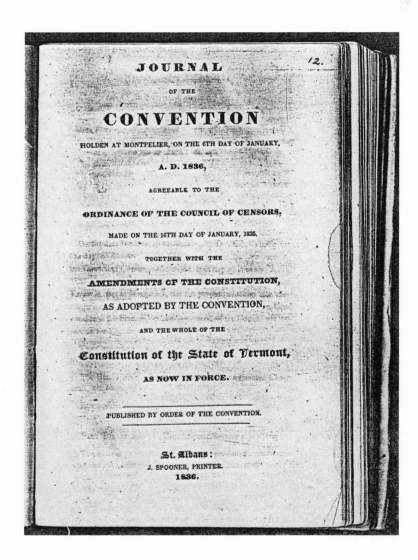

JOURNAL

OF THE

CONVENTION

HOLDEN AT MONTPELIER, ON THE 6TH DAY OF JANUARY,

A. D. 1836,

AGREEABLE TO THE

ORDINANCE OF THE COUNCIL OF CENSORS,

MADE ON THE 16TH DAY OF JANUARY, 1835,

TOGETHER WITH THE

AMENDMENTS OF THE CONSTITUTION,

AS ADOPTED BY THE CONVENTION,

AND THE WHOLE OF THE

Constitution of the State of Vermont,

AS NOW IN FORCE.

PUBLISHED BY ORDER OF THE CONVENTION.

St. Albans:
J. SPOONER, PRINTER.
1836.

stitutional amendment that abolished the Governor's Council and created the Vermont State Senate in 1836. A greater equality of representation based upon population and the fact that the Council was being ignored by the Assembly were other factors contributing to the change.

ANTI-SLAVERY SENTIMENT

The Whigs occupied the statehouse for almost twenty years beginning with Silas Jenison in 1835, with the Democrats winning only one election, in 1853. In addition to the Whigs, Democrats and Anti-Masons, a splinter party had come upon the Vermont political scene. The Liberty party grew out of the organized anti-slavery movement in the state, which had begun with the founding in Middlebury of an Anti-Slavery Society in 1834.

The society, in its first annual report, declared, "We therefore proclaim war with slavery, our weapon is truth— our basis, justice—our incentive, humanity—our force, moral power—our watchword, onward—our hope of success, in God." Abolitionist speakers were met with resistance, in some cases. In 1835 anti-slavery lectures by Samuel May were broken up in Montpelier and Rutland.[8]

Quaker woman protects Reverend Samuel J. May at an anti-slavery meeting in Montpelier in 1835. (NL)

FREEMAN EXTRA.

COME UP TO FREEDOMS' GATHERINGS.

COUNTY

LIBERTY

CONVENTIONS,

Will be holden at

WATERBURY, TUESDAY,	October 27 1846, commencing precisely at 10 o'clock, A. M.			
DANVILLE, THURSDAY,	do	29,	do	do
LYNDON CENTRE, FRIDAY,	do	30,	do	do
BARTON, SATURDAY,	do	31,	do	do
CAMBRIDGE (Jeffersonville,) Tuesday, November 3,			do	do
MORRISTOWN, Wednesday,		do	4, do	do
CALAIS, Friday,		do	6, do	do

Which conventions will be addressed by

A. Judson Rowell, Esq.

(Of Troy—Liberty candidate for Representative to Congress,)

And also by the ## Hon. JACOB SCOTT - of Barre -

And other able advocates of the Liberty Cause.

FREEMEN of the Fourth District! the time has come for ACTION—vigorous, determined, successful action. The time for words has passed—DEEDS will alone suffice! If our beloved country is ever to be rescued from the dominion of the Slave-Power, now is the time to begin. Our countrymen are in chains! In the nation's capital they are articles of merchandise! In the councils of this nation, which our Fathers shed their blood to make Free, slave-holding tyrants bear sway; the President is the owner of 100 MEN and WOMEN! The Senate has a majority of similar tyrants! All but one of our full ministers abroad are robbers of the poor—oppressors of the 'hireling in his wages!' Every department of the government is managed by slaveholders—and as might be expected, tyranny and oppression thrive under it, while freedom languishes, and seems about to give up the ghost.

Now, in view of these undeniable facts, will not the freemen of the several counties—the Men, Women and Children—come up to these conventions, to probe this plague-spot to the bottom, and devise means to apply that Remedial *Power* which, thank God! yet rests in the hands of an Uncorrupted *People*!

☞ It is particularly desirable that *every* *Town* should be fully represented at these convent'ons, as it is designed to mature plans for a vigorous winter campaign.

October 20, 1846.

By order of *DIST. & CO. COMMITTEES.*

Liberty Party poster 1846. (UVM)

(UVM)

FREE SOIL
UNION
CONVENTION!

The Freemen of the Fourth District,

Without regard to party, opposed to *extending* and *perpetuating* the curse of *slavery* in any territory under the control of the Federal Government, and opposed to the election of Cass and Taylor, are requested to meet in Mass Convention at SOUTH HARDWICK, Wednesday, Aug. 30, at 10 A. M.

L. P. POLAND, Esq. of Morristown, and *A. J. ROWELL, Esq.* of Troy, with others, will address the Freemen.

By order of the PEOPLE.

*William Slade, Vermont Governor
and Congressman from Cornwall
who tried to make his Whig Party
adopt a stronger anti-slavery
stance.*

In 1837 the society resolved that "American slavery in principle is under all circumstances a flagrant sin." In 1840 the society resolved that "the ministers who . . . oppose the cause of emancipation or remain silent on the subject, are unworthy of support or confidence as religious guides or teachers."

During the late 1830s abolitionist petitions poured into the United States Congress. Most of the petitions related to the existence of slavery in the District of Columbia, and the domestic slave trade. As a result, a "gag rule" was adopted by Congress that required that petitions on the subject of slavery be laid on the table without action.

Congressman William Slade, who had received many such petitions from his constituents in Vermont, rose to address the U.S. House of Representatives and said:

> We must not bury these petitions. And let me say to you gentlemen, that such a policy will certainly defeat itself. You cannot smother investigation of this subject. The spirit of free inquiry is the master spirit of the age.[10]

Vermonters submitted many petitions, prompting angry replies from southern politicians. Governor Wise of Virginia said: "We cannot reason with the heads of fanatics, nor touch hearts fatally bent upon treason." The Georgia House resolved: "That His Excellency the Governor be and is hereby requested to transmit the Vermont resolutions to the deep, dank and fetid sink of social and political iniquity from whence they emanated, with the following unequivocal declaration inscribed thereon: Resolved, That Georgia standing on her constitutional palladium, heeds not the maniac ravings of hellborn fanaticism, nor stoops from her lofty position to hold terms with perjured traitors."[11]

The Georgia Senate, not to be outdone, requested President Franklin Pierce "to employ a sufficient number of able-bodied Irishmen to proceed to the State of Vermont, and to dig a ditch around the limits of the same, and to float 'the thing' into the Atlantic."[12]

Feeding southern resentment was Vermont's participation in the underground railroad, the secret system of helping fugitive slaves escape from their masters and flee to the North and Canada. Vermont was on the border, it served as a "trunk" route north. There are still some houses in the state which have secret passageways and trap doors that were built to hide runaway slaves. [13]

Those interested in the anti-slavery movement during the pre-Civil War period often were involved in the temperance crusade. The Montpelier anti-slavery paper, *Voice of Freedom* saw this relationship. "The temperance and anti-slave causes go well together. In fact I do not know of any moral or religious enterprise which can prosper without temperance being its companion. It was this which prepared the way for me to be an abolitionist, and I trust it has been so with thousands of others."

As early as 1806, the Council of Censors warned about the problems of intoxicating liquor: "No crime is, perhaps, attended with more evil consequences to society and individuals, than that of drunkeness. In proportion as this vice prevails, the morals of old and young appear to be affected. If there be any reformation on this head, we rejoice and are glad."[14]

Towns throughout Vermont petitioned the General Assembly to prohibit the sale of liquor. Many people signed such a petition in Charlotte in 1836 which said, in part:

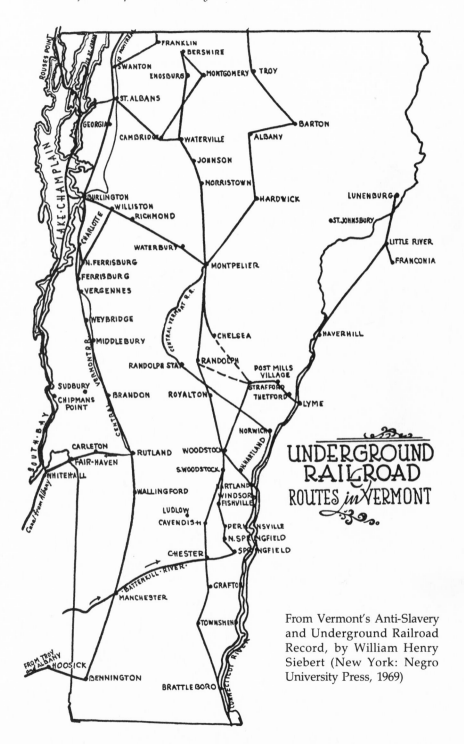

UNDERGROUND RAILROAD ROUTES *in* VERMONT

From Vermont's Anti-Slavery and Underground Railroad Record, by William Henry Siebert (New York: Negro University Press, 1969)

To intemperance is owning a large proportion of the pauperism and the crime, which prevail in the community. Minute and extended examinations make the amount from three-fourths to nine-tenths of both. It is adverse in various ways to the productive industry of the public; it generates habits of improvidence and profusion, and hence leads on to poverty. It tends to dethrone reason and conscience; it exasperates and often goads to madness the base passions of our nature, and hence a vast preponderance of the acts of outrage and violence, and especially of violence done to life, are perpetrated under an excitement derived from ardent spirits. For other species of felony, men are trained by habits of intemperance.

Addison County granted no liquor permits in 1843. In 1844 former Congressman Slade in his successful campaign for governor, proposed local option. No licenses would be granted in any town that did not "in town meetings warned for that purpose, pass a resolution specially requesting the county court to grant licenses for the sale of intoxicating liquors in that town." This was the gist of the law signed by Governor Slade in 1844.[15]

In 1852, the General Assembly passed a prohibition law that required a referendum vote. With over 40,000 votes cast, statewide prohibition passed by only 521 votes. All of the counties west of the Green Mountains favored the new law, while the counties to the east were opposed, with the exception of Caledonia.[16]

The organizational techniques successfully used to enact a prohibition law were also employed in the anti-slavery movement. The Sudbury Anti-Slavery Society recommended "the use of these means which have been most effectual in removing intemperance" to liberate slaves.[17]

POLITICAL POWER OF ABOLITION

During the course of the temperance crusade another anti-slavery organization was formed, the Free Soil party. The party was formed in 1848, when dissenters from the Democratic and Whig parties, believing a stronger anti-slavery stance was needed, ran former President Martin Van Buren as a presidential candidate. (Jackson had won elec-

To the General Assembly of the State of Vermont to be convened in October, 1837:

The undersigned, inhabitants of *the town of Peacham* appeal to you, as guardians of the public morals, and as the preservers of the public weal, and beg leave respectfully to represent—That we believe the vending of ardent spirits is demonstrated to be the cause of more crime, vice, pauperism and misery in our community, than are produced from any other source whatever; that the licensing the sale is conferring exclusive privileges upon a certain class of men, at the expense and great injury of all others; and that it is thus subverting the first principles of legislation by encouraging the cause of those very evils which it prohibits and condemns.

Statistics have been collected which show conclusively, that at least three fourths of all the crime and pauperism in our land is produced directly through the influence of ardent spirits. This may be charged directly as the effect of the present license system; and the result is, that the vender of ardent spirits is enabled to pursue a lucrative trade, at the expense of public morals, private rights, and individual happiness. The vender is made rich by the traffic, while the community is loaded with burdensome taxes, to defray the expenses of criminal prosecutions, and to support the victims of intemperance. We humbly represent, that we cannot view it otherwise than *unjust*, that we should thus be subjected to onerous taxation for the support of a privileged class, which is preying upon the vitals of community.

We would further represent that in our view a great part of the distress experienced the past year, by the poorer class of community, from the extreme scarcity and high price of bread-stuffs is chargeable indirectly to the license system. The sale encourages the manufacture; and it is believed, that if the amount of grain distilled, and thus worse than destroyed, had been saved, instead of a deficiency, there would have been a large surplus of bread-stuffs in the country; and while plenty would have prevailed in the poor man's abode, thousands of dollars of his hard earnings would have been saved.

We would further represent that from data gathered in many towns, we are led to believe that the cost of ardent spirits consumed in this State, annually, is equal to the share of the national revenue coming to Vermont the present year; and if the traffic were interdicted, each town would save yearly, as much as it is to receive under the distribution bill of the last legislature.

We appeal to you for aid in counteracting this giant evil, from motives of philanthropy and patriotism. The happiness and welfare of our country in an eminent degree is placed in your hands. It is for you to say whether this blighting and consuming traffic shall continue, shall increase, or shall cease. If it is to continue, will probably increase, and we may expect in time to see our country borne down by this withering evil, as depressed and degraded Ireland is at this day, where it is estimated, from evidence taken before a parliamentary committee, that forty millions of dollars are annually paid by the consumers, for spirious liquors, and many millions of bushels of bread-stuffs are annually destroyed.

The voice of public opinion has carried forward the temperance reform thus far; but those now engaged in the traffic are principally such as disregard its mandates. Your petitioners, believing that public sentiment is opposed to the traffic and that the public good imperiously demands that it should cease; in view of the premises, pray your honorable body, to repeal the present statutes in regard to licenses, and to pass laws wholly interdicting the traffic in ardent spirits.

The town of Peacham in 1837 petitions the Vermont General Assembly to "wholly interdict the traffic in ardent spirits." (SS)

tion in 1828 and 1832; Van Buren, his hand-picked successor, won in 1836 but lost to a Whig, William Henry Harrison in 1840.) The Free Soil party saw that a powerful new party could be built around the slavery issue. The old parties were trying to appease northern and southern members by straddling the slavery issue, a strategy which satisfied no one.

William Slade, recognized the appeal of the Free Soil and Liberty parties. He hoped to discourage the formation of an anti-slavery "third" party and encouraged his own party, the Whigs, to advocate abolitionism more strongly. Yet he realized the limitations of the anti-slavery appeal: "The public mind is not prepared to have an abolition candidate for the Presidency; nor to have an abolition President. What possible good can come to abolition . . . by now bringing the question into the presidential election [of 1840]"? William Lloyd Garrison, the famous abolitionist, praised Slade for his position on emancipation and for his position against the formation of an anti-slavery party. Garrison spent part of his career in Bennington, where he was the editor of the *Journal of the Times*.[18]

ELECTION OF 1840

The campaign of 1840 was one of the most spectacular ever waged in Vermont. More people voted (56,117) than in any previous Vermont election. Not until 1868 would the vote be exceeded (57,978).

The 1840 Whig State Convention was held in Burlington on June 25. It was reported to be the largest ever held in New England. Attendance was estimated between 15,000 and 25,000 and placards, banners and log cabins were features of a huge parade for "Tippecanoe and Tyler too." Tippecanoe was a famous battle won by William Henry Harrison's troops.[19]

Some of the colorful placards during the campaign of 1840 read:

> Hard cider, preferred to hard times —
> Addison County

RUTLAND  HERALD.

[WHITE, HENDERSON & CO.]   "He comes, the Herald of a noisy world, with news from all nations."   [PUBLISHERS.

VOL. XLVI.]   RUTLAND, VT. TUESDAY, SEPTEMBER 1, 1840.   [NO. 35.

The People's Ticket and the People's Choice.

TO THE RESCUE!!

For President of the United States

W. H. Harrison

For Vice President of the United States

JOHN TYLER.

State Officers.

For Governor

Silas H. Jenison.

For Lieutenant Governor.

David M. Camp-

For Treasurer.

HENRY F. JANES.

For State Senators

ISAAC NORTON, ORSON CLARK, ANDERSON G. DANA.

For Congress, Second District,

WM. SLADE.

Old Orange—Old Tip—we'll try—
Orange County

All farmers, all Whigs—Jericho

Is he honest, is he capable? He is, he is, and
the people know it—Washington County

Genuine Democracy—Van Buren's don't
pass in Enosburg

Let the people teach these palace slaves to
respect log cabins—Essex County[20]

On July 8 a crowd estimated at 10,000-15,000 gathered on Stratton Mountain to hear Daniel Webster speak of the need to hold the Union together by electing the Whigs.[21]

The convention and parade were a harbinger of the election results. Vermont gave the Whigs the greatest proportionate vote in the nation. In that year the Liberty party at-

Daniel Webster speaks to Vermonters at Stratton Mountain in 1840. (NL)

tracted only 319 votes in Vermont and only 7,000 in the nation. One year later the Liberty party received more than 3,000 votes. This deprived the Whig candidate of a popular majority, forcing the election into the General Assembly.

Many Vermont Whigs now realized that slavery could not be ignored. Slade continued his attempts to "abolitionize the Whig party." In 1842 he wrote the editor of the *New Haven Palladium:*

> The great mass of abolitionists think that every just purpose of abolition may be better accomplished without, than within, a distinct political organization. They think, indeed, that so far as political action is concerned, that action may be rendered more safe and effectual by incorporating abolition . . . into all parties . . . than by a separate organization.[22]

The Whig platform of 1842 labeled slavery as a "moral and political evil which ought to be removed by all just and proper means consistent with the Constitution." This tactic was successful, and in 1842 the Liberty party vote dwindled.[23]

FREE SOIL PARTY

The great issue of the presidential campaign of 1844 was the annexation of Texas. Vermonters feared that Texas would become another slave state. Henry Clay, the Whig candidate, tried to avoid the issue. This led the Whigs in Vermont to question Clay's position on slavery.

TO THE HONORABLE, THE SENATE AND HOUSE OF REPRESENTATIVES OF THE STATE OF VERMONT:

THE undersigned, inhabitants of the town of . *Starksboro, and* State of Vermont, respectfully request your honorable body to instruct the Senators and request the Representatives in Congress from this State, to use all constitutional measures to procure the abolition of slavery and the slave-trade, in the District of Columbia and the several Territories; and also the abolition of the inter-state slave-trade.

Also to remonstrate, in the name of the people, and as a sovereign State, against any abridgement of, or infringement upon, the right of petition, by refusing to receive petitions, important in their nature and respectful in their language, or having received, to deny them a proper consideration and answer.

And to remonstrate against the admission of Texas, or any new State, into the Union, with constitutions permitting the existence of slavery.

Anti-slavery petition to the Vermont General Assembly from Starksboro and vicinity opposing the admission of Texas. (State Archives)

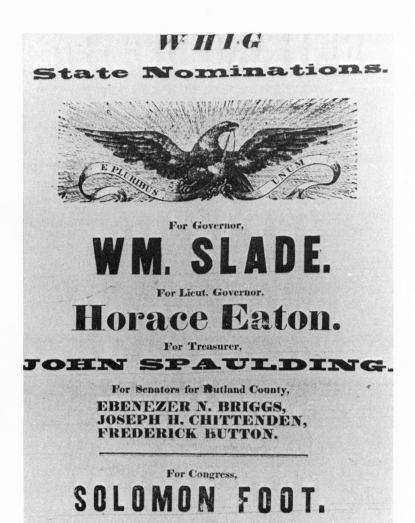

To overcome this handicap the Vermont Whigs nominated Slade for governor and adopted an unequivocal anti-slavery stance at the state level. They won handily in Vermont, with Slade polling a majority of the votes. Despite Clay's ambivalence on the Texas issue, he won a majority of Vermonters' votes. The nation, however, elected James K. Polk, a dark horse Democratic candidate from Tennessee.

The annexation of Texas was featured in Slade's Inaugural Address of 1844. If Texas were annexed he said "it would

Caledonian Office, St. Johnsbury, March 25, 1844.

The following Call has been handed to us with a request that it be printed. It has been called forth by the fact, recently come to light, that a secret negociation has for some time been pending between our Government and the Government of Texas with the view of annexing the latter to the United States ; and the plan has been so far matured it was confidently expected at the date of our latest advices from Washington that a Treaty would be immediately laid before the Senate for its ratification. It does then seem to be a fitting time for all opposed to adding more slave territory to the Union to enter their solemn protest against the consummation of the measure.

NOTICE.

The undersigned request a meeting of the citizens of the towns in the vicinity at the meeting house on St. Johnsbury Plain, on Friday the 29th inst. at 1 o'clock P. M. for the purpose of remonstrating to the U. S. Senate against the ratification of the pending Treaty for annexing Texas to the U. States.
March 23, 1844.

ERASTUS FAIRBANKS,	O B Partridge,	N C Bacon,	Samuel Sias,
HULL CURTIS,	John Morrill,	Horace Fairbanks,	H H Deming,
MOSES KITTREDGE,	Luther Green,	Joel Owen,	Orange Smith,
E A SNOW,	Abel Shorey,	Abel Willard,	I A Stevens,
JAMES HARRIS,	Benj West,	H H Flint,	David Boynton,
DYER DOWNING,	Russel Hallett,	Alvin Flint,	Wm H Leighton,
E A PARKS,	Freeman Hallet,	Wm M C Dinkerman,	Ferdinand Evans,
C JEWETT,	Benj Hutchinson,	L M Wright,	Lucius Barnes,
W C BOARDMAN,	Hiram Knapp,	Jerry Dickerman,	S B Mattocks,
LEVI FULLER,	John Drew,	George Pierce,	J R Delano,
W WOOD,	J K Colby,	Isaac Denison,	G B Chandler,
JOHN BARNEY,	William Aldrich,	W F Morris,	J Boler,
E P MATTHEWS,	J P Fairbanks,	John Bacon,	E Alexander,
IRA WHIPPLE,	B S Webster,	Ezra Ide,	C W Porter,
LUTHER CLARK,	Henry Lovejoy,	Edmund Hallet,	H C Babcock,
LEVI P PARKS,	Noah Eastman,	C A Harris,	J Morrill,
JOHN A PARKS,	Francis Bingham,	John Morse,	Salma Trussell,
STEVENS WOODS,	Wm P Pierce,	Abel Pierce,	L Kingsbury,
JOHN C IDE,	John Underwood,	John Kelley,	C P Carpenter,
EZRA BRIGHAM,	D G Smith,	Willard Hawkins,	Ephraim Jewett,
JOHN IDE,	J C Bingham,	George Ramsey,	Huxham Paddock,
J K REMICK,	John Page,	Abel Willey,	B P Worcester,
DAVID BILSBY,	Nathan Wetherbee,	W Wright, jr	Luther Jewett,
ZENAS WOODS,	N P Dean,	Hiram Pierce,	Elisha Peck,
CURTIS FELCH,	J C Crossman,	Simeon Stevens,	George Drew jr
C LAWRENCE,	A C Morse,	Nathaniel Gout,	G. W. Brown,
I P POPE,	Augustus Sanborn,	Charles Martin,	E Perry,
CHARLES FROST,	Thaddeus Fairbanks,	B P Cheate,	Alexander Osgood,
EZEKIEL CUTLER,	D P Hall,	J G Allen,	John Fry jr
S C Brackett.	D C Kimman,	Fordyce Lothrop,	Joseph Ide.

(UVM)

be the duty of Vermont to . . . have no connection with the new union thus formed without her consent and against her will."[24] Following Slade's lead, the Vermont Legislature opposed the annexation of Texas on a 120-48 vote, because such an act would be "unconstitutional, inexpedient and unjust."[25]

The annexation of Texas led to the Mexican War, which was opposed by Whig Governor Horace Eaton, Slade's successor. Eaton said "that Vermont has seen nothing in the progress of the contest to change her sentiment, either in regard to the insufficiency of the ground on which the war was commenced, or the unworthiness of the purpose for which it was waged."

Eaton and Slade were also involved in Vermont school reform. In addition to the Texas question, Slade emphasized the importance of education in his inaugural address.

> Great political responsibilities rest on our people involving the necessity of a high state of general intelligence. They are the judge not only of the personal qualifications of candidates for office, but of the character and the tendency of measures and the force in bearing of great principles. They must be able to correct errors of fact, detect false reasoning, and put demagogues to silence.[26]

As a result of the work of Slade and other reformers, the General Assembly passed a comprehensive education act in 1845, which created three new offices: the town superintendent, county superintendent and state superintendent. The first state superintendent of education under the new law was Horace Eaton.

Eaton, who was concurrently state superintendent and governor from 1846-1848, said Vermont's 2,750 school districts were far too many; that thirty-seven pupils per district were too few. He said that schoolhouses were in miserable condition and challenged each town to erect "a well-located, well-planned, and well-constructed schoolhouse." Eaton criticized the teaching apparatus and said that many schools were not even equipped with blackboards. One superintendent said that the blackboards he observed were not "very large nor very black." "This presents the condition of things truly alarming; we might say absolutely appalling." Eaton said the state of affairs was due "to the failure of parents to estimate the immense influence which the instruction children receive at school is to exert upon the character and destinies of their children."[27]

Two years later, in 1847, Governor Eaton in his inaugural address had praise for the new school law.

> It is a source of much gratification to me to be able to express my firm and decided convictions, that, under the regulations

FIRST

ANNUAL REPORT

OF THE

STATE SUPERINTENDENT

OF

COMMON SCHOOLS,

MADE TO THE LEGISLATURE

OCTOBER, 1846.

MONTPELIER, VT.:
EASTMAN & DANFORTH, PRINTERS.

recently adopted for the supervision of our common schools, and the efforts made in connection with that supervision to improve these institutions and extend their influence, a palpable advancement has been made.[28]

Educational reform did not preclude concern over national issues. In the presidential campaign of 1848, Vermont Whigs expressed their keen displeasure with Whig slave owner Zachary Taylor, the hero of the Mexican War. The Vermont Democrats found themselves in a similar situation with presidential candidate Lewis Cass of Michigan, a "Northern man with southern principles," or a "doughface," as such politicians were called.

Slade finally gave up his efforts to make the Whigs into an abolition party and jumped to the Free Soil party." In the name of God, let us be united now—standing firmly and immovably, upon the platform of no more slave states—no more slave territory—Free Soil for Free Men," he proclaimed as he took over leadership of the party in Vermont.[29]

In August 1848 a Free Soil convention in Middlebury nominated a member of the Liberty party for governor, a Democrat for lieutenant governor and a Whig for treasurer. One of the resolutions expressed the reasons for discontent with the national organizations: "That the Democratic and Whig parties in this State, by passing resolutions in their State Conventions, pledging themselves to oppose the extension of Slavery into Free Territory, while they recommend the support of candidates . . . for president who are . . . pledged to the South . . ., insult the intelligence and honesty of the members of those parties and stamp their own conduct with the strangest inconsistency."[30]

The Whig candidate, Carlos Coolidge (a distant ancestor of Calvin Coolidge), won the governorship in 1848. Despite what his party's national candidates might say or do, Coolidge advocated abolition and said Vermonters were united on the issue: "In performing their part of the work of destroying slavery, her people will not falter at which they can rightfully do. Hostility to slavery is, in Vermonters, an instinct."[31]

The political instability of the period was highlighted by

WHIG
MEETING!

FREE SOIL! FREE SPEECH! AND FREE MEN!

The Whigs of the town of Tunbridge
and the neighboring towns, and all who
are in favor of

FREE SOIL!
FREE SPEECH,
AND
FREE MEN!

and of course opposed to the further EXTENSION
OF *SLAVERY*, are requested to meet at the Town
House in

Tunbridge Centre,
ON
SATURDAY, SEPT. 2, 1848,

at 1 o'clock, P. M., to take counsel together as to
*their duties as freemen, in the present condition of
our public affairs.*
Hon. Jacob Collamer and Hon. Wm.
Hebard will address the meeting.
Other Whig speakers will also address the meeting, should
there be time.
J. K. PARISH,
for Co. Committee.

Tunbridge, Aug. 23, 1848.

(VHS)

Democratic Caucus.

The Democrats of Northfield are hereby notified to meet in Caucus at the Inn of Isaac W. Brown, on SATURDAY, August 28, 1852, at 7 o'clock, p. m., to nominate a suitable person to be supported by them for

TOWN REPRESENTATIVE

at the coming election ; also, to nominate Justices of the Peace for the ensuing year.

All who are in favor of the election of PIERCE

and KING, and are conscious that the servitude of a large portion of our own neighbors and friends, if not equal to Southern Slavery, approximates too nearly to it, and is a subject as well as that which demands our consideration and who are in favor of adopting measures to ameliorate the condition of that class of persons by the passage of a law limiting the time laborers shall be required to work, except in cases of special contract to the contrary, to ten hours in each day and who generally are in favor of protecting the rights of the masses of our own citizens of whatever faction, name, or party, are respectfully invited to attend.

By order of Committee.

Northfield, August 23, 1852.

(VHS)

the election and non-election of 1853. It took thirty-one ballots by the General Assembly to elect a speaker and twenty to elect a governor, Democrat John Robinson. The Assembly was not able to elect a United States senator. Hardly an election passed during this period when the constitutional requirement of a majority was reached. Under these circumstances, the General Assembly had the responsibility of selecting the governor and other state officials.[32]

THE GRAND OLD PARTY IS BORN

The Democratic party in Vermont lost any abolitionist support it still had in 1854, when Illinois Senator Stephen Douglas (a native of Brandon) proposed the Nebraska Act, which allowed new states in the Nebraska territory to decide for themselves whether they wanted to allow slavery. Douglas was described as a "steam engine in breeches" and a "fountain of tobacco juice and spread-eagled oratory." Economic expansion, thought Douglas, would help the nation forget the issue of slavery.

Douglas had not anticipated the vehemence of the opposi-

PATRIOT OFFICE,
Montpelier, Vt., Friday, Oct. 28.

The Star has "sot."

We have the satisfaction of announcing that Vermont is democratic at last, and that, too, without trade or bargain with anybody.

Yesterday afternoon, the General Assembly made choice of

JOHN S. ROBINSON,

democrat, Governor, by the following vote:

JOHN S. ROBINSON, dem,   120
Erastus Fairbanks, whig, 104
L. Brainard, f. s.,   15
                                                  ——119
                                                  ——
                                                      1

*Democrat John Robinson was elected by the General Assembly in 1853
by one vote. During the pre-Civil War period, few governors were able
to win by a majority popular vote. Under those circumstances, the governor was chosen by majority vote. From 1836-1853, eight gubernatorial
elections were decided by the General Assembly. (See chart.)*

tion. He was assailed throughout the North by "Anti-Nebraska" groups, and Vermont was no exception. The *Montpelier Watchman* called his actions a

> Deed of Darkness.
> . . . The deed was fitly done in darkness—for it was an evil deed. . . Every vote in the affirmative we regard as a stain upon the personal integrity of the man who casts it. Let no such man be trusted.[33]

Stephen Douglas, Democratic presidential candidate of 1860 against Lincoln; a native of Brandon.

PRESIDENTIAL VOTING RETURNS 1836 TO 1853

Year	Total	Whig %	Democratic %	Liberty %
1836	36,630	55.8	44.0	–
1837	39,979	55.7	44.3	–
1838	43,952	56.3	43.7	–
1839	46,902	52.5	47.4	
1840	56,452	59.2	40.1	.7
1841	47,942	48.7	44.4	6.3
1842	53,398	50.9	45.1	4.1
1843	50,921	48.7	43.5	7.5
1844	54,847	51.5	38.2	10.3
1845	48,402	47.4	38.6	13.5
1846	48,703	48.5	36.7	14.6
1847	48,080	46.8	38.7	14.4

Year	Total	Whig %	Democratic %	Democratic-Free Soil
1848	50,405	43.7	27.7	29.6
1849	52,845	49.6	6.4	44.0
1850	47,607	51.4	8.8	39.8
1851	44,355	51.1	15.2	33.7
1852	50,199	51.3	29.8	18.9
1853	47,415	44.0	38.0	18.0

Rutland-born Vermont Congressman James Meacham opposed the Nebraska Bill on the floor of the House. "The people are absolutely struck dumb by the audacity of the proposition. If this bill passes there will be raised in the north a more bitter and prolonged anti-slavery excitement than ever." All four Vermont congressmen voted against the bill.[34]

At March town meetings the Nebraska Bill was condemned. Charlotte censured Douglas, the bill's sponsor. The town of Springfield declared that "we will vote for such men, and such men only, as will use their vote and influence to protect this territory from the encroachments of slavery." Mass meetings protesting the Kansas Nebraska Act were held in Rutland, Chittenden and Franklin counties.[35]

The Democratic party was undermined further by the nomination of New Hampshire's Franklin Pierce for president. Pierce supported the Nebraska Act and favored returning runaway slaves to their southern masters under the Fugitive Slave Law.

The time was ripe for the rise of a new party that would gather under one stand the disaffected members of the various established parties. The Republican party in Vermont was organized on July 13, 1854, when about 600 to 800 people gathered at the state house in Montpelier. Vermont was the second state to organize the party, preceeding national organization by two years. [36]

A person who played an important role in the creation of the new party was the crusading editor of the *Vermont Watchman*, Ezekiel P. Walton. In June of 1854, Walton, disappointed that the Whig Convention had not taken a stronger stand against slavery, editorially called for a mass state convention. Invited were "all persons who are in favor of resisting . . . the usurpations of the propagandists of Slavery." The meeting was set for July 4. The date was later changed to July 13 in order to mark "the anniversary of the Ordinance of 1787, which dedicated to Freedom all territory northwest of the Ohio River."[37]

Had the Convention met on July 4, Montpelier, Vermont would have been given recognition as the birthplace of the new Republican party. As it turned out, the honor went to Jackson, Michigan.

The convention agreed to call their new party Republican. Those attending resolved

. . . in as much as there are now no great measures of Legislation . . . , dividing political parties, except that of slavery . . . we do as Whigs, Free Soldiers, and Democrats, freely relinquish our former party associations and ties, to form a new party organization . . . we propose, and respectfully recommend to the friends of freedom in other States to cooperate and be known as REPUBLICANS.[38]

The Republican platform stated unequivocally: "Our rallying cry shall henceforth be the repeal of the Fugitive Slave

Stephen Royce, first Republican Governor of Vermont, elected in 1854; a native of Tinmouth.

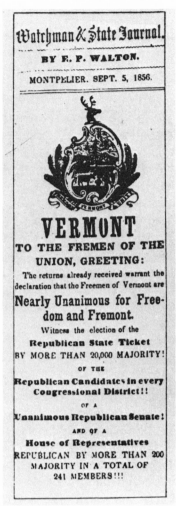

Watchman & State Journal.

BY E. P. WALTON.

MONTPELIER. SEPT. 5, 1856.

VERMONT

TO THE FREMEN OF THE UNION, GREETING:

The returns already received warrant the declaration that the Freemen of Vermont are

Nearly Unanimous for Freedom and Fremont.

Witness the election of the

Republican State Ticket

BY MORE THAN 20,000 MAJORITY!

OF THE

Republican Candidates in every Congressional District!!

OF A

Unanimous Republican Senate!

AND OF A

House of Representatives

REPUBLICAN BY MORE THAN 200 MAJORITY IN A TOTAL OF 241 MEMBERS!!!

Vermont election returns in 1856.

Law . . ., the abolition of slavery in the District of Columbia, the prohibition of slavery in all the Territories of the United States, and the admission of no more slave states into the Union."[39]

The Republicans' success came quickly. That fall their candidate, Stephen Royce, won the governorship.

The new Republican party spread quickly throughout the North. In 1855 a Republican was elected speaker of the U.S. House. And in 1856 Republicans ran their first presidential

Hiland Hall wrote a history of Vermont and served as Governor from 1858-1860. (UVM)

Abraham Lincoln, first Republican President, elected in 1860.

candidate, John Fremont. He lost to the Democrat, James Buchanan, but in 1860 the GOP took over the White House with Abraham Lincoln and stayed there until 1888.

The depth of Vermont's concern for abolition was no better expressed than in a report by a committee of the Vermont Senate in 1855: "Born of a resistance to arbitrary power — her first breath that of freedom — her first voice a declaration of equal rights of man — how could her people be otherwise than haters of slavery — how can they do less than sympathize with every human being and every community which asserts the rights of all men to blessings like their own?"[40]

Vermont's resistance to the concept of slavery, from the constitution of 1777 to the formation of the Republican party, shaped the state's commitment to the Civil War.

"In the course of the war, Vermont had 34,328 men under arms, mostly volunteers. That was more than twice the number of Vermonters who fought in World War I. Vermont had a greater proportion of her men killed in battle than any other northern state. Her troops were the first to entrench on Confederate soil, and the first to attack Confederate for-

Democratic National Ticket.

FOR PRESIDENT,
STEPHEN A. DOUGLAS.

FOR VICE PRESIDENT,
HERSCHEL V. JOHNSON.

ELECTORS
For President and Vice President.

ISAAC B. BOWDISH, of Burlington,

PAUL DILLINGHAM, of Waterbury,

JOHN CAIN, of Rutland,

AMASA PAINE, of Lowell,

E. M. BROWN, of Woodstock.

Democratic Ticket 1860. (UVM)

DOUGLAS IN BURLINGTON

CHAMPION OF THE PEOPLES' RIGHTS!

SENTINEL OFFICE, JULY 28, 1860.

We take pleasure in announcing to the citizens of Burlington and vicinity, that the

Hon. Stephen A. Douglas

WILL ARRIVE IN BURLINGTON

On Monday next, 30th inst., at 9½ A. M.

Our citizens are invited, without distinction of party, to unite in giving a hearty welcome to this DISTINGUISHED SON OF VERMONT.

Mr. DOUGLAS and his estimable lady will spend the day in Burlington, and such arrangements will be made as to give to those who desire it, an introduction to

THE GREATEST STATESMAN OF THE DAY!

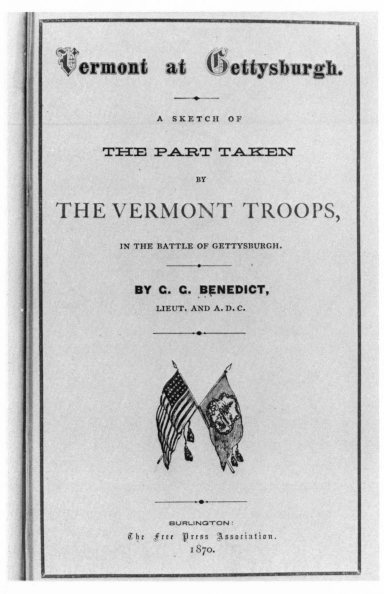

G. G. Benedict was Vermont's best known Civil War historian. (UVM)

"*Put the Vermonters Up Front.*" (UVM)

Battle of Cedar Creek, Virginia. Vermont troops distinguished themselves as the South made one last attempt to invade the North. (VDD)

Civil War Governor Erastus Fairbanks. (UVM)

tifications. This was an extraordinary record for a small, rural state."[41] An oft-quoted order by a Union general to "Put the Vermonters ahead and keep the column well closed up" seemed to summarize Vermont solders' strength in battle. The order came during the first day of the Battle of Gettysburg on July 1, 1863. The New York Times wrote, two days later, "A Vermont brigade held the key of the position at Gettysburg and did more than any other body of men to gain the triumph which decided the fate of the Rebellion."[42]

NOTES

1. *Second Annual Report of the Vermont Anti-Slavery Society* 1836 as cited by Ludlum, *Social Ferment in Vermont* p. 135.
2. *Governor and Council*, vol. 6, p. 543.
3. *Ibid.* p. 539.
4. *Vermont Advocate*, vol. 2, Editorial, "The Election", (November 26, 1828), p. 2, col. 2 as cited by David W. Barry, *Vermont State Politics 1812-1888* (New York: St. John's University: unpublished thesis 1961) p. 12.
5. *Governor and Council*, vol. 7, p. 478.
6. Crockett, *History of Vermont*, p. 258.
7. *Ibid.* p. 269-270.
8. J. Kevin Graffagnino, *Vermont Attitudes Towards Slavery: The need for a Closer Look, Vermont History*, vol. 45, No. 1 (Winter 1977), pp. 31-34. According to Graffagnino there was "significant diversity" among Vermonters relating to the slavery issue. "That only a few 'low fellows' in Vermont differed with the anti-slavery majority ... is not the case. The fact that a segment of Vermont's population in the first half of the nineteenth century at least tolerated, if not supported slavery, needs further examination."
9. *Register of Debates in Congress*, Twenty Fourth Congress, First Session ... 1836, XII, 2062 as cited by Ludlum, *Social Ferment in Vermont* p. 153.
10. Crockett, *History of Vermont* p. 444.
11. *Ibid.* p. 444.
12. *Ibid.*
13. Wilbur Siebert, *Vermont's Anti-Slavery and Underground Railroad Record* (New York: Negro University Press, 1937)
14. Ludlum, *Social Ferment in Vermont*, p. 63.
15. *Acts and Resolves passed by the Legislature of the State of Vermont*. 1844, pp. 14-18.
16. Ludlum, p. 85.
17. *Ibid.* p. 71.
18. *Ibid.* p. 126.
19. T.D. Semour Bassett, Vermont Politics and the Press in the 1840's Vermont History, vol. 47, no. 3 (summer 1979), p. 196.
20. *Ibid.* pp. 196-197
   Bassett concludes that "By the 1840's politics in Vermont had developed its own set of habits. Politics had become a dominant pastime woven deeply into the social structure of the state. The country press served as a handmaiden to the politicians and their parties. The press was not only indispensable to politicians, radical or regular; it was also the most widespread form of popular education and propaganda, a potentially profitable business and the best reflection of village society." For another description of politics during this period see also Wilbur Siebert, *Vermont's Anti-Slavery and Underground Railroad* (New York: Negro University Press, 1937) pp. 35-45.

21. Martha R. Wright, "The Log Cabin Convention of 1840 sixty years later: Vermonters Correct the Record" Vermont History vol. 40, no. 4 (Autumn 1972) pp. 237-240. A whig song denounced President Van Buran as a drinker of wine: Let Van from his cooler of silver drink wine, and lounge on his cusioned settee our man on a buckeye bench can recline content with hard cider is he.

22. *Ludlum, Social Ferment,* p. 182.

23. *Ibid.* p. 183.

24. *Journal of the House of Representatives of the State of Vermont,* 1844 (Montpelier: E.P. Walton, 1845) p. 25.

25. *Ibid.* p. 154.

26. William Slade, *Journal of the House of Representatives,* 1844 p. 12.

27. *First Annual Report of the State Superintendent of Common Schools Made to the Legislature.* October 1846, pp. 16-17.

28. Horace Eaton, *Inaugural Address, Journal of the Senate* 1847, p. 17.

29. *Ludlum, Social Ferment,* p. 195.

30. *Ibid.*

31. Carlos Coolidge, *Journal of the Senate,* 1848, pp. 27-32.

32. Crockett, *History of Vermont,* vol. 3, p. 412.

33. *Vermont Watchman and State Journal,* March 10, 1854.

34. Crockett, *History of Vermont,* vol. 3 pp. 419-420.

35. *Ibid.* p. 422-423.

36. *Ibid.* pp. 425-426.

37. *Ibid* p. 425.

38. Platform of the Montpelier Mass Meeting, July 13, 1854, *The Vermont Watchman and State Journal.* July 18, 1854. See also Edward P. Brynn, "Vermont's Political Vacuum of 1846-1856 and the Emergence of the Republican Party," *Vermont History* 38 (Spring 1970): pp. 113-123, Brynn Wrote: Not only did the Republican Party gain the allegiance of the greater percentage of voters in Vermont than in any other state, but its formation was more than simply a reaction to the moral dilemma posed by slavery. Indeed, the Republican Party as it emerged in 1855 in Vermont was an expression of intense moral conviction on a somewhat wider front, while the support it obtained was due at least in part to hostile reaction to the maneuvering for votes which had characterized the Whigs, Democrats, and Free Soilers during the previous decade. Vermont Republicanism represented "right thinking" on slavery, but it also put an end to incessant sparring by three parties for power and patronage and restored a measure of calm to politics in the Green Mountain state.

39. *Ibid.*

40. "Report of a Select Committee," Journal of the Senate 1855, p. 295.

41. Edmund Fuller, *Vermont: A History of the Green Mountain State* (Montpelier: State Board of Education, 1952) p. 165.

42. *Ibid.* p. 165.

CHAPTER VIII

The First Half Century of Republican Control

THE REPUBLICAN PARTY DOMINATED VERMONT POLITICS for more than a century. From 1856 until 1964, Vermont supported every Republican candidate for president. Republicans held every major office in Vermont until the election of William Meyer as United States Representative in 1958, the election of Philip Hoff as governor in 1962 and the election of Patrick Leahy as United States Senator in 1974. Identification of Vermont with Republicanism was as strong as that of southern states with Democratic politics. Nothing seemed to typify the image more than the fact that in 1912 and 1936 Vermont was one of only two states to vote Republican in the presidential election.

After the Civil War, the Democratic party in Vermont had little support and never became a haven for dissident Republicans. In an article entitled "The Future of Democracy in Vermont", Charles Davenport, a son of a Democratic candidate for governor, had this to say about the party:

> The cause for this condition of affairs may be said to be several but really resolve themselves into one. The people of the state are peculiarly moveable by the force of moral ideas. They live largely upon the patriotic memories of the war with the true mountaineers' hatred of slavery. They remember the time when the Democratic Samson was beguiled into the lap of the Delilah of the South, and it has not been brought home to them that the Democracy of today stands for anything better. So far as has been shown to them, the party in the state lived only to hold federal offices when there is a Democratic administration.[1]

141

GRAND REPUBLICAN RALLY

AT BENSON, V.T.,

Tuesday, August 27th at 2 o'clock P. M.

Civil War General Ulysses S. Grant ran for re-election in 1872; Henry Wilson was his running mate. The first Grant administratin was tinged by scandal, but he easily beat his Democratic opponent, Horace Greeley. This broadside is from the election.

(VHS)

Samuel Tilden was an unsuccessful Democratic presidential candidate in 1876 losing to Rutherford B. Hayes. At that time the rooster not the donkey was the Democratic symbol and Vermont had five electoral votes instead of today's three. (UVM)

ADMINISTRATIVE REFORM.

For President,

SAMUEL J. TILDEN,

OF NEW YORK.

For Vice President,

THOMAS A. HENDRICKS,

OF INDIANA.

For Presidential Electors,

LUCIUS ROBINSON,
HENRY L. RODIMAN,
GEORGE L. WATERMAN,
AMOS ALDRICH,
STEPHEN L. GOODELL.

ATTENTION
GREENBACKERS.

Gen. Horace Binney Sargent,

OF BOSTON.

Will address the people of Burlington and vicinity

ON THE SUBJECT OF

FINANCE *and* POLITICS

AT THE

CITY HALL,

THIS FRIDAY EVENING,

August 23d, 1878.

ALL ARE INVITED TO ATTEND

DEMOCRATIC CAUCUS!

THE DEMOCRATS OF
MONTPELIER, VT.,

are requested to assemble in Caucus at

Village Hall,

MONDAY EVENING, SEPT. 4th, 1876,

At 7.80 o'clock.

ALL ARE DESIRED TO BE PRESENT.

Per Order of Town Committee.

(VHS)

The Greenback Party wanted to put more paper money in circulation. (VHS)

Robert Mitchell, senior editor and publisher of the *Rutland Herald*, wrote that the post-Civil War Democrats were more interested in organizational control than winning elections:

> The Democratic Party is tightly controlled from the top by a group of five or six men. The same candidates run repeatedly in election after election and newcomers have difficulty breaking into this exclusive coterie of losers. As a result, some disgruntled young Democrats feel that the leadership of their party is more interested in maintaining its control of the organization than it is in conducting a winning election campaign against the Republicans.[2]

Abraham Lincoln's election in 1860 precipitated the southerners' attack on Fort Sumter in South Carolina. The Democrats were seen as the party of the South. In the first election after the start of the Civil War, the Democratic party in Vermont received only eleven percent of the total vote for governor. From 1854 to 1934 the Democratic gubernatorial vote was less than 40 percent in every election.

SOLIDIFYING SUPPORT

Nothing succeeds like success, and once the Republican party was established, it developed a solid base of support around the state. The only way to succeed in Vermont politics was to be a Republican. Issues on which Vermont Republicans built their power included tariffs that protected the state's dairy, wool and marble industries, and a policy of "hard money" currency that appealed to Vermonters' perceived self interest. One of Vermont's greatest statesmen, United States Senator Justin Morrill, sponsored the Protective Tariff Act of 1861 and was a strong proponent of "sound money."

Mitchell suggested some of the reasons for the Republicans' success:

> Vermont is dominated politically by the voters of non-industrial towns and cities. The state is primarily supported by a dairying economy. Consequently the voters of the State have always demanded and obtained tariff protection against Canadian milk. The same type of tariff protection has been sought by the sheep raisers and the marble industry. The Republican Party has consistently answered this need.

Justin Morrill, elected six times to the U.S. Senate whose Morrill Act of 1862 established the nation's land grant colleges.

The residents of the Green Mountain State have been since 1852 seriously interested in the temperance and prohibition movement. Even today local option is still in force throughout the State. Though neither of the major political parties have been the exclusive champions of prohibition on the national level, such a policy has been more in line with Republican than Democratic pronouncements.

The fact that Vermont is not a large state has helped the Republicans as well. Public activity can be scrutinized with greater care in a small area of governmental administration - this factor prohibits extensive graft and corruption in politics. The Republican officeholders' records have been high and relatively free from scandal, so the voters do not feel compelled to shift their allegiance to another party.[3]

Republicans also recognized that east-west regional sentiments were strong in Vermont, and alternated major state and federal offices between the two regions. This deliberate sharing of offices has been termed "mountain rule" because the spine of the Green Mountains was the dividing line between the regions.

Once in power the Republicans were determined to bring a measure of order and stability through constitutional change. From 1841-1853 eight gubernatorial elections had been decided by the Vermont General Assembly. It would

GRAND
DEMOCRATIC RALLY!

TWO GRAND MEETINGS

will be given

AT MONTPELIER,

under the auspices of the

TILDEN AND HENDRICKS CLUB,

On Thursday Evening, August 24th,
and Monday Evening, August 28, 1876.

THURSDAY EVENING

Addresses will be delivered by

Hon. HENRY O. KENT,

of New Hampshire.

A. N. MERCHANT, Esq.,

of Burlington.

ON MONDAY EVENING

Address by

Hon. E. J. PHELPS,

of Burlington, from whom the people may expect a rare
treat as he is one of the most accomplished and cultivated speakers in the State.

Music will be Furnished by

THE MONTPELIER CORNET BAND,

and Singing by the

TILDEN AND HENDRICKS GLEE CLUB!

The Speaking will be in Village Hall.

All are cordially invited to listen to a candid exposition of the
issues of the day. Reserved seats for Ladies.

Per order Executive Committee.

(VHS)

be almost fifty years before the General Assembly would
decide another gubernatorial election.

In 1870 a Republican-controlled Constitutional Convention approved a proposal that increased the term of the governor, state officers, and the General Assembly from one year
to two. The two-year term had the effect of diminishing op-
portunities for political controversy and gave a measure of
stability that had been lacking prior to the Civil War.

Another important change related to amending the constitution. Before 1870, the amendment process began with
the Council of Censors. The Council consisted of thirteen
people who ran for election statewide. If they felt that the
constitution needed to be amended, they had the power to
make proposals and to call a constitutional convention. The
Council had fallen into disfavor because of its identification
with attempts to re-apportion the Vermont General
Assembly. In 1870 a convention was called and the Council
was abolished. The power to amend the Vermont Constitution was given to the General Assembly, subject to ratification by the people.

The Republican party controlled access to state politics,
and there was a succession route to different offices and rotation of those in office. Governors served only single, two-
year terms, making difficult the building of a power base
within the party. An exception to this was the Proctor family and organization, which were a force in Republican politics
for generations. Then, as now, the Republican State Committee did not dominate Republican politics. In making appointments, for instance, governors did not usually consult
the party chairmen.

One of the ways to become prominent in the party was
to run a railroad (railroads exerted tremendous power in the
post-Civil War era) or run the marble industry, another
mainstay of the Vermont economy. For many years the path
from president of the Central Vermont or Rutland railroads
to the governor's office was well-trod. But it was the founder
of the Vermont Marble Company, Redfield Proctor, who used
his business interests to build a solid political base in the state.
The Proctor family was a major force in Vermont Republican

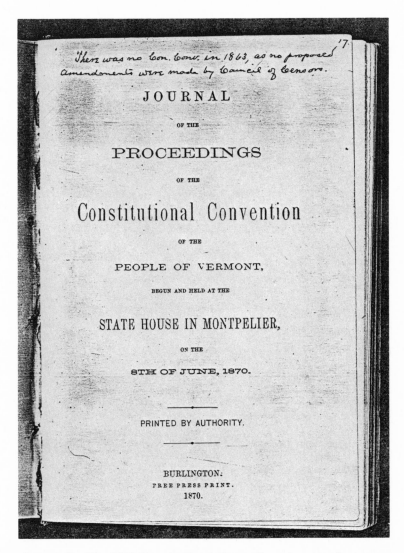

As a result of the 1870 Constitutional Convention, the term of governor, state officers, and the General Assembly was increased from one year to two. The Council of Censors was also abolished. (VSL)

politics for a half-century, and family members served in government for 100 years. All four Proctors who became governors were also presidents of the family marble business. Other company officials also held political office.[4]

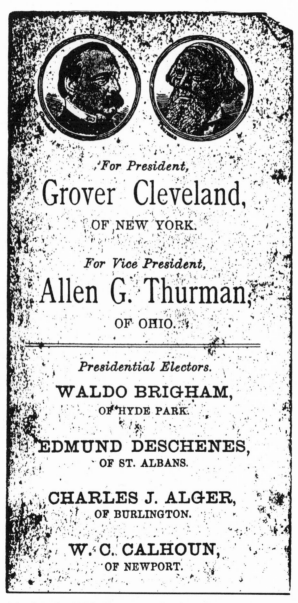

Democratic slate in 1888. Democrat Grover Cleveland lost this election but was successful in 1884 and 1892. (VHS)

HEADQUARTERS OF
◄Randolph Republican Club►

——◄◇◇◇◄——

August 31, 1888.

Dear Sir:—We enclose herewith the address of the Republican State Committee to the Voters of Vermont, and we invite your careful attention to the earnest appeal therein made.

Will you not be present at the polls next Tuesday before 3 o'clock (sickness alone excepted), and cast the enclosed ballot, which is the Regular Republican Ticket.

We want *at least 25,000 majority* for the State ticket.

Our majority in 1886 was less than 20,000, in 1884 less than 22,000. To reach 25,000 this year every Republican Voter must go to the pools and vote.

We depend upon you without fail.

Very truly yours,
THE EXECUTIVE COMMITTEE,
Randolph Republican Club.

(VHS)

THE PROCTOR FAMILY

Proctor, a Civil War veteran, developed his organizational base within the Republican party around returning Civil War veterans, a group that maintained its identity for years after the war. It has been claimed that the Proctor organization had a veteran in every Vermont community who could be relied upon for support and getting out the vote.

As governor, Proctor took an interest in prison reform, juvenile delinquency and state taxation. In 1880, Proctor noted that based on his familiarity with corrections work, "congregating a large number of youthful delinquents together is now admitted by the best authorities to be a failure." And on taxation, he said towns were "miniature republics in themselves. One great cause of the present unequal assessment of taxes is that we have a town system for levying the state tax and each town is afraid that its neighbor will make a lower appraisal than itself and so gain an advantage."[5]

As a United States Senator, Proctor played an important role in the nomination of Benjamin Harrison at the Republican National Convention in 1888. And in 1898, he went to Cuba, at his own expense, for a firsthand look at how the Spanish were ruling the country. Proctor was appalled by the "spectacle of a million and a half of people, the entire native population of Cuba, struggling for freedom and deliverance from the worst misgovernment of which I have ever had knowledge."[6] His report, given on the Senate floor, was given wide publicity and helped fan the flames of war. He was the chairman of the Senate committee that awarded federal building contracts to make sure government edifices were made of marble—Vermont marble.

THE DYNASTY CHALLENGED

Three Proctors served as governors after the turn of the century. Fletcher, Redfield's son, served from 1906-1908; Redfield Proctor Jr. served from 1923-1925; and Mortimer Proctor, son of Fletcher Proctor Jr. served from 1945-1947.

The Proctor influence was weakened in the election of 1902, when Percival V. Clement of Rutland ran against General J.G. McCullough of Bennington and Fletcher Proctor, for the Republican gubernatorial nomination. McCullough won the nomination, but the Local Option League, which advocated towns' rights in deciding if liquor should be sold within the town, put Clement on the ballot as a third-party candidate. A Republican candidate was deprived of a majority for the first time since 1854; the election was thrown into the General Assembly and McCullough was chosen. In response to the Clement challenge, local option was adopted during McCullough's term. The Clement threat was dissipated and in 1906 he was soundly defeated by Fletcher Proctor.[7]

From 1906 to 1908 Governor Fletcher Proctor advocated a progressive forestry policy, urged court reorganization and was given credit for the formation of a commission that regulated the utilities and railroads. In 1912 on the national

*Redfield Proctor, founder of
Vermont Marble Company who
capitalized on his business interests
to build a family dynasty within the
GOP. Governor 1878-1880. U.S.
Senator 1891-1908.*

*Fletcher D. Proctor, Governor
1906-1908.*

*Redfield Proctor, Jr., Governor
1923-1925. (UVM)*

*Mortimer Proctor, Governor
1945-1947.*

John G. McCullough, Governor
1902-1904. (UVM)

Percival W. Clement, Governor
1919-1921. (UVM)

License Local-Option Ticket.

For Governor:

PERCIVAL W. CLEMENT,

OF RUTLAND.

For Lieutenant-Governor :

FRANK W. AGAN,

OF LUDLOW.

For Secretary of State :

FREDERICK G. FLEETWOOD,

OF MORRISTOWN.

For State Treasurer:

JOHN L. BACON,

OF HARTFORD.

For State Auditor :

HORACE F. GRAHAM,

OF CRAFTSBURY.

The Local Option Movement.

The Vermont State Local Option Convention at Burlington, on July 16, nominated Percival W. Clement of Rutland, for Governor and Frank W. Agan of Ludlow, for Lieutenant-Governor. The convention also nominated for Secretary of State, State Treasurer and State Auditor, respectively, Frederick G. Fleetwood of Morristown, John L. Bacon of Hartford, and Horace F. Graham of Craftsbury, the Republican candidates for these positions.

· The purpose of the Local Option Convention in putting in the field independent candidates for the two executive positions in the list of State officers elected by the people was

(1) To protest against the methods of the political machine of the Republican organization.

(2) To advocate in the most effective manner the repeal of the prohibitory law and the substitution of a high license, local-option enactment, And finally

(3) To force the issue of a reform of State finances by doing the public business on business principles. 2674

The Republican Party ruled national and Vermont politics after the Civil War, but the election of 1912 split the party. Former President Theodore Roosevelt, denied his party's nomination in favor of incumbent President William Taft, ran as the Progressive Party candidate. The split allowed the Democrat, Woodrow Wilson, to win. Vermont voted narrowly for Taft, and also turned back the state Progressive candidate for governor. Both Taft and Roosevelt visited Vermont during the campaign. Here "TR," looking fit as a bull moose, speaks from a platform by the Barre Opera House. (APL)

level, ex-President Theodore Roosevelt bucked the Republican party's nomination of President William Taft for re-election and ran on his own Progressive, or "Bull Moose," party ticket. Vermont Republicans divided between Taft and Roosevelt. Vermont Progressives ran pastor-politician Fraser Metzger of Randolph for governor. Nationally, Roosevelt gained enough votes from Taft to allow the Democrat, Woodrow Wilson, to win the presidency. Vermont voted for Taft, but Roosevelt was a scant 1,200 votes behind. In the gubernatorial race, Allen Fletcher, a Proctor relative, won forty-three percent of the vote and Metzger twenty-five percent. There was no majority, once again the election was thrown into the House, where mainline Republican Fletcher was chosen. During Fletcher's administration many new laws

The Vermont Senate in the early 1900's. (VHS)

were enacted including workmen's compensation and measures relating to the conservation of natural resources.

One of the leaders in the state Progressive movement was Ernest W. Gibson, who went to the 1912 Republican national convention as a Roosevelt delegate. Gibson later served in the U.S. House and Senate as a Republican from 1923-1940. He was succeeded in the Senate by George Aiken, who served a total of six terms. Opposition to the Proctor faction within the party was often referred to as the Aiken-Gibson wing. A final showdown between the two wings came in 1946, when Gibson's son, Ernest, successfully challenged incumbent Governor Mortimer Proctor. By the mid-1950s, the Proctor influence had virtually disappeared. By the late 1970s the family had even lost its interest in the marble company and sold it to a Swiss company.

VERMONT POLITICIANS "ABROAD"

It has been said that Vermont's greatest export is its people, and this is no less true for its political figures. Vermonters who have served their state in Washington, and the natives

Ernest W. Gibson, U.S. Congressman and Senator from 1923-1940. (EWG III)

Progressive Party of Vermont.

Believing in the Principles of the Progressive Party as set forth in the recent campaign, and believing that the fight should be continued until these principles shall have fully triumphed, I hereby promise to give, or to secure from others, the sum of $ ...., the same to be used for the campaign of the Progressive Party of the State of Vermont for the year 1913. This subscription is payable in two equal parts, the first part on or before January 1, 1913, the second part on or before April 1, 1913.

Signed ....

Address ....

Checks should be made payble to **ERNEST KELLEY**, Treasurer Salisbury, Vt.

(UVM)

The three Ernests—last being the current Supreme court judge. Three generations of Gibsons—from left, Ernest Sr., Ernest Jr. and Ernest III.

"WOMAN'S PLACE IS IN THE HOME." YES, BUT HOW ABOUT WOMEN WHO MUST WORK TO HAVE A HOME

Placard of a meeting of women from New Hampshire and Vermont in 1912.

IN ALL EQUAL SUFFRAGE STATES AN AVERAGE OF 83 1-3% OF WOMEN VOTE

Placard of a meeting of women from New Hampshire and Vermont in 1912.

VERMONT
PROHIBITION CONVENTION

A MASS CONVENTION
of the Prohibition Party of Vermont

is hereby called to Meet in the

MEMORIAL ROOM   -   -   CITY HALL

MONTPELIER, VT., SEPTEMBER 12th, 1916.

AT ONE O'CLOCK P. M.,

For the purpose of adopting a Platform, Nominating Candidates for the several State Offices, Electing a State Committee and doing any other appropriate business.

Some Interesting Speaking is Expected.

All adherents of the Prohibition Party, men and women, are entitled to participate in the Convention upon Registering at the Bureau of Information and Registration in the CITY HALL, First Floor.

THE SPECIAL ATTENTION OF THOSE WHO HAVE SIGNED THE VOTER'S PLEDGE THAT:

"No POLITICAL PARTY CAN HAVE MY VOTE THAT DOES NOT DECLARE FOR STATE AND NATIONAL PROHIBITION OF THE LIQUOR TRAFFIC", IS CALLED TO THE FACT THAT ALL THE OTHER PARTIES ARE ACTIVELY SILENT ON THAT ISSUE AND THAT THE PROHIBITION PARTY AFFORDS THE ONLY OPPORTUNITY TO VOTE IN HARMONY WITH THEIR PLEDGE.

A VOTE FOR ANY OTHER PARTY IS A VOTE FOR THE CONTINUANCE OF PRESENT CONDITIONS.

ALL VOTER'S PLEDGE SIGNERS ARE CORDIALLY INVITED TO THIS CONVENTION.

A large and Representative Attendance is desired.

The State Committee will be pleased to meet any of the party for an informal Conference in the Convention Hall between ten and twelve o'clock in the forenoon.

The Convention will open for Business at 1 o'clock P. M.

For further information address Dr. L. W. Hanson, Chairman, Montpelier, Vt.

PLEASE EXTEND NOTICE AND INVITE OTHERS.

(VHS)

*U.S. Senator George Edmunds,
served from 1866 to 1891.
Played a major role in settling
the Hayes-Tilden presidential
controversy. (UVM)*

who left Vermont and served in other states, have been part
of an unusually large group of highly regarded public figures
from one of the country's smallest states.

One such person was Strafford-born Justin Morrill. His
political career spanned forty-four years, including six terms
in the United States Senate. He angered the South by his
sponsorship of the protective tariff in 1861 and is perhaps
best known for the Morrill Act of 1862, which established
the nation's land grant colleges. He advocated civil service
reform and opposed territorial expansion and the Spanish
American War. His position on the war brought him into
conflict with Redfield Proctor. He was also influential in helping promote the Library of Congress and the Washington
Monument.

Another Vermonter who served with distinction in
Washington was George Edmunds from Richmond. Elected
four times to the U.S. Senate, Edmunds played a major role
in the Hayes-Tilden presidential controversy of 1876. Tilden
won the most popular votes in the election, but not enough
in the Electoral College. A dispute over the electors' creden-
tials led to the establishment of an electoral commission to
settle the disagreement. Edmunds was the sponsor of the
bill setting up the commission. Many felt that the establish-

OUR ROYAL RULERS (BY DIVINE RIGHT) IN SECRET SESSION.

An 1886 cartoon attacking Senator Edmunds for holding secret U.S. Senate sessions. Edmunds is portrayed as King Charles I of England.

George Perkins Marsh, three-term Congressman, leading figure in the early conservation movement.

Thaddeus Stevens led the fight for constitutional amendments guaranteeing rights to all and helped establish the Freedman's Bureau which provided food and education for ex-slaves.

ment of the commission helped avert another Civil War. For his efforts, Edmunds was honored by the Republican conventions of 1880 and 1884 by having his name placed in nomination for the presidency.

Another prominent lawmaker was Luke Poland, born in Westford, Chief Justice of the Vermont Supreme Court and a five-term Congressman. Poland was the chairman of the committee that investigated the Credit Mobilier Scandal during the Grant administration and led an investigation of the Ku Klux Klan. As chairman of the committee, Poland reported that "this country is fast becoming filled with gigantic corporations, wielding and controlling immense aggregations of money and thereby commanding vast influence and power."[9]

Three-term Whig congressman George Perkins Marsh from Burlington, who served for twenty-one years as the nation's first minister to Italy, was a leading figure in the early conservation movement. His book, *Man and Nature*, was a

Levi P. Morton, born in Shoreham.
Morton was a Congressman, U.S.
Minister to France, Vice-President
in 1888 and Governor of New
York in 1894.

Chester Arthur, Vermont native
who became President when James
Garfield was assassinated in
~~*1882.*~~ *1881.*

seminal work in the movement that eventually blossomed
into the environmental efforts of the 1960s and 1970s.

Thaddeus Stevens, born in Danville, achieved his political
success in Pennsylvania, and was perhaps the best-known
of the so-called "radical" Republicans of the Civil War era.
Stevens was a militant abolitionist and a leader in the
organization of the Republican party. He continually exerted
pressure on the Republicans to provide services to freed
blacks and was an outspoken opponent of Lincoln. Whereas
Lincoln, and to some extent Andrew Johnson, stressed compassion toward the defeated confederacy once the war
ended, Stevens stressed retribution, which won him the
nickname of "The Scourge of the South." He pushed for
passage of Constitutional amendments guaranteeing rights
to all regardless of race and helped establish the Freedman's
Bureau, which was designed to provide food and education
for ex-slaves.

The Democrats had argued that the Republican administration needed a house cleaning. In this cartoon they are dejected when their entrance to Washington is blocked by President Arthur's Civil Service reform legislation.

Levi Morton, born in Shoreham, was governor of New York, served in Congress, was United States minister to France and served as vice-president from 1888-1892.

Fairfield-born Chester Arthur, who taught school in Pownal before leaving the state, became president when a disappointed office-seeker assassinated James Garfield in 1881. Arthur pioneered Civil Service reforms while in office.

Dorman Kent, in his 1937 book "Vermonters," reviewed the 1890 edition of "Who's Who In America" and found at that time Vermont provided the United States with a greater number of statesmen and judges, proportation to its size than almost any other state in the Union. Vermonters serving out-of-state included forty-six state supreme court judges, fourteen United States senators, one hundred United States congressmen and twenty-two governors.[10]

Republican Ticket in 1880. (UVM)

NOTES

1. Charles H. Davenport, "The Future of Domocracy in Vermont", *The Quill* September, 1890, p. 54. See also, *History of Vermont Politics* by Davenport, The Vermonter, November, 1901, pp. 378-394.
2. Robert W. Mitchell, "Unique Vermont," *The American Mercury*, LX (March, 1945), pp. 337-340.
3. *Ibid.*pp. 337-340.
4. *Rutland Daily Herald*, October 7, 1976.
5. Redfield Proctor, Inaugural Address.
6. Crockett, Vol. 4, 264.
7. Mason A. Green, *Nineteen-Two in Vermont - the Fight for Local Option*, (Rutland: The Marble City Press, 1912)
8. Alan Jeffrey, "Vermont's Pastor-Politician: Fraser Metzger and the Bull Moose Campaign of 1912", *Vermont History*, Vol 38, No. 1 (Winter, 1970) pp. 58-69.
9. Crockett, Vol. 4, p. 62.
10. Dorman B.E. Kent, *Vermonters* (Montpelier: Vermont Historical Society, 1937) pp. 7-8.

Chester Arthur's birthplace in Fairfield.

CHAPTER IX

The Rise of the Modern Republican Party

THE GENERAL ASSEMBLY OF 1915, WHICH ENACTED the direct primary, was considered a "progressive" group. Progressive legislation included Vermont's initial workmen's compansation act, court reform, regulation of narcotics and the establishment of farm labor and agricultural marketing bureaus. The Senate passed a constitutional proposal providing for women's suffrage but the measure was killed in the House. The direct primary was referred to the people and passed by slightly over 3,000 votes. Dissatisfaction with the existing caucus procedures by which party nominations had taken place was a basic reason for the adoption of the new primary law.[1]

Percival Clement, owner of the Rutland *Herald*, was one of the first to benefit from this change. He had unsuccessfully challenged the Republican organization in 1902 and 1906 as a candidate for governor. In 1918, after the convention system was abandoned, he won the nomination – and of course the general election, because he was the Republican.

In 1920 James Hartness, a self-educated inventor, engineer and political novice, used the primary to capture the governorship. Hartness believed management systems brought to government would produce efficiency and economy. Speaking before the General Assembly in 1921 he said: "It is supremely necessary for the workers and executives in our industries to get the fullest possible conception of principles governing life and engineering, so that they can see

Charles W. Gates, served as Governor from 1915-1917. (UVM)

James Hartness, inventor, engineer and Governor from 1921-1923. (UVM)

Edna Beard, the first woman to serve in the Vermont General Assembly.

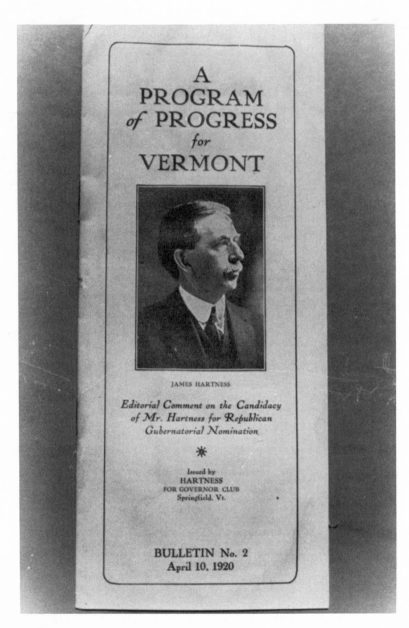

Start Making Vermont Better for All
By Nominating Hartness

READ IT ALL!

THE DRIVE
Issued in the Interest of a Progressive Vermont

VOL. 1. No. 2.   SPRINGFIELD, VERMONT

The Women of Vermont May Vote at the State Primaries

Adoption by Thirty-six States of the Woman's Suffrage Amendment Makes It Possible for Women to Vote in Vermont Sept. 14th Without Any Further Legislation, Declares Attorney General Archibald.

(Special to The Drive.)

Montpelier.—"The proclaiming of the equal suffrage amendment to the United States Constitution automatically makes women voters and no additional legislation is needed in Vermont to allow them to participate in state and federal elections."

With these words Attorney General Frank C. Archibald answered the question, "Can women in Vermont vote at the primaries and at the election?"

Mr. Archibald's affirmative answer means that the way is open for the women, for the first time in the history of the state, to vote for candidates in the primaries and for state and federal officers at a general election.

There is no longer any distinction between men and women politically, said Mr. Archibald. The state laws which recognize such a distinction no longer prevail, he said.

In order to vote at the primaries women have to do exactly what men have to do; no more, no less.

There is absolutely no tax qualification. It is not necessary that men or women be tax payers in order to vote in state or federal primaries or elections. The tax requirement holds only for town meetings.

THINGS WOMEN VOTERS MUST DO.

There are just two things women must do to qualify:—

1st. You must get your name placed with the men voters on the check-list. This list of men voters is now posted in your town or city clerk's office. You have the right to have your name placed on that list if you are at least twenty-one years of age, have lived in this state at least a year before September 14 and are an American citizen.

2nd. See to it that you swear to the following oath, called the Freemen's Oath, before either your town clerk, a justice of the peace, or one of your selectmen.

"You solemnly swear (or affirm) that whenever you give your vote or suffrage, touching any

matter that concerns the State of Vermont, you will do it so as in your conscience you shall judge will most conduce to the best good of the same, as established by the Constitution, without fear or favor of any man."

Your town or city clerk and your selectmen, or similar officers if you live in a city, with certain others, are charged with the duty of placing the names of all legal voters (and you are one of them now) on the check list. Apply to them immediately. They can help you and tell you when and where you should go to have these two things done.

THINGS WOMEN VOTERS ARE NOT REQUIRED TO DO.

There are certain things not required of women to become voters:—

1. The fact that you have or have not paid a tax this year has nothing to do with your right to vote at the primary election September 14, 1920.

2. The fact of having your name placed on the check list as a voter and your voting does not make you a tax payer, or make you liable to a poll tax, or bind you to pay any tax.

The extent to which women play a part in the coming primaries depends in large measure on women as individuals. They are not placed on the check list automatically. Women must attend to this matter themselves. They must appear in person before the town clerk and the board of civil authority and make claim of the right of suffrage.

It is a very easy matter, only it must be attended to personally. Because of the newness of it all, some town clerks or boards of civil authority may themselves be confused as to the process. Some may say that a woman must first be a tax payer. Such, however, is not the case. Attorney General Archibald is authority for this statement, and any women who encounters an official who says payment of a tax is necessary, should inform him to the contrary and has a perfect right to cite the attorney general.

(Continued on Fourth Page.)

What the Newspapers Say About Hartness

All Admit His Remarkable Ability and His Honesty of Purpose to Aid Vermont.

Rutland Herald.—During the war Mr. Hartness was an active worker. He was appointed United States food administrator for Vermont, which position he later resigned because his time and

of the Royal Astronomical Society of London, a fellow of the Aeronautical Society and a member of the Royal Societies Club. He is one of the few civilian aviators in the state and is predicted entrance of Mr. Hartness is ex-

can possibly be performed for our commonwealth.

St. Albans Messenger.—The Messenger welcomes James Hartness, of Springfield, into the contest for the Republican nomination to the office of governor. This paper feels that he is the type of executive of which the state stands in need.

Manchester Journal.—If Mr. Hartness should bring the same degree of energy and ability to the office of governor of this state that he has shown in his private affairs he should make a good governor.

Middlebury Register.—The entrance of Mr. Hartness in Springfield, in many ways the

thought in his upbuilding of the Jones & Lamson company, in his encouragement and assistance in the starting of all the other industries that have been, in a way, offshoots of the parent plant, and also in his farsighted efforts to place Vermont on the aerial map.

Burlington Free Press.—We thoroughly and honestly believe that the Hon. James Hartness of Springfield would do more to get Vermont out of its rut than any other man who could be made governor at this time. This is our whole gospel for the Vermont state election of 1920.

Rutland News.—The neighbors of James Hartness of Springfield, in many ways the

As Primary Day Approaches Hartness

All Sections of State Support Springfield Candidate Predicted by a Washington

JAMES HARTNESS, OF S

(Special to The Drive.)

Montpelier.—The political situation in Vermont, so far as the Republican nomination for the governorship is concerned, has undergone some rapid changes since the first issue of THE DRIVE, changes that have been featured by the development of Hartness strength, an increase which is admitted by that section of the opposition which is inclined to be frank. For instance, The Brattleboro Reformer, a supporter of Frederick H. Babbitt, admitted editorially August 26 that "There is no doubt that the Hartness campaign has been making noticeable progress of late". This paper sees the real contest to be between Hartness and Babbitt. The Burlington Free Press, on the other hand, predicts the final clash to be between Hartness and Agan.

In many ways the Hartness campaign has been unique and unusual for Vermont. Whereas Mr. Babbitt had long been aiming at the governorship and had built up his machine as much as possible for this one end, and whereas Mr. Emery, being a practiced politician with a wide acquaintance among politicians who might aid him according to the old political standards, Mr. Hartness started out without these "assets" (which have turned into liabilities) and went directly to the people with his "Program of Progress for Vermont".

HARTNESS' DIRECT APPEAL TO THE PEOPLE.

Hartness was a leader in the women's right to vote movement. Hartness published his own newspaper during his gubernatorial campaign. (UVM)

what must be done to promote their own success and also to know what is deadly to their own interests and the interests of the state."

Hartness capitalized on another reform of the era—giving women the right to vote. He had been a leader on a state committee to ratify the nineteenth amendment to the United States Constitution, the women's suffrage amendment. When Hartness gave his Inaugural Address in 1921, sitting as a member of the House was Edna Beard, of Orange, a former school superintendent. She was the first woman ever elected to the Vermont House. In the beginning of his presentation Hartness said: "Women's coming into full equality suffrage bodes well for humanity. . . . We have a thousand other reasons for being glad that woman has been granted equality in controlling and shaping the destiny of our State and Nation."[2]

CALVIN COOLIDGE

A few days after Hartness's Inaugural address, Vice President-Elect Calvin Coolidge addressed the General Assembly. A native of Plymouth Notch, the Republican Coolidge had made his mark in Massachusetts politics and had gained national recognition during the Boston police strike of 1919, when he made the famous pronouncement that "There is no right to strike against the public safety by any body, any time, any where." Coolidge was chosen as Vice President to balance the Warren G. Harding ticket. Few suspected that within two years he would be in the White House, upon Harding's death.

Paying a tribute to his State, Coolidge said:

The State House of Vermont holds an interest for me that no public building can ever exceed. This hall of the House of Representatives has a fascination that is unapproachable. Here my father sat as a member of the Legislature and his father before him. At an age so early that my memory holds no previous recollection, I was brought here by my mother and my grandfather to visit my father, and among other experiences, seated in the chair of the Chief Executive with a veneration which has forever marked for me the reverence due that righteous authori-

Calvin and Grace Coolidge, photograph by Charles McCormick from the Coolidge Family Papers at the Vermont Historical Society.

President and Mrs. Coolidge standing in auto at Burlington, Vermont. (UVM)

Coolidge's country bumpkin image was created by photographs such as this, taken at the family farm in Plymouth Notch.

ty which is vested in a government over which the people are supreme. Compared with that visit no other journey will ever seem of equal importance. No other experience will ever touch in like manner and in like degree my imagination. Here I first saw that sacred fire which lights the altar of my country.[3]

Coolidge's administration, from 1923-1929, has traditionally been characterized as strongly pro-business. Coolidge himself helped create this impression with his oft quoted utterance, "The business of America is business." His taciturn

Campaign sticker from the 1924 presidential campaign.

Homestead of our 30th President, Calvin Coolidge, Plymouth, Vermont. (VDD)

THE OFFICIAL
CAMPAIGN SONG *OF THE* HOME TOWN COOLIDGE CLUB
OF
PLYMOUTH, VERMONT

KEEP COOL AND KEEP COOLIDGE

MUSIC BY BRUCE HARPER   WORDS BY IDA CHEEVER GOODWIN

BAND, ORCHESTRA,
MALE QUARTET & MIXED QUARTET,
ARRANGEMENTS MAY BE OBTAINED FROM THE PUBLISHERS

PUBLISHED BY
HOME TOWN COOLIDGE CLUB, PLYMOUTH, VERMONT
COPYRIGHT MCMXXIV by W.S. TUTTLE
PRINTED IN U.S.A.

(UVM)

Keep Cool And Keep Coolidge

(UVM)

VERMONT

FROM THE SPEECH OF

∽ PRESIDENT COOLIDGE ∾

AT BENNINGTON, SEPTEMBER 21, 1928

"Vermont is a state I love.

"I could not look upon the peaks of Ascutney, Killington, Mansfield and Equinox without being moved in a way that no other scene could move me.

"It was here that I first saw the light of day; here I received my bride; here my dead lie pillowed on the loving breast of our everlasting hills.

"I love Vermont because of her hills and valleys, her scenery and invigorating climate, but most of all, because of her indomitable people. They are a race of pioneers who have almost beggared themselves to serve others. If the spirit of liberty should vanish in other parts of the union and support of our institutions should languish, it could all be replenished from the generous store held by the people of this brave little state of Vermont."

To the Vermont Historical Society,

Calvin Coolidge.

*Porter H. Dale, served in the U.S. House from
1914-1922 and as a U.S. Senator from
1922-1933. (UVM)*

nature led many to believe he was simply a caretaker president, who let others – both from within government and outside of it – run the country. More recent historians have mentioned Coolidge's shrewdness, and his ability to hold the Republican party together in the aftermath of the Harding scandals. He also stressed reducing the national debt.

The Coolidge years represented a calm before the storm, which broke right after he left office. Although he probably could have gained re-nomination in 1928 Coolidge declined the opportunity – in what is possibly the shortest statement ever given on such a subject, "I do not choose to run for President in 1928." Herbert Hoover received the nomination, and within less than a year, the stock market had collapsed and the nation was in its worst depression.

WASHINGTON COUNTY RALLY

Barre City Opera House
Saturday Evening, October 6
At 8 O'clock

HON. PORTER H. DALE
Of ISLAND POND

The Leading Republican Candidate for
THE UNITED STATES SENATE
Will address the Rally on

THE ISSUES OF THE CAMPAIGN

INCLUDING: BOLSHEVISM, THE
SOLDIER BLOC, THE FARMER
BLOC, THE MOTHER BLOC, THE
VOLSTEAD ACT.

MUSIC BY THE BARRE CITY BAND

DON'T MISS THIS GREAT
POLITICAL EVENT

Rally for U.S. Senator Porter H. Dale, 1923 at the Barre City Opera House.

SAMPLE COPY.

IN DEFENSE
Of The Volstead Act and
The Dry Candidates

Read first the position of the candidates on the wet and dry issue, then read the facts concerning the Volstead Act on the last three pages and you will learn that this act of Congress does not need to be "humanized" or is it lacking in "reason and common sense."

Congressman Dale
AND
Congressman Greene

Both Voted for the Volstead Act

We submit that our Congressmen, after hearing every phase of the "Enforcement Act" discussed, concluded it was sufficiently "humanized" to deal with "King Alcohol" and that the code did contain the elements of "reason and common sense," therefore, they supported the Act to make the Eighteenth Amendment effective in Vermont and the Nation.

The Dry Candidates are Strong Men
VOTE FOR THEM

For Additional Copies to Distribute address
THE VERMONT ANTI - SALOON LEAGUE
Burlington, Vermont

The constitutional amendment which prohibited the manufacture and sale of alcoholic beverages was ratified in 1919 and repealed in 1933. The Volstead Act was prohibition's enforcement statute. (UVM)

WHO SAYS
The Enforcement Act
Is Too Drastic?

The Brewer

The Distiller

The Bootlegger

The Ex-Saloon Keeper

The Liquor Smuggler

The Blind Pig Proprietor

The Anti-Prohibition League

The Personal Liberty League

The Vermont Local-Option
     League

The Wet Candidates

The Modification Candidates

and a few others.

What law-abiding citizen
wants to add his name to
the above list?

National Life Building, Montpelier, Vermont, flood 1927. (UVM)

THE FLOOD OF 1927

It was the flood of 1927, and not the Depression, however, that first led Vermont through a period of great change. The flood caused massive damage around the state, wiping out highways and railroads and sweeping buildings off their foundations. Hoover, then Secretary of Commerce, came to the state to view the damage, remarking he had seen "Vermont at her worst, but Vermonters at their best." Much of Vermont was inaccessible except for air travel. Barnstorming pilots whose aid delivered medical supplies to remote parts of Vermont were the real heroes of the flood.

Before the flood, individual towns were largely responsible for the repair of bridges and roads, but the flood damage was so massive that they alone could not finance all the repairs. At a special session in November 1927, the General Assembly voted an $8.5-million bond issue. The state assumed further responsibility for highway maintenance, and it was symptomatic of the need to shift power from the local to the state level. The repair program also brought Vermont into the automobile age. Some damaged railroads were never restored and most of the public funds went to new highways. Cars and trucks increasingly replaced trains and horses.[4]

The flood also caused changes in the state's dependence on the federal government. Contrary to popular belief, Vermont did accept federal money to help it rebuild after the flood. Vermont's congressional delegation asked for and received more than $2.5 million to repair highways and bridges within Vermont.

The flood played a role in breaking the "single-term" tradition. In 1928, Governor John E. Weeks won re-election and became the first governor to serve two terms since the Vermont Constitution was amended in 1870 to provide for a two-year term. Weeks stressed that re-election was necessary to have continuity in the flood recovery program.

State government grew to meet the new demands placed upon it by the disaster, and it needed more money. In 1931 the Legislature passed the state's first income tax and established a system of state highways.

The state realized a need for a flood control program. As a result Vermont accepted federal dollars to build dams at East Barre, Middlesex, and Waterbury. The dams were built by the Civilian Conservation Corps and Army Corps of Engineers.

Studies by scholars such as Professor Frank Bryan of the University of Vermont have shown that Vermont is one of the most centralized of all the states. One reason for this is that counties play a relatively insignificant role compared to that in other states. Some argue that centralization took place years before the flood.

During the post-Civil War period the smaller agricultural towns looked for greater state services. In 1869 The Vermont Dairymen's Association fought for a greater participation in the fluid milk market. Transporting milk requires open roads and Vermont became one of the first states to establish state aid to highway programs. In addition National Highway legislation required state supervision over federal grants. Promotion of the dairy industry had implications for a greater state interest in health and education.

Centralization was supported by both conservatives who were concerned about mounting governmental costs and by progressives who thought that centralization meant greater efficiency. In 1917 administrative supervision was tightened under a Board of Control. In the same year, the General Assembly consolidated a myriad of conservation and agricultural activities under a new Commissioner of Agriculture. Activities relating to workmen's compensation and arbitration were placed under a Commissioner of Industries.

The first full-scale state governmental reorganization took place under the leadership of Redfield Proctor in 1923. All governmental activities were consolidated into seven departments: agriculture, education, finance, highways, public service, public welfare, and public health. In the 1960s Governor Philip Hoff fought for governmental reorganization, and under Governor Deane Davis partial reorganization took place.

THE DEPRESSION

The Depression accelerated the forces of centralization, although the New Deal's power came from the federal and not the state level. As the state had begun to be involved directly in the day-to-day affairs of its people, so too, did the federal government under Roosevelt move into Americans' daily lives. In April 1933 Governor Stanley Wilson wrote President Franklin D. Roosevelt that the thrust of Roosevelt's programs was to attack what he perceived as national problems that state and local governments alone could not solve. It was a sharp departure from the limited role government played in the Coolidge and Hoover years.

Despite Vermont's eighty-year tradition of voting Republican, Roosevelt was not willing to write off the state in the 1932 election. He came here in September of 1932 and was greeted warmly at the Vermont State Fair in Rutland. Predicting that he would carry Vermont, Roosevelt said "All sections of the country are related and should receive equal benefits from the government. Neither city nor farm can be prosperous without either being prosperous."

Franklin D. Roosevelt visited Rutland Fair in 1932. President from 1933 to 1945.

His foray was unsuccessful, though. He defeated Hoover nationally, but in Vermont he lost by 20,000 votes out of about 135,000 cast. (Norman Thomas, the socialist candidate, received 1,500 votes.) The only bright note for the Democrats in Vermont was that the Republican victory represented the narrowest margin since the party was split in the 1912 election.

Stanley C. Wilson served as Governor from 1931 to 1935. (UVM)

George Aiken, Vermont Governor and long-time U.S. Senator.

AIKEN'S ASCENDANCE

Vermont Democrats were not able to capitalize on the economic disarray and make serious inroads into Republican power. Part of the reason was the leadership provided the Republicans by George Aiken, who was a legislator, House speaker and Lieutenant Governor before running successfully for governor in 1936. Among Aiken's strongest supporters were Sterry Waterman (later a federal judge), president of the Young Republicans in Vermont and Aiken's 1936 campaign manager, and Ernest Gibson Jr.[4]

Aiken shrewdly rejected the philosophy of the New Deal

This Man Aiken

What About Him?

GEORGE D. AIKEN
1931 Representative   1933 Speaker of the House
Present Lieutenant Governor
President Windham County Farm Bureau
School Director, 15 years
A Granger since 1907

Candidate for the Republican Nomination

FOR GOVERNOR OF VERMONT

AT THE PRIMARY ELECTION

September 8, 1936

(VHS)

Federal Judge Sterry Waterman, Aiken's campaign manager in 1936. (VHS)

while accepting the money and benefits provided by many of its programs. He supported Social Security and recreation and conservation programs, and as United States Senator was the architect of the current Food Stamp program, which he saw as a way to help both the poor get food and farmers to sell it. Aiken did not oppose New Deal reforms simply because they were proposed by Democrats. But he did not like the way the federal government had become the dominant power in people's lives. In his book *Speaking from Vermont* written in 1938, Aiken termed the New Deal a "tragedy." He wrote, "Helping folks in their own homes, in their own localities, in a quiet and unobtrusive way, has been exchanged for a nationwide ballyhooed machine with its propaganda agents, its circus poster, and high-pressure advertising methods."[5]

After the 1936 election one Vermont newspaper said that the nation "follows strange gods" and recommended that the national government "run excursions from the rest of the country into Vermont to show what a Republican looks like."

As one of only four Republicans who were elected governor in the Democratic landslide of 1936, Aiken was thrown into the national spotlight. He had attacked the New Deal as "that visible and invisible government in Washington, whose thoughts and actions are so alien to the free-thinking people of Vermont and of the nation." He said the Roosevelt administration was an attempt "for more and more control of all of us and our possessions and resources, public and private."[6]

That was the kind of rhetoric the Republicans liked to hear. His attacks on the New Deal's attempt to control hydro power rights in Vermont gave him a stage from which to try to rally Republicans. He did not, however, see the New Deal as the sole cause for Republican problems. In December 1937 Aiken, in an attempt to rejuvenate the Republican party and broaden its appeal, suggested to the Republican National Committee that the party "reject decisively the use of enormous expenditures and special benefits as a political expedient for attracting agriculture, industrial groups, and other workers to our Party. We can never outbid our opponents and we should be ashamed to try. . . . Instead of offering a place at the feed-troughs, invite . . . the nation . . . to work together to produce . . . a larger volume of goods and services for more people of this nation. Emphasize what we can give and do—not what we can get."[7]

Toward the end of 1937 Vermonter Leo Casey, publicity director of the Republican National Committee, organized an Aiken presidential campaign. The high point was a nationally broadcast speech to the National Republican Club's 1938 Lincoln Day Dinner in New York City. True to his candid style, Aiken began his radio address with a bombshell: "The greatest praise I can give Lincoln . . . is to say he would be ashamed of his party's leadership today."[8] The speech was reported favorably in *Newsweek,* and *The Christian Science Monitor,* but Aiken's bid got nowhere. Wendell Wilkie won the Republican nomination, but then lost to Roosevelt in 1940 when the popular president ran for a third term.

In 1940 Senator Gibson died. Aiken subsequently defeated Ralph Flanders, like Hartness an engineer, for the Republican nomination and went on to win the general election. It was the beginning of a thirty-six-year tenure in the Senate.

AFTER THE ELEPHANT HEARD FROM VERMONT

Elderman in The Washington Post and Page in The Louisville Courier-Journal

Comments following the letter from George D. Aiken, G. O. P. Governor of Vermont, assailing party leaders. At the left, "How far down can you read?"   At the right, "His baby."

(VHS)

THE LAST PROCTOR

Aiken was succeeded in the statehouse by William Wills, and then in 1944 by the last of the Proctors, Mortimer. In 1946 Proctor was challenged by Ernest Gibson, Jr. Gibson was just back from World War II, where he had fought with distinction with the forty-third Division commanded by General Leonard Wing of Rutland.

Gibson attacked Proctor for his "Old Guard" connections, called his administration a "study in still life," and asked Vermont voters to break the "rule of succession," which since 1930 had allowed the lieutenant governor to succeed to the governorship. He charged that a relatively small clique of people chose governors nearly ten years in advance, "supporting them up a series of political steps to the highest office."

Ernest Gibson is treated for a head wound during a Japanese air raid in the Pacific during World War II.

VOTE ON AUGUST 13

No Political Entanglements

"For nearly 20 years the rule of succession has dominated Vermont politics. Under this rule a relatively small clique of people choose Governors nearly 10 years in advance, supporting them up a series of political steps to the highest office. Because of this, able men at the height of their ability who have not followed the rule of succession hesitate to seek this high public office. . . . To stop this unwholesome practice, to promote a greater democracy and to make economic security march hand in hand with political liberties in Vermont is the challenging reason for my candidacy. . . . I stand wholly on my own merits and ask no person to vote for me who does not believe, deep in his heart, that I can give better leadership to Vermont than can the opposing candidate."

ERNEST W. GIBSON

FOR GOVERNOR

ERNEST W. GIBSON

Ernest W. Gibson, Jr. of Brattleboro served as Governor from 1947-1950. This is part of his 1947 campaign brochure. (VHS)

Although Proctor had the advantage of incumbency, Gibson won the primary by 8,000 votes and easily won the general election. During his first term in office governmental services in the areas of education, health, welfare and highways were greatly increased. Interestingly, he felt the greatest problem facing his administration was "equalizing educational opportunity and distributing the costs as equally as possible among the towns and school districts of the state."[9]

Gibson asked for what was then the highest budget in Vermont history, thirty-one million. To raise the necessary funds, he pushed for and won an increase in the state income tax. Gibson turned back a challenge from his lieutenant governor, Lee Emerson, in 1948, and served until 1950, when he resigned to become a federal district judge.

Gibsons have continued to hold state and national political offices. Ernest Gibson, Jr.'s eldest son, Ernest III, served in the Vermont House, was appointed public service commis-

(UVM)

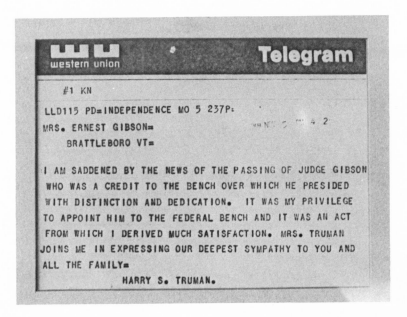

western union   **Telegram**

#1 KN

LLD115 PD=INDEPENDENCE MO 5 237P=

MRS. ERNEST GIBSON=

    BRATTLEBORO VT=

I AM SADDENED BY THE NEWS OF THE PASSING OF JUDGE GIBSON WHO WAS A CREDIT TO THE BENCH OVER WHICH HE PRESIDED WITH DISTINCTION AND DEDICATION. IT WAS MY PRIVILEGE TO APPOINT HIM TO THE FEDERAL BENCH AND IT WAS AN ACT FROM WHICH I DERIVED MUCH SATISFACTION. MRS. TRUMAN JOINS ME IN EXPRESSING OUR DEEPEST SYMPATHY TO YOU AND ALL THE FAMILY=

    HARRY S. TRUMAN.

(VHS)

sioner by Governor Philip Hoff and is currently a supreme court judge. Another son, Robert, has served as secretary of the state senate since 1963, and the youngest son, David, has been a state's attorney from Windham County and a state senator.

Proctor's defeat by Gibson was the first time a Republican incumbent had been defeated in a primary. The traditions that had served the party well were no longer in place. Mortimer Proctor's election in 1944, for example, had marked the first Republican break from the mountain rule. From now on, the Republicans could not rely upon the rule to limit the pool of candidates nor could incumbents be assured of nomination.

NOTES

1. Winston Allen Flint, *The Progressive Movement in Vermont* (Washington, D.C.: American Council on Public Affairs) pp 61-73. Flint wrote that the strongest defense of the direct primary ... "was that it conformed to the general principle of democratic control of government. This defense was especially true in Vermont, a one-party state, whose democratic control of nominations is much more significant than popular control of the final election."

2. James Hartness, *Inaugural Address*, Vermont Senate Journal, 1921, pp. 668-669. See John A. Neuenschwader, "An Engineer for Governor: James Hartness in 1920", *Vermont History*, Vol. 38, No. 2 (Spring 1970)

3. Crockett, Vol. 4, pp. 558-559.

4. Samuel B. Hand, "The Erosion of Republican Hegemony in Vermont, 1927-1974." A manuscript and prospectus for a research project funded by the National Endowment for the Humanities, pp. 1-2. Hand wrote:

   > During the 1930's an organized group of dissidents, the Young Republicans, wrenched significant concessions from the party and were major contributors to the primary victories of like-minded Republicans. The 1936 election of Governor George Aiken is the most celebrated instance of this strategy. It was not until after World War II, however, that this element, in the person of Ernest Gibson, Jr., was able to achieve state-wide electoral victory in its own right. Gibson, running on a primary ticket that included such other former Young Republicans as Sterry Waterman and Winston Prouty, successfully challenged the established order by defeating Governor Mortimer Proctor, who was seeking the second term traditionally awarded incumbents.

5. George Aiken, *Speaking From Vermont*, (New York: Frederick Stokes, 1938) p. 196.

6. H. Nicholas Muller and Samuel B. Hand, *In A State of Nature: Reading In Vermont History*, (Montpelier, Vermont: Vermont Historical Society 1982) p 329.

7. Aiken, p. 219.

8. D. Gregory Sanford, "You Can't Get There From Here: The Presidential Boomlet for Governor George D. Aiken, 1937-1939, *Vermont History*, Vol. 4, (Fall 1981) p. 205.

9. Ernest W. Gibson, *Inaugural Address To the General Assembly and the People of Vermont*, January 9, 1947, p. 6.

CHAPTER X

The Democrats Finally Gain Power

IN MANY WAYS GEORGE AIKEN TYPIFIED the Republican rule that had held sway in Vermont for a century. He was able to appeal to a wide range of Vermonters because of his strong, native ties to the state – his solid base of political support built over a number of years of service to the state – and his down-to-earth style. Aiken served six consecutive terms in the United States Senate.

When he finally retired in 1975, he was one of the most respected men in the Senate. He was the ranking Republican on the Agriculture and Foreign Relations committees. One of his greatest achievements was his fight for the St. Lawrence Seaway and its related power project, which brought to Vermont cheap hydroelectricity.

Aiken's popularity was so great that he claimed he never had to ask for a vote. "Get into the community and find out what the problems are. That's the best politics," he said. When Aiken retired at eighty-two, he said he would miss his friends in the capital, but not Washington. "I've never been at home in Washington. . . . Home's up on the mountains in Vermont where I always lived." To Putney, and his orchard and wildflowers, he returned.[1]

Aiken's senatorial career eclipsed those of most of his other Vermont colleagues. Among those serving with him during his long tenure were Warren Austin, Winston Prouty, and Ralph Flanders and Robert Stafford. Austin and Flanders achieved perhaps the greatest recognition. Austin was this country's first ambassador to the United Nations.

Warren Austin

Warren Austin (UVM)

Ralph Flanders served in the U.S. Senate from 1947-1959. (UVM)

Senator Ralph Flanders visiting the camp of the 206th Field Artillery Battalion, A.P. Hill Military Reservation. (UVM)

Harold J. Arthur became Governor when Ernest Gibson resigned in January, 1950 to become a U.S. District Judge. (UVM)

In a letter to a little Swanton girl on the meaning, of his native state, Austin wrote:

> I love Vermont because it was there I was born and . . . prepared for . . . the opportunity to qualify to humbly serve in the greatest cause mankind has ever known—in the relations of nations, to hasten that day when 'men shall beat their swords into plowshares' and live in security and peace.[2]

Flanders, an inventor and philosopher, self-educated and the son-in-law of former Governor James Hartness, stood up to Senator Joseph McCarthy's bullying communist "witch-hunts." Flanders's congressional resolution censuring McCarthy did much to galvanize opposition to the "red-baiter" and helped lead to his downfall. Flanders said, "It became clear that in the outside world McCarthy was the United States and the United States was McCarthy. The conviction grew that something must be done about this, even if I had to do it myself."[2]

In 1948 Prouty was the Speaker of the Vermont House, leader of the Gibson forces in that chamber, and candidate for lieutenant governor. He wrote Governor Gibson about "a widespread story . . . that some of your friends were insisting that I stay out of the picture in order that you might team up with Harold [Arthur] in an all-veterans ticket." Prouty predicted that if Arthur won "you will have a lieutenant governor whose political philosophy is greatly at variance with yours, and who has more or less opposed your administration."[3] Arthur, who had served in the military, bested Prouty in the primary. In 1950 Arthur became governor when President Harry S. Truman appointed Gibson a Vermont Federal District Judge.

DEMOCRATS' RISE

By the 1950s, Vermont's Republican politics was no longer ruled by a family dynasty or even one faction. Ernest Gibson, Jr.'s successful challenge to Mortimer Proctor for governor in 1946 undermined the Proctor's power. He was part of an anti-Proctor faction in the Republican party that served as a focus for progressives within the party. By the end of the 1950s, the Republicans seemed to be conducting "free-for-alls" during their primaries. In 1958, six candidates ran for the Republican congressional nomination; four ran for lieutenant governor.

Contributing to the Republican disarray was the "reform" that Gibson had used to defeat Proctor. He had campaigned against grooming successors for the governor's office and this left the Gibson Republicans disorganized and with no plan of how to stay in power. Primaries became "slugfests," and the Republicans often emerged splintered from the first round of elections.

Democrats saw the cracks in the party's armor. They also saw the way in which Vermont was changing, a change that accelerated greatly during the 1960s and 1970s. Vermont's population had shown little growth from 1900-1950, but the tide turned in the 1960s when there was an influx of new residents from outside the state. The 1970 census showed that one-fourth of the permanent residents had been born elsewhere. Many came from Massachusetts, Connecticut, New York and New Jersey. Along with their love of rural areas, they brought with them their political affiliations, which in many cases were Democratic.

Vermont's 246 member house. In 1965 the number of members was reduced to 150.

The Democrats began improving their organizational techniques in the early 1950s. They also were able to attract some Gibson Republicans because Democratic programs more clearly reflected their views. The Democrats' platform in 1958, for instance, was written with Gibson Republicans in mind. And in 1965 Vermont was forced to reapportion its representatives to reflect the one person-one vote rule. The most populous areas of the state, most often Democratic, benefitted.

The Democrats were a force to be taken seriously as early as 1952. In that year, Democrat Robert Larrow won thirty-nine percent of the gubernatorial vote in a race with Republican Lee Emerson of Barton, the incumbent governor who had become governor by beating two Gibsonites in the Republican primary in 1950.[4]

In 1954, Democratic nominee state Senator Frank Branon of Franklin County received forty-seven percent of the vote in the governor's race and ran another strong race in 1956 both times against Joseph Johnson. Finally, in 1958, Vermont Democrats won their first major office in a century, the state's congressional seat. Forester William Meyer defeated the Republican, Harold Arthur, by more than 3,000 votes. Meyer ran a low-key grassroots campaign that brought him into contact with Vermonters around the state. A technique that impressed voters.

Also in 1958, Bernard Leddy, the Democratic nominee for governor, came within eight hundred votes of victory over Republican Robert Stafford and forced an unprecedented recount of a Vermont gubernatorial election.

PHILIP HOFF ARRIVES

In 1962 came the big break. Burlington attorney Philip Hoff, one of the so-called "Young Turks" in the 1960 General Assembly (the bipartisan group also included Republicans Richard Mallary, Sanborn Partridge, Ernest Gibson III and Franklin Billings), ran successfully against incumbent Republican Governor F. Ray Keyser, Jr. Hoff claimed Vermont had been hurt by a century of Republican dominance. Keyser was hurt in the Northeast Kingdom by his proposal

Governor Lee Emerson
1951-1955

Joseph B. Johnson, Governor
1955-1959. (UVM)

FOR GOVERNOR

what he stands for

● Highway program:
  (a) Matching Federal funds.
  (b) Building other roads as needed.
  (c) Bonding for adequate program.
  (d) Ending diversion of highway funds.
  (e) Roads where needed, not where politics dictates.
● Increase in Old Age Assistance.
● Care for chronically ill and aged.
● Collective bargaining and minimum wage law.
● Increased workmen's compensation benefits.
● State hospitalization program.
● New industries for Vermont.
● Cheaper power for Vermont users.
● Expansion of farm markets.
● Cooperation between farmers, producers and consumers.
● Increased income tax exemptions.

Vote Branon

FRANK BRANON

★ *a real Vermonter* ★

Frank Branon, Democratic candidate for governor ran strong races in 1954 and 1956. (UVM)

Consuelo Bailey, Republican elected Lieutenant Governor in 1955, the first woman in the nation elected to a state's second-highest office. (UVM)

Governor F. Ray Keyser, Jr. 1961-1963

Governor Philip Hoff 1963-1969 (UDD)

to eliminate Lyndon State College. He was also hurt by the defection of some fellow Republicans, including T. Garry Buckley and Luke Crispe, a former Gibson law partner who formed the Independent party and endorsed Hoff. The three thousand votes the Independents gathered were important—Hoff's margin of victory was fewer than fifteen hundred votes.

The significance of Hoff's election was lost on no one. A report by the Associated Press described Hoff's victory night this way: "The deliriously joyful people in Winooski filled the streets of their small city on election night in November 1962 when the tall, blond lawyer from across the river in Burlington arrived for the victory celebration. They lifted him on their shoulders. Philip Henderson Hoff grinned at the sea of French/Canadian faces as he celebrated with them his election as Vermont's first Democratic governor since the founding of the Republican Party. 'One hundred years of Republican bondage—broken'! Hoff shouted. The roar of the crowd echoed off the grimy buildings of the mill city . . . one of the most faithful to the Democratic party."[5]

Winooski's vote released late in the evening provided Hoff with the winning margin. (PH)

Philip H. Hoff crowned king of Winooski election night 1962. (PH)

The election of 1964 marked another Democratic turn-around. Lyndon Johnson, the Democratic presidential candidate, beat Republican Barry Goldwater with sixty-six percent of the vote. Hoff beat his opponent, Ralph Foote, with a nearly equal sixty-five percent of the vote. The Democrats made further inroads by winning the offices of lieutenant governor, treasurer, auditor and secretary of state.

The Democrats' surprise at their successes was perhaps best summed up by the winning candidate for treasurer, eighty-one-year-old Peter Hincks. He said of his ousted incumbent: "George Amidon has done a good job as treasurer and he's a fine guy. I was awfully surprised about being elected and I hadn't expected to be taking his job away."[6]

Governor Robert Stafford
1959-1961

Governor on the ski trail with his wife Helen and family.

Lyndon B. Johnson with Lieutenant Governor Daley and Governor Philip Hoff.

Hoff, who also won re-election in 1966 against House member Richard Snelling of Shelburne, brought Vermont into the age of federal largesse. He brought eighty federally funded programs to Vermont, including development, manpower training, education and welfare.

Hoff's appeal was based upon more than his stands on political issues, however. He was an energetic leader who knew how to make people enthusiastic about their state and themselves. Elbert Moulton, a Republican, served under Hoff as his development commissioner, and held him in high regard. Hoff, he explained, fostered "a climate of stimulating courage, enthusiasm and faith, making people more self-confident."[7]

Hoff also attempted to reduce the number of school districts in Vermont. "With a population of 400,000 persons," declared Hoff, "Vermont has 800 school directors, 246 road commissioners, and 246 overseers of the poor. It's ludicrous, utterly ridiculous and wasteful. It may be political suicide but I am determined to end this sort of provincialism." Hoff suggested that the state have twelve school districts. He argued that the regionalization of highway and taxing districts would be less costly and avoid duplication.[8]

The Boston Globe depicted Philip Hoff as a re-incarnated saint in this 1962 political cartoon. St. Michael is one of the seven archangels of Christianity and is regarded as the leader among the angels in battle with Satan. Hoff was the first Democrat governor elected in modern times. (PH)

Hoff was influential toward moving Vermont toward a two-party state. "I think we opened up the State of Vermont to new ideas, new ways of doing things, that hadn't been heard in the state for a long, long time."

In his third term Hoff turned to national issues. He came

to oppose the Vietnam War and was the first Democratic governor to break with President Lyndon Johnson and support Senator Robert Kennedy for president. After Kennedy's assassination, he supported Senator Eugene McCarthy. In 1970 Hoff ran for the United States Senate, but it was not for him to break the Republican strangle hold. He lost to Winston Prouty in a hard-fought campaign.[9]

THE DAVIS YEARS

The Democrat who tried to follow in Hoff's gubernatorial shoes failed. John Daley of Rutland was beaten in 1968 by Deane C. Davis, former president of National Life Insurance Company of Montpelier and long-time Republican. Davis who possessed wit and charm combined a person-to-person campaign with imaginative television ads and promised to place Vermont on a sound fiscal basis. Once in office he realized that to accomplish that the state needed more revenue, so

"The boat ad was created during my second campaign to counter the low ratings I endured because of the sales tax. In the ad, a voice-over explains that I didn't want to impose a sales tax but had to in order to provide funds for the state's burdened budget. It was an instant success and has since been called the most effective television ad in the history of Vermont politics."
(From Deane C. Davis's Autobiography)

"Well, We'll Have To Begin With Our Last Resort — A Sales Tax!"

Rutland Herald

"My first inaugural address became fodder for my first political cartoon. The press seemed to ignore the dozens of times during the campaign that I had said that I would not hesitate to propose a sales tax if Vermont needed additional revenue to meet its obligations. It was a rough start to my first term." (From Deane C. Davis's Autobiography)

he fought for and won the state's first general sales tax. Davis supported the three percent sales tax in order to pay the mounting costs of welfare.

Davis is best-remembered, however, for his reorganization of state government by combining agencies, boards and commissions (which he termed "islands of unaccountability") into a cabinet system; and for his strong environmental stands, including support for Act 250. It was obvious to him that Vermont was in for trouble "unless we did something about the invasion of the state by people and the type of quick development that was going on to make a fast buck. As I studied the development in Windham County, I realized that the so-called second homes before too long turned out to be first homes and when they are first homes, there are children in the home, schools have to be taken care of, roads have got to be built to them and they were building $200,000 houses on dirt roads up on the mountain where the soil was

Deane Davis of Montpelier, Republican Governor who helped push through Act 250, the state's landmark environmental control law. In this photograph Governor Davis gives a riding exhibition at the Barton Fair in 1968. (DCD)

Governor Davis on the campaign trail.

fragile." Act 250 was one of the most progressive pieces of
legislation to emerge from the Vermont General Assembly,
and to this day it is known as a model of sound environmental
and social planning.[10]

THE SALMON YEARS

The Democrats were able to recapture the governorship
in 1972 under Thomas Salmon, a Rockingham attorney. He
was no doubt helped by a blood-letting Republican primary
fight between victor Fred Hackett and James Jeffords. Salmon
continued the environmental work begun by Davis; one of
his main themes was to slow development and keep "Vermont for Vermonters."

Perhaps Salmon's greatest accomplishment was his property tax relief program. In his farewell address to the 1977
Vermont General Assembly, Salmon said, "By our decision in 1973 to commit state revenue sharing money and
land gains tax money to refund to local taxpayers on income
criteria, we have made the most regressive tax in the country, the local property tax, more progressive."[11] Salmon was
also remembered for his fiscal conservatism during the recession in the mid-seventies in Vermont. In 1980, "The Vermont
Business World" wrote, "Thomas Salmon campaigned as
a liberal in the 1972 election but economic conditions forced
him to preside over a large decline in real estate expenditures.

Thomas Salmon, Democratic Governor and unsuccessful senatorial candidate.

If statistics alone were used to measure political sentiment, he would go down in the books as the most conservative governor in modern Vermont history."

Salmon was a popular governor, and he could well have received the Democratic nomination for the United States Senate seat vacated by George Aiken in 1974. But Salmon said he had more work to do in Vermont before trying to

Walter (Peanut) Kennedy, Speaker
of the House of Representatives
and Republican nominee in 1974.

(UVM)

move on to Washington, and he said he wanted no part of the "unprecedented political jockeying in the wake of Senator Aiken's announced retirement." This cost Salmon a Senate seat. Chittenden County prosecutor Patrick Leahy won the Democratic nomination and beat the Republican nominee, Richard Mallary. Salmon ran again for the governorship in 1974, winning handily over Walter "Peanut" Kennedy, of Chelsea and waited until 1976 for his shot at the Senate seat held by incumbent Robert Stafford (Stafford, governor from 1958-1961, had been elected senator upon Winston Prouty's death in 1971) Stafford defeated Salmon in a hard-fought campaign, dashing the Democrats' hopes for winning both Senate seats.

The Democrats made significant gains on other levels of government. In 1975, Timothy O'Connor of Brattleboro was

U.S. Senator Patrick Leahy first elected in 1974.

U.S. Senator Winston L. Prouty 1959-1971.

Robert Stafford, former Attorney General, Governor, Congressman, elected to the U.S. Senate in 1971.

Richard Mallary, former Speaker of the House of Representatives and U.S. Congressman 1971-1974.

elected Speaker of the House, and in 1976 the Democrats won a working majority in that chamber. They almost repeated the feat in the Vermont Senate in 1980, when they won fourteen of that chamber's thirty seats. And in 1978 Democrat Madeleine Kunin of Burlington was elected lieutenant governor, the second woman elected to that job (Consuelo Bailey, a Republican, was the first in 1955 and was also the first female lieutenant governor in the nation).

It wasn't until the state itself and its people changed that changes occurred in politics. Television, the interstate highway system and the migration to Vermont of former metropolitan residents made the state into something different than it had been for the past century. It was becoming more like the rest of the country, and so did its politics.

NOTES

1. Neal R. Peirce, *The New England States* (New York: W.W. Norton, 1976) p. 284.
2. *Ibid.* p. 269.
3. Samuel Hand, et al, *Vermont's New Dealing Yankee: Governor Ernest Gibson, Jr. of Brattleboro* (Burlington: Center for Research on Vermont), p. 8.
4. L. Samuel Miller, *The Vermont Democratic Party and The Development of Intra-Party Responsibility* (Burlington: unpublished paper, 1960), pp. 32-33. Miller wrote: "The eight years prior to 1952 might well be termed a period of gestation. The culmination came when Robert W. Larrow told the National Committeeman, Robert Ready, that he was willing to run for governor and that he really meant to campaign. Campaign he did! Up and down the State, stumping hard in the known Democratic strongholds, Larrow received thirty-nine percent of the total vote! This was better than any gubernatorial candidate had done in the preceding three decades with the exception of 1934. In that year the gubernatorial candidate, James P. Leamy, picked up 42.1 percent of the total vote but with 5,892 fewer votes than Larrow. Never before in the history of the State had any Democratic gubernatorial candidate polled more than 60,000 votes, and this in a banner Republican year! Only Roosevelt, in 1936 and 1940, and Fred C. Martin, 1934 candidate for the U.S. Senate, had received more than 60,000 votes.
   Larrow's showing was a "shot in the arm" and the surprised Democrats rallied. Democratic enthusiasm was widely evident and the initiative of party leaders was apparent in intraparty fights such as the Rutland-Burlington split over the election of William I. Ginsburg of Rutland, who was elected National Committeeman in 1956."
5. Peirce, p. 272.
6. *Ibid.* p. 273.
7. *Ibid.* p. 247.
8. *Ibid.* p. 273.
9. *Ibid.* p. 274.
10. *Ibid.* pp. 255-256.

CHAPTER XI

The Equilibrium

THE SNELLING ERA

The Republicans recaptured the governorship in 1976 through Richard Snelling. Snelling had campaigned on a platform of providing more jobs to Vermonters and running government more efficiently, which apparently appealed to Vermonters as they returned him to the governorship in 1978, 1980 and 1982. He gained national attention through his advocacy of changes in federal-state relations and as chairman of the National Governors Association. Richard Snelling became the second governor in twenty years to be elected to a third term.

Snelling's re-election to his fourth term earned him a place in political record books as one of the longest-serving chief executives in Vermont history. (Only three governors have served more than six years: Thomas Chittenden, 1778-1789 and 1790-1797; Isaac Tichenor, 1797-1807 and 1808-1809; and Jonas Galusha, 1809-1813 and 1815-1820.)

During his long tenure, Snelling strongly supported equality of opportunity for women, and he took the lead in amending Vermont's Constitution to include the Equal Rights Amendment. Acquisition of low cost Canadian power was another major accomplishment of the Snelling years. At the national level he was the leading proponent of federalism. The high quality of his appointments, aggressive leadership and a progressive vision of the future were other characteristics of his administrations.

(UVM)

James Jeffords, first elected to Congress in 1974.

Richard Snelling of Shelburne, four-term Republican Governor known for his businesslike approach to government.

In his last formal message to the Vermont General Assembly Snelling said:

> I believe leadership requires us all to act upon the truth when we believe we know it, and to do that which we believe the people of the State of Vermont would have us do in the light of what we have learned ....
>
> Vermonters love the past, but they love the future far more. We have never sacrificed the future. We shall not do it. We do not sacrifice it for the comfort of the moment; we cannot do it. Vermont is moving. Our people rightfully have a sense that we here have the best combination of any people of this country of a wholesome place in which to live and a decent access to the financial circumstances which permit us to enjoy our natural surroundings.

THE ELECTION OF 1984

In the 1984 election the Democrats made substantial gains and reaffirmed that Vermont was a two party state. Madeleine Kunin, elected Vermont's first woman governor interpreted

Madeleine Kunin and campaign worker Beth Sachs give the thumbs up signal to drivers on the Winooski Bridge. The sign in French says, "This time Madeleine." (AP, Toby Talbot)

her narrow victory over John Easton as an indication that "independence is alive and well in the State of Vermont." Easton carried over 140 towns while Kunin captured almost every city. For the first time in history the Democrats gained control over the Vermont Senate. In addition, the Democratic party made gains in the House of Representatives.

While President Ronald Reagan won an impressive victory in Vermont his coattails were not long enough to help win the governorship or legislature seats. However, Republican incumbents were re-elected to the other statewide offices and newcomer Jeffrey Amestoy won a decisive victory in his race for attorney general. The presidential race was marked by visits to Vermont by both vice-presidential candidates, George Bush and Geraldine Ferrarro.

THE ELECTION OF 1986

The 1986 election featured a three way race between former Republican Lieutenant Governor Peter Smith, Governor Kunin and Independent Bernard Sanders, Mayor of Burlington, who received 15% of the vote. Governor Kunin was reelected with 47% of the vote. For the first time since 1912, a gubernatorial candidate failed to receive a majority. The Legislature decided the election as required by the Vermont Constitution and Kunin, who led in the popular vote, received an overwhelming legislative majority.

Democrat Howard Dean captured the Lieutenant Governorship defeating Republican Majority Leader Susan Auld. It was the second time in Vermont history that a Democratic Lieutenant Governor has served with a Democratic Governor. For the first time ever, the Democrats gained a numerical advantage in the House of Representatives. They re-elected Ralph Wright as Speaker. The Democrats also increased their margin in the Senate to 19-11.

The contest for the U.S. Senate pitted Senator Patrick Leahy against former Governor Richard Snelling. Many thought this would be the race of the century, but the result was a two to one victory for Leahy. The election was another indication of the value of incumbency and an additional reminder that Vermont is no longer a rock-ribbed Republican state.

The campaign expenditures for the U.S. Senate race established a new record of 2.3 million dollars. The race for governor cost approximately 1 million dollars, the same as in 1984. The Equal Rights Amendment to the Vermont Constitution was narrowly defeated after having been approved by the Vermont General Assembly.

THE KUNIN YEARS

During the Kunin years emphasis was placed upon the environment, children, mental health services and education. In her Farewell Address before the Vermont General Assembly in 1991, Governor Kunin said:

> As I look back, it is when we worked together that we were at our best.
>
> That is how we have come so far in these six years, moving

Madeleine Kunin is joyful on election night after learning that Peter Smith had conceded the election to her. November, 1986. (AP, Toby Talbot)

to the head of the class in so many important areas; today, Vermont is the #1 state in the country for children's services, for the environment, and for mental health services. And we are ranked 1 of the top 10 education states in the nation.

Tomorrow's jobs will go to those states who have developed their brain power, and Vermont will be ready because in good economic times, we invested our wealth in our children, and it is they who will bring us the greatest rewards.

An excellent government is a humane government, one that makes choices based on truth, justice and compassion.

To achieve that, I have learned that passion counts. Passionate conviction makes the difference between what happens and what doesn't.

That there is only one reason to be a political person—to translate belief into action, to create change for the better—whenever, wherever, and however one can.

Governor Kunin should be credited for giving key appointments in her administration to women and, in general, broadening the base of women in politics.

THE ELECTION OF 1990

In 1990 Vermonters continued their independent thinking by electing Independent Bernard Sanders to Congress, Republican Richard Snelling Governor and Democrat Howard Dean Lieutenant Governor.

Snelling won the gubernatorial race by six percentage points over Democrat Peter Welch. Snelling received about 52 percent of the vote; Welch, 46 percent. Snelling was the first governor since the Civil War to win nonconsecutive terms in office. Snelling's campaign expenditures were about $450,000 while Welch spent about $280,000.

On what was a cold and windy Election Day, the largest number of voters in a nonpresidential year cast their ballots. In the race that attracted the most interest, Sanders defeated Congressman Peter Smith by 16.5 percent. And the Independent candidate's coattails were evident in many sections of the state. The turnout in Vermont was the seventh largest in the nation with 215,970 or 61.7 percent of those registered voting.

The election of Brooklyn-born Sanders made him the first Independent to be elected to a statewide office in Vermont history and made up for a narrow defeat to Smith in a three-way congressional race in 1988.

On election night, Sanders told his supporters in Burlington's Memorial Auditorium, "Tonight I'm proud. I'm proud of the people of this state who showed the courage in going outside the two-party system and standing up to

INDEPENDENT VICTOR—Independent candidate Bernie Sanders raises his hands in victory after upsetting incumbent Republican Peter Smith for the Vermont Congressional seat. Sanders is the first socialist elected to the House in nearly half a century. (photo by Vyto Starinskas, Rutland Herald) 1990

the President, and Vice-President and every multi-national corporation in America and saying that something is fundamentally wrong in Washington."[1]

Sanders, who capitalized on an anti-incumbent sentiment, said that he has been espousing anti-establishment ideas for 20 years, "but the time's caught up with me in a sense . . . and the climate for my candidacy became far better."[2]

"The message we're bringing to Congress is not a message they're going to be overjoyed to hear," said Sanders, "but they're going to have to hear it. The message is that they are out of touch with the needs of ordinary Americans, that there is no excuse to have a situation in which two-thirds of the people don't vote and 98 percent of the incumbents get re-elected—that's not what democracy is about.

"We need campaign finance reform. We need to break the hold that wealthy people have over the political process. We

GOVERNOR AGAIN—*Former Vermont Governor Richard Snelling enters the Days Inn in Montpelier with his wife Barbara for his victory party. (AP Toby Talbot) 1990*

need major cuts in military spending, and the wealthy have to start paying their fair share of taxes."[3]

What was extraordinary about the election of 1990 was the magnitude of Sanders' victory. Sanders was aided by a strong registration drive which added over 6,000 people since the September primary, half of which resided in Chittenden County. He conducted a strong grassroots campaign that could leaflet virtually every home in Vermont during a two-day period. Door-to-door visits by volunteers were augmented by targeted phone calls. Sanders' visibility was enhanced by attendance at pot luck suppers, visits to senior citizen centers and interviews with local newspapers around Vermont. During this period Smith had to spend most of his time in Washington struggling with the federal budget and other national issues.

Sanders' campaign—stressing personal contact—is known as "retail politics," which until recently had been a tradition in Vermont. Snelling's Campaign Manager Tom Moore reflected: "What the Sanders' victory tells me is that Vermont is still a 'retail politics' state. I think we got away from that type of campaign in Vermont the last few years. It's a lesson we've all re-learned with this election."[4]

220 DAYS

In his Inaugural Address in 1991 beginning his fifth term, Governor Snelling stressed the need to put Vermont's fiscal house in order:

> My oath has been sworn, and I must begin discharging my obligations now by telling you frankly and clearly that Vermont faces an immediate and urgent need to limit its public spending to a rate which can be supported by reasonable levels of taxation even in years of average economic activity.
>
> Our state General Fund budget is being driven by a very small number of very expensive programs, all of which are escalating in cost remarkably faster than either the United States or the Vermont economy can be expected to support on a dependable and sustainable basis. Just seven (7) programs - Welfare, State Aid to Education, (including retirement funds and aid to higher education), Property Tax Relief, Use Tax reimbursements, Corrections, Medicaid and Debt Service are together responsible for about 490 million dollars.
>
> This is nearly 80% of the approximately 630 million dollar estimated spending for 1991. To those who wonder where the money is going, let it be clear that it is not going to hundreds of hidden items. It is not dust in the corners of the bureaucracy. It is mountains in the center of the public policy stage.[5]

As a result of Snelling's leadership, the Legislature, almost evenly divided between Democrats and Republicans, increased the sales, room and meals and income taxes with the provision that they be sunseted. The intent of the tax increase was to put into place a plan that would eliminate Vermont's fiscal deficit. Just before the Legislature adjourned in May, Snelling praised that body for "enacting an expansive new package" and putting Vermont "on the road to a solid recovery."[6] Although he fought for the largest tax increase in Vermont history, 65 percent of Vermonters gave him a favorable rating and Vermont was able to retain its AA bond rating.

A Vermont State Police Honor guard passes by the front of the Statehouse at the beginning of a memorial service for Gov. Richard Snelling, who had died in office three days earlier. (AP Craig Line, August 16, 1991)

Governor Snelling saw the temporary tax increases as a short term response to the deficit. His long term goal was to create sustainable programs and to that end began a substantive review of the functions and activities of all of government. Unfortunately, less than three months after the legislative session ended, Governor Snelling died of a heart attack on August 13, 1991. He was the first governor to die in office since 1870 and Lieutenant Governor Dean became the Chief Executive.

Over 2,000 Vermonters came to Montpelier to pay tribute at his service. A *Rutland Herald* editorial commented that: "At a time when many states faced critical financial and other problems, Vermont under Governor Snelling's leadership had been recognized for superior handling of its difficulties during a recession."[7] The *Burlington Free Press* said: "His death stopped a great governor, a man who continued to take risks, to follow his heart, to protect and serve the Vermont he loved." Snelling had observed, "I don't want to be in the position of having it said about me only that 'he was governor.' I would like to have it said that I was a good governor or I accomplished some things—and that requires taking risks."[8]

Four days later thousands of Vermonters celebrated Vermont's Statehood Bicentennial. The *Burlington Free Press* reported that: "The Statehouse's six pillars were decorated with red, white and blue bunting. Above, red and blue balloons flew from the statue of Ceres, the Goddess of Agriculture." Governor Dean asked for a moment of silence in Snelling's memory. Barbara Snelling said, "Happy birthday Vermont and Vermonters, and a toast to the future."[9]

Two hundred years ago a convention in Bennington ratified the Constitution of the United States in order to become the fourteenth state in the Union. In his Inaugural Address in January, 1991, Dick Snelling quoted Thomas Chittenden who told the Vermont Legislature in 1791:

> The Constitution, gentlemen, groped in the dark for days, months and years, but now it shines with pure lustre. By it our lives, properties, liberties and privileges, civil and religious, are protected: By it we retain a right to choose our own rulers and that from among ourselves; — by it we are rescued from submit-

A view of the Vermont Statehouse during the Bicentennial Celebration held for the state's 200th birthday. (AP Craig Line, August 17, 1991)

ting to the edicts of any foreign power, or neighboring government, while every civil officer is annually taught his
dependence.[10]

During a period of 220 days Snelling successfully rallied
Vermonters to his vision of responsible government, helping to renew faith in state government as Vermont entered
its third century.

THE ELECTION OF 1992

The Democratic party made substantial gains in the election of 1992. Arkansas Governor Bill Clinton won by a com-
fortable margin and was the only Democrat to carry Vermont
since Lyndon Johnson in 1964. Ross Perot received 23% of
the vote. The campaign was a well coordinated one embrac-
ing Clinton, Senator Patrick Leahy, Governor Howard Dean
and other statewide candidates. Another campaign plus was
Clinton's appearance in Burlington where he attracted 6,000
people. His running mate, Al Gore was also favorably received
during his two visits. The Democrats had a technical ad-

*BURLINGTON, Vermont—Democratic candidate Bill Clinton greets sup-
porters during a campaign stop along the shores of Lake Champlain on
Sept. 26. (AP photo by Craig Line, 1992)*

"Governor Richard Snelling joins Robert Chittenden, great, great, great, great, great grandson of Vermont's first governor to ring the bell at the Old First Church in Bennington on March 4, 1791." (photo by Vyto Starinskas, Rutland Herald)

Bennington schoolchildren on March 4, 1991 wait to ring bells commemorating a Bennington Convention vote on March 4, 1791 that ratified the United States Constitution. (photo by Vyto Starinskas, Rutland Herald)

𝕿𝖍𝖊 𝕭𝖚𝖗𝖑𝖎𝖓𝖌𝖙𝖔𝖓 𝕱𝖗𝖊𝖊 𝕻𝖗𝖊𝖘𝖘

Clinton wins

He's the first Democrat in 28 years to carry Vermont

vantage with up-to-date computerized voter list that increased from 30,000 pro-Democratic voters to 75,000 from 1986 to 1992. Curiously, the Democrats did not support congressional nominee Lewis Young who received only 8% of the vote.

Sam Hemingway, Burlington Free Press staff writer, stressed the importance of the "coordinated campaign":

> In the past, a cult of personality marked the path to victory for Democrats from Phil Hoff to Madeleine Kunin to Leahy. Each built campaigns outside of the party apparatus, leaving it to focus on legislative contests.

Jubilant Dean with wife and daughter on election night, 1992. (AP photo by Toby Talbot)

Not this year, though. Instead, Leahy's and Clinton's campaigns were run out of the same South Winooski Avenue office in Burlington and their campaign aides met weekly with Dean representatives.

The Democrats made significant gains in the Vermont House of Representatives adding 17 seats for a total of 90 and solidifying Speaker Ralph Wright's control. On the other hand, the Republicans ran a strong campaign in the State Senate which resulted in their control of that chamber for the first time since 1984. The Republicans won their first Senate seat in Franklin County in almost forty years and ran strongly in Chittenden, Washington and Rutland counties. The Democrats made senatorial gains in Windham, Bennington and Lamoille.

Another Republican bright spot was the election of Barbara Snelling for Lieutenant Governor defeating State Senator David Wolk by ten percentage points. Dhyan Nirmegh (Rock Man) also ran for lieutenant governor as a write-in candidate after protesting the removal of ledges on the Interstate highway.

Successful Lieutenant Governor candidate Barbara Snelling hugs three of her grandchildren in Colchester after it became apparent that she had won the election over Democrat David Wolk, late on election night. (AP photo by Craig Line, 1992)

Dhyan Nirmegh sits atop a rock outcropping in Waterbury on Labor Day, 1992 to protest the removal of the ledges by the state. After gaining support for his cause from Vermonters, including Gov. Howard Dean, Nirmegh mounted a write-in campaign for Lieutenant Governor. (AP photo by Craig Line, 1992)

Eggs played a major role in the battle of television ads between Jim Douglas and Patrick Leahy in the campaign of 1992. (AP photo by Toby Talbot)

Independent Bernard Sanders had little difficulty retaining his Congressional seat. Other Progressives, however, had little success gaining only one member in the House of Representatives and losing Senate challenges in Washington, Chittenden and Windham counties. In Chittenden county, John Franco endorsed by the Burlington Free Press and considered a strong challenger finished twelfth out of thirteen senate candidates.

Dean won a 3 to 1 victory over Kirby Republican and State Senator John McClaughry. Voters viewed Dean as a moderate who did a good job after the unfortunate death of Richard Snelling. Leahy survived a challenge from Secretary of State Jim Douglas, who ran more strongly than was anticipated, and was re-elected for a fourth term. This race was characterized by imaginative television advertisements.

The 76% turnout in 1992 was the strongest since 1964 when over 79% of those registered voted. Thousands of new voters were registered in October of 1992 and helped produce a record turnout of almost 293,000.

"Republican U.S. Senate candidate James Douglas (left), compares a smaller Social Security cost-of-living increase to a larger Senate cost-of-living increase in questioning a pay-raise vote by Sen. Patrick Leahy (right) during a Vermont ETV debate. Freedom for Larouche Party candidate Michael Godeck (center) watches." (Marvin Hill Jr., Burlington Free Press)

GENERAL ELECTIONS

NUMBER OF REGISTERED VOTERS, 1940-1992 AND TURNOUT

Date	Total	No	%
Nov. 5, 1940	191,273	145,289	76.0
Nov. 3, 1942	176,951	61,424	34.7
Nov. 7, 1944	183,517	126,744	69.1
Nov. 5, 1946	180,822	74,743	41.3
Nov. 2, 1948	191,521	124,749	65.1
Nov. 7, 1950	189,665	90,778	47.3
Nov. 4, 1952	201,000	156,923	78.0
Nov. 2, 1954	194,198	116,179	59.8
Nov. 6, 1956	200,381	156,973	78.3
Nov. 4, 1958	196,279	125,461	64.0
Nov. 8, 1960	206,034	169,438	82.2
Nov. 6, 1962	199,141	120,747	61.0
Nov. 3, 1964	209,225	166,049	79.4
Nov. 8, 1966	208,221	137,994	66.3
Nov. 5, 1968	222,024	163,955	73.8
Nov. 3, 1970	230,148	155,705	67.6
Nov. 7, 1972	273,056	194,215	71.1
Nov. 5, 1974	266,649	144,556	54.2
Nov. 2, 1976	284,294	193,655	68.1
Nov. 7, 1978	286,275	127,849	44.7
Nov. 4, 1980	311,919	215,500	69.1
Nov. 2, 1982	315,767	172,084	54.5
Nov. 6, 1984	333,778	235,140	70.4
Nov. 4, 1986	328,466	198,616	60.5
Nov. 8, 1988	348,682	247,075	70.9
Nov. 6, 1990	350,349	215,970	61.6
Nov. 3, 1992	383,371	292,797	76.37

This was the year of the woman and Vermont was no exception. A record sixty women were elected to the Vermont General Assembly in 1992. Eleven women were elected to the Senate, also a new record and forty-nine to the House.

Since the House was reapportioned in 1966 from 246 to 150, the percent of women legislators has risen from 13% to 33%. In the 30 member Senate the percent has increased from 7% to 37%. Of the six member Chittenden county senatorial delegation, five are women. Vermont now ranks fifth in the nation in the percentage of women elected to a state legislature.

Number of Women In Vermont General Assembly, 1966-1991

| | No. of Women | |
Biennium	House	Senate
1966	21	2
1967-69	19	2
1969-71	18	3
1971-73	18	3
1973-75	17	3
1975-77	20	2
1977-79	24	2
1979-81	33	3
1981-83	35	4
1983-85	29	4
1985-87	43	4
1987-88	43	3
1989-90	51	6
1991-92	48	7
1993-1995	49	11

For the second time in Vermont history the Democrats captured the statewide offices of Auditor, Treasurer and Secretary of State. The Republicans now hold only the office of Lieutenant Governor and Attorney General.

During the past three decades, the Vermont political scene has resembled more closely the national scene—two active parties vying for power, with wins and losses on both sides. That is a major departure from the years 1854-1958, when winning the Republican nomination for office was tantamount to winning the election.

For many years, Vermont governors alternated from east and west—the mountain rule. In modern times, a new trend

seems to be developing. Since 1961, Vermonters have alternated the office of governor between Republican and
Democrat.

Since 1977 all Vermont governors have come from Chittenden County which comprises approximately 25% of the
population of Vermont

   F. Ray Keyser (R) 1961-1963
   Philip H. Hoff (D) 1963-1969
   Dean C. Davis (R) 1969-1973
   Thomas P. Salmon (D) 1973-1977
   Richard A. Snelling (R) 1977-1985
   Madeleine Kunin (D) 1985-1991
   Richard A. Snelling (R) 1991
   Howard Dean (D) 1991

As the above chart indicates, politics in Vermont has reached
an equilibrium. The party that fields the best candidates and
provides the best technical resources can win in any given
year. Hopefully this competition will serve the best interests
of all Vermonters.

1. Burlington Free Press, November 7, 1990.
2. Boston Globe, November 11, 1990.
3. Burlington Free Press, November 8, 1990.
4. Sam Hemingway, *Sanders' Win Perplexes Both Parties*, Burlington Free
Press, November 14, 1990. Assisting in the preparation of the Election of
1990 were Professor Eric Davis, Middlebury College; Professors Garrison
Nelson, and Sam Hand, University of Vermont; Professor Frank
Smallwood, Dartmouth College; Sam Hemingway, Burlington Free Press;
Christopher Graff, Associated Press; Steve Terry, Green Mountain Power,
students at Johnson State College; State Senator Vincent Illuzzi; and Alan
Gilbert, free lance writer.
5. Journal of the Senate, January 10, 1991, p. 865.
6. Ibid., May 19, 1991, p. 836.
7. Rutland Herald, August 17, 1991.
8. Burlington Free Press, August 15, 1991.
9. Burlington Free Press, August 18, 1991.
10. Journal of the Senate, January 10, 1991, p. 864.
11. Assisting in the preparation of the election of 1992 were Professors
Garrison Nelson and Sam Hand, University of Vermont; Sam Hemingway,
Burlington Free Press; Frank Smallwood, Dartmouth College; Christopher

Graff, Associated Press; Paul Gillies, Deputy Secretary of State; Gregory Sanford, State Archivist; Ryan Cotton, Montpelier City Manager; Stuart Seidel, Vermont News Letter; Paul Silver and students at Johnson State College.

The ice jam flood of 1992 caused over five million dollars in damages and resulted in Montpelier being designated a federal disaster area. The rebuilding of the community was noteworthy for the close cooperation by the public and private sector. (Vyto Starinskas, Rutland Herald)

A spectacular fireworks display celebrating Vermont's Statehood Bicentennial at the Statehouse in Montpelier, August 17, 1991. (photo by Sandy Macys, courtesy Vermont Bicentennial Commission and Vermont State Archives)

POPULATION OF VERMONT BY COUNTIES
1791-1990

COUNTY	1791	1800	1810	1820	1830	1840	1850
Addison	6,420	13,417	19,993	20,469	24,940	23,583	26,549
Bennington	12,206	14,617	15,893	16,125	17,468	16,872	18,589
Caledonia	2,277	9,377	18,730	16,669	20,967	21,891	23,595
Chittenden	4,718	12,778	18,120	16,272	21,765	22,977	29,036
Essex	567	1,479	3,087	3,284	3,981	4,226	4,650
Franklin	2,454	8,782	16,427	17,192	24,525	24,531	28,586
Grand Isle	–	–	3,445	3,527	3,696	3,883	4,145
Lamoille	–	–	–	–	–	10,475	10,872
Orange	7,663	18,238	25,247	24,681	27,285	27,873	27,296
Orleans	134	1,439	5,830	6,976	13,980	13,634	15,707
Rutland	15,590	23,813	29,486	29,975	31,294	30,699	33,059
Washington	–	–	–	14,106	21,378	23,506	24,654
Windham	17,572	23,581	26,760	28,457	28,748	27,442	29,062
Windsor	15,740	26,944	34,877	38,233	40,625	40,356	38,320
TOTAL	85,341	154,465	217,895	235,966	280,652	291,948	314,120

COUNTY	1860	1870	1880	1890	1900	1910	1920
Addison	24,010	23,484	24,173	22,277	21,912	20,010	18,666
Bennington	19,436	21,325	21,950	20,448	21,705	21,378	21,577
Caledonia	21,408	22,235	23,607	23,436	24,381	26,031	25,762
Chittenden	28,171	36,480	32,792	35,389	39,600	42,447	43,708
Essex	5,786	6,811	7,391	9,511	8,056	7,384	7,364
Franklin	27,231	30,291	30,225	29,755	30,198	29,866	30,026
Grand Isle	4,276	4,082	4,124	3,843	4,462	3,761	3,784
Lamoille	12,311	12,448	12,684	12,831	12,289	12,585	11,858
Orange	25,455	23,090	23,525	19,575	19,313	18,703	17,279
Orleans	18,981	21,035	22,083	22,101	22,024	23,337	23,913
Rutland	35,946	40,651	41,829	45,397	44,209	48,139	46,213
Washington	27,612	26,520	25,404	29,606	36,607	41,702	38,921
Windham	26,982	26,036	26,763	26,547	26,660	26,932	26,373
Windsor	37,193	36,063	35,196	31,706	32,225	33,681	36,984
TOTAL	315,098	330,551	332,286	332,422	343,641	355,956	352,428

COUNTY	1930	1940	1950	1960	1970	1980	1990
Addison	17,952	17,944	19,442	20,076	24,266	29,420	32,953
Bennington	21,655	22,286	24,115	25,088	29,282	33,307	35,845
Caledonia	27,253	24,320	24,049	22,786	22,789	25,814	27,846
Chittenden	47,471	52,098	62,570	74,425	99,131	115,588	131,761
Essex	7,067	6,490	6,257	6,083	5,416	6,300	6,405
Franklin	29,975	29,601	29,894	29,474	31,282	34,800	39,980
Grand Isle	3,944	3,802	3,406	2,927	3,574	4,593	5,318
Lamoille	10,947	11,028	11,388	11,027	13,309	16,769	19,735
Orange	16,694	17,048	17,027	16,014	17,676	22,763	26,149
Orleans	23,036	21,718	21,190	20,143	20,153	23,455	24,053
Rutland	48,453	45,638	45,905	46,719	52,637	58,332	62,142
Washington	41,733	41,546	42,870	42,860	47,659	52,371	54,928
Windham	26,015	27,850	28,749	29,776	33,074	36,878	41,588
Windsor	37,416	37,862	40,885	42,483	44,082	50,882	54,055
TOTAL	359,611	359,231	377,747	389,881	444,330	511,272	560,029

APPENDICES

Appendix A

VERMONT DECLARATION OF INDEPENDENCE

In Convention of the representatives from the several counties and towns of the New Hampshire Grants, holden at Westminster, January 15, 1777, by adjournment.

Whereas the Honorable the Continental Congress did, on the 4th day of July last, declare the United Colonies in America to be frée and independent of the crown of Great Britain ; which declaration we most cordially acquiesce in : And whereas by the said declaration the arbitrary acts of the crown are null and void, in America, consequently the jurisdiction by said crown granted to New York government over the people of the New-Hampshire Grants is totally dissolved:

We therefore, the inhabitants, on said tract of land, are at present without law or government, and may be truly said to be in a state of nature ; consequently a right remains to the people of said Grants to form a government best suited to secure their property, well being and happiness. We the delegates from the several counties and towns on said tract of land, bounded as follows : South on the North line of Massachusetts Bay ; East on Connecticut river ; North on Canada line ; West as far as the New Hampshire Grants extends :

After several adjournments for the purpose of forming ourselves into a distinct separate state, being assembled at Westminster, do make and publish the following Declaration, viz. :

" That we will, at all times hereafter, consider ourselves as a free and independent state, capable of regulating our internal police, in all and every respect whatsoever—and that the people on said Grants have the sole and exclusive and inherent right of ruling and governing themselves in such manner and form as in their own wisdom they shall think proper, not inconsistent or repugnant to any resolve of the Honorable Continental Congress.

" *Furthermore,* we declare by all the ties which are held sacred among men, that we will firmly stand by and support one another in this our declaration of a state, and in endeavoring as much as in us lies, to suppress all unlawful routs and disturbances whatever. Also we will endeavor to secure to every individual his life, peace and property against all unlawful invaders of the same.

" *Lastly* we hereby declare, that we are at all times ready, in conjunction with our brethren in the United States of America, to do our full proportion in maintaining and supporting the just war against the tyranical invasions of the ministerial fleets and armies, as well as any other foreign enemies, sent with express purpose to murder our fellow brethren, and with fire and sword to ravage our defenceless country.

" The said state hereafter to be called by the name of NEW CONNECTICUT."

Extract from the minutes.   IRA ALLEN, *Clerk.*

Appendix B

PREAMBLE

Whereas, all government ought to be instituted and supported for the security and protection of the community as such and to enable the individuals who compose it, to enjoy their natural rights, and the other blessings which the Author of existence has bestowed upon man; and whenever those great ends of government are not obtained, the people have a right, by common consent, to change it, and take such measures as to them may appear necessary to promote their safety and happiness.

And whereas, the inhabitants of this State have, (in consideration of protection only) heretofore acknowledged allegiance to the King of Great Britain, and the said King has not only withdrawn that protection, but commenced, and still continues to carry on, with unabated vengeance, a most cruel and unjust war against them; employing therein, not only the troops of Great Britain, but foreign mercenaries, savages and slaves, for the avowed purpose of reducing them to a total and abject submission to the despotic dominion of the British parliament, with many other acts of tryanny (more fully set forth in the declaration of Congress), whereby all allegiance and fealty to the said King and his successors, are dissolved and at an end; and all power and authority derived from him, ceased in the American Colonies.

And whereas, the territory which now comprehends the State of Vermont, did antecedently, of right, belong to the government of New Hampshire; and the former Governor thereof, viz. his excellency Benning Wentworth, Esq., granted many charters of lands and corporations, within this State, to the present inhabitants and others. And whereas, the late Lieutenant Governor Colden, of New York, with others, did, in violation of the tenth command, covet those very lands; and by a false representation made to the court of Great Britain (in the year 1764, that for the convenience of trade and administration of justice, the inhabitants were desirous of being annexed to that government), obtained jurisdiction of those very identical lands, ex-parte; which ever was, and is disagreeable to the inhabitants. And whereas, the legislature of New York, ever have, and still continue to disown the good people of this State, in their landed property, which will appear in the complaints hereafter inserted, and in the 36th section of their present constitution, in which is established the grants of land made by that government.

They have refused to make re-grants of our lands to the original proprietors and occupants, unless at the exorbitant rate of 2300 dollars fees for each township; and did enhance the quitrent, three fold, and demanded an immediate delivery of the title derived before, from New Hampshire.

The judges of their supreme court have made a solemn declaration, that the charters, conveyances, &c., of the lands included in the before described premises, were utterly null and void, on which said title was founded; in consequence of which declaration, writs of possession have been by them issued, and the sheriff of the county of Albany sent, at the head of six or seven hundred men, to enforce the execution thereof.

They have passed an act, annexing a penalty thereto, of thirty pounds fine and six months imprisonment, on any person who should refuse assisting the sheriff, after being requested, for the purpose of executing writs of possession.

The Governors, Dunmore, Tryon and Colden, have made re-grants of several tracts of land, included in the premises, to certain favorite land jobbers in the government of New-York, in direct violation of his Britannic majesty's express prohibition, in the year 1767.

They have issued proclamations, wherein they have offered large sums of money, for the purpose of apprehending those very persons who have dared boldly, and publicly, to appear in defence of their just rights.

They did pass twelve acts of outlawry, on the 9th day of March, A. D. 1774, impowering the respective judges of their supreme court, to award execution of death against those inhabitants in said district that they should judge to be offenders, without trial.

They have, and still continue, an unjust claim to those lands, which greatly retards emigration into, and the settlement of, this State.

They have hired foreign troops, emigrants from Scotland, at two different times, and armed them, to drive us out of possession.

They have sent the savages on our frontiers, to distress us.

They have proceeded to erect the counties of Cumberland and Gloucester, and establish courts of justice there, after they were discountenanced by the authority of Great Britain.

The free Convention of the State of New-York, at Harlem, in the year 1776, unanimously voted, "That all quit-rents formerly due to the King of Great Britain, are now due and owing to this convention, or such future government as shall be hereafter established in this State."

In the several stages of the aforesaid oppressions, we have petitioned his Britannic majesty, in the most humble manner, for redress, and have, at very great expense, received several reports in our favor; and in other instances, wherein we have petitioned the late legislative authority of New-York, those petitions have been treated with neglect.

And whereas, the local situation of this State, from New-York, at the extreme part, is upwards of four hundred and fifty miles from the seat of that government, which renders it extreme difficult to continue under the jurisdiction of said State,

Therefore, it is absolutely necessary, for the welfare and safety of the inhabitants of this State, that it should be, henceforth, a free and independent State; and that a just, permanent and proper form of government, should exist in it, derived from, and founded on, the authority of the people only, agreeable to the direction of the honorable American Congress.

We the representatives of the freemen of Vermont, in General Convention met, for the express purpose of forming such a government, confessing the goodness of the Great Governor of the Universe (who alone, knows to what degree of earthly happiness, mankind may attain, by perfecting the arts of government), in permitting the people of this State, by common consent, and without violence, deliberately to form for themselves, such just rules as they shall think best for governing their future society; and being fully convinced that it is our indispensable duty, to establish such original principles of government, as will best promote the general happiness of the people of this State, and their posterity, and provide for future improvements, without partiality for, or prejudice against, any particular class, sect, or denomination of men whatever: Do, by virtue of authority vested in us, by our constituents, ordain, declare, and establish, the following declaration of rights, and frame of government, to be the Constitution of this Commonwealth, and to remain in force therein, forever, unaltered, except in such articles, as shall, hereafter, on experience, be found to require improvement, and which shall, by the same authority of the people, fairly delegated, as this frame of government directs, be amended or improved, for the more effectual obtaining and securing the great end and design of all government, herein before mentioned.

CHAPTER I

A DECLARATION OF THE RIGHTS OF THE INHABITANTS OF THE STATE OF VERMONT

I. That all men are born equally free and independent, and have certain natural, inherent and unalienable rights, amongst which are the enjoying and defending life and liberty; acquiring, possessing and protecting property, and pursuing and obtaining happiness and safety. Therefore, no male person, born in this country, or brought from over sea, ought to be holden by law, to serve any person, as a servant, slave or apprentice, after he arrives to the age of twenty-one years, nor female, in like manner, after she arrives to the age of eighteen years, unless they are bound by their own consent, after they arrive at such age, or bound by law, for the payment of debts, damages, fines, costs, or the like.

II. That private property ought to be subservient to public uses, when necessity requires it; nevertheless, whenever any particular man's property is taken for the use of the public, the owner ought to receive an equivalent in money.

III. That all men have a natural and unalienable right to worship Almighty God, according to the dictates of their own consciences and understanding, regulated by the word of God; and that no man ought, or, of right, can be compelled to attend any religious worship, or erect, or support any place of worship, or maintain any minister, contrary to the dictates of his conscience; nor can any man who professes the protestant religion be justly deprived or abridged of any civil right as a citizen, on account of his religious sentiment, or peculiar mode of religious worship, and that no authority can, or ought to be vested in, or assumed by, any power whatsoever, that shall in any case, interfere with, or in any manner control, the rights of conscience, in the free exercise of religious worship; nevertheless, every sect or denomination of people ought to observe the Sabbath, or the Lord's day, and keep up, and support, some sort of religious worship, which to them shall seem most agreeable to the revealed will of God.

IV. That the people of this State have the sole, exclusive and inherent right of governing and regulating the internal police of the same.

V. That all power being originally inherent in, and consequently, derived from, the people; therefore, all officers of government, whether legislative or executive, are their trustees and servants, and at all times accountable to them.

VI. That government is, or ought to be, instituted for the common benefit, protection, and security of the people, nation or community; and not for the particular emolument or advantage of any single man, family or set of men, who are a part only of that community; and that the community hath an indubitable, unalienable and indefeasible right to reform, alter, or abolish government, in such manner as shall be, by that community, judged most conducive to the public weal.

VII. That those who are employed in the legislative and executive business of the State, may be restrained from oppression, the people have a right, at such periods as they may think proper, to reduce their public officers to a private station, and supply the vacancies by certain and regular elections.

VIII. That all elections ought to be free; and that all freemen, having a sufficient evident common interest with, and attachment to, the community, have a right to elect officers, or be elected into office.

IX. That every member of society hath a right to be protected in the enjoyment of life, liberty and property, and therefore, is bound to contribute his proportion towards the expense of the protection, and yield his personal service, when necessary, or an equivalent thereto; but no part of a man's property can be justly taken from him, or applied to public uses, without his own consent, or that of his legal representatives; nor can any man who is conscientiously scrupulous of bearing arms, be justly compelled thereto, if he will pay such equivalent; nor are the people bound by any law, but such as they have in like manner, assented to, for their common good.

X. That, in all prosecutions for criminal offences, a man hath a right to be heard, by himself and his counsel—to demand the cause and nature of his accusation—to be confronted with the witnesses—to call for evidence in his favor, and a speedy public trial, by an impartial jury of the country; without the unanimous consent of which jury he cannot be found guilty; nor can he be compelled to give evidence against himself; nor can any man be justly deprived of his liberty, except by the laws of the land or the judgment of his peers.

XI. That the people have a right to hold themselves, their houses, papers and possessions free from search or seizure; and therefore warrants, without oaths or affirmations first made, affording a sufficient foundation for them, and whereby any officer or messenger may be commanded or required to search suspected places, or to seize any person or persons, his, her or their property, not particularly described, are contrary to that right, and ought not to be granted.

XII. That no warrant or writ to attach the person or estate of any freeholder within this state, shall be issued in civil action, without the person or persons, who may request such warrant or attachment, first make oath, or affirm, before the authority who may be requested to issue the same, that he, or they, are in danger of losing his, her or their debts.

XIII. That, in controversies respecting property, and in suits between man and man, the parties have a right to a trial by jury; which ought to be held sacred.

XIV. That the people have a right to freedom of speech, and of writing and publishing their sentiments; therefore, the freedom of the press ought not to be restrained.

XV. That the people have a right to bear arms for the defence of themselves and the State; and, as standing armies, in the time of peace, are dangerous to liberty, they ought not to be kept up; and that the military should be kept under strict subordination to, and governed by, the civil power.

XVI. That frequent recurrence to fundamental principles, and a firm adherence to justice, moderation, temperance, industry and frugality, are absolutely necessary to preserve the blessings of liberty, and keep government free. The people ought, therefor, to pay particular attention to these points, in the choice of officers and representatives, and have a right to exact a due and constant regard to them from their legislators and magistrates, in the making and executing such laws as are necessary for the good government of the State.

XVII. That all people have a natural and inherent right to emigrate from one State to another, that will receive them; or to form a new State in vacant countries, or in such countries as they can purchase, whenever they think that thereby they can promote their own happiness.

XVIII. That the people have a right to assemble together, to consult for their common good—to instruct their representatives; and to apply to the legislature for redress of grievances, by address, petition or remonstrance.

XIX. That no person shall be liable to be transported out of this State, for trial, for any offence committed within this State.

CHAPTER II

PLAN OR FRAME OF GOVERNMENT

SECTION I

The Commonwealth or State of Vermont, shall be governed here-after, by a Governor, Deputy Governor, Council, and an Assembly of the Representatives of the Freemen of the same, in manner and form following.

SECTION II

The supreme legislative power shall be vested in a House of Representatives of the Freemen or Commonwealth or State of Vermont.

SECTION III

The supreme executive power shall be vested in a Governor and Council.

SECTION IV

Courts of justice shall be established in every county in this State.

SECTION V

The freemen of this Commonwealth, and their sons, shall be trained and armed for its defence, under such regulations, restrictions and exceptions, as the General Assembly shall, by law, direct; reserving always to the people, the right of choosing their colonels of militia, and all commissioned officers under that rank, in such manner, and as often, as by the said laws shall be directed.

SECTION VI

Every man of the full age of twenty-one years, having resided in this State for the space of one whole year, next before the election of representatives, and who is of a quiet and peaceable behaviour, and will take the following oath (or affirmation), shall be entitled to all the privileges of a freeman of this State.

I .... solemnly swear, by the ever living God (or affirm in the presence of Almighty God), that whenever I am called to give my vote or suffrage, touching any matter that concerns the State of Vermont, I will do it so, as in my conscience, I shall judge will most conduce to the best good of the same, as established by the constitution, without fear or favor of any man.

SECTION VII

The House of Representatives of the Freemen of this State, shall consist of persons most noted for wisdom and virtue, to be chosen by the freemen of every town in this State, respectively. And no foreigner shall be chosen, unless he has resided in the town for which he shall be elected, one year immediately before said election.

SECTION VIII

The members of the House of Representatives, shall be chosen annually, by ballot, by the freemen of this State, on the first Tuesday of September, forever (except this present year), and shall meet on the second Thursday of the succeeding October, and shall be stiled the General Assembly of the Representatives of the Freemen of Vermont; and shall have power to choose their Speaker, Secretary of the State, their Clerk, and other necessary officers of the house—sit on their own adjournments—prepare bills and enact them into laws—judge of the elections and qualifications of their own members—they may expel a member, but not a second time for the same cause—They may administer oaths (or affirmations) on examination of witnesses—redress grievances—impeach State criminals—grant charters of incorporation—constitute towns, boroughs, cities and counties, and shall have all other powers necessary for the legislature of a free State; but they shall have no power to add to, alter, abolish, or infringe, any part of this constitution. And for this present year the members of the General Assembly shall be chosen on the first Tuesday of March next, and shall meet at the meeting-house, in Windsor, on the second Thursday of March next.

SECTION IX

A quorum of the house of representatives shall consist of two thirds of the whole number of members elected; and having met and chosen their speaker, shall, each of them, before they proceed to business, take and subscribe, as well the oath of fidelity and allegiance hereinafter directed, as the following oath or affirmation, viz.

I .... do solemnly swear, by the ever living God (or I do solemnly affirm in the presence of Almighty God), that as a member of this assembly, I will not propose or assent to any bill, vote or resolution which shall appear to me injurious to the people; nor do or consent to any act or thing whatever, that shall have a tendency to lessen or abridge their rights and privileges, as declared in the Constitution of this State; but will in all things, conduct myself as a faithful, honest representative and guardian of the people, according to the best of my judgment and abilities.

And each member, before he takes his seat, shall make and subscribe the following declaration, viz.

I do believe in one God, the Creator and Governor of the universe, the rewarder of the good and punisher of the wicked. And I do acknowledge the scriptures of the old and new testament to be given by divine inspiration, and own and profess the protestant religion.

And no further or other religious test shall ever, hereafter, be required of any civil officer or magistrate in this State.

SECTION X

Delegates to represent this State in Congress shall be chosen, by ballot, by the future General Assembly, at their first meeting, and annually, forever afterward, as long as such representation shall be necessary. Any Delegate may be superceded, at any time, by the General Assembly appointing another in his stead. No man shall sit in Congress longer than two years successively, nor be capable of re-election for three years afterwards; and no person who holds any office in the gift of the Congress, shall, thereafter, be elected to represent this State in Congress.

SECTION XI

If any town or towns shall neglect or refuse to elect and send representatives to the General Assembly, two thirds of the members of the towns that do elect and send representatives (provided they be a majority of the inhabited towns of the whole State), when met, shall have all the powers of the General Assembly, as fully and amply as if the whole were present.

SECTION XII

The doors of the house in which the representatives of the freemen of this State, shall sit, in General Assembly, shall be and remain open for the admission of all persons, who behave decently, except only, when the welfare of this State may require the doors to be shut.

SECTION XIII

The votes and proceedings of the General Assembly shall be printed, weekly, during their sitting, with the yeas and nays, on any question, vote or resolution, where one third of the members require it; (except when the votes are taken by ballot) and when the yeas and nays are so taken, every member shall have a right to insert the reasons of his votes upon the minutes, if he desire it.

SECTION XIV

To the end that laws, before they are enacted, may be more maturely considered, and the inconveniency of hasty determination as much as possible prevented, all bills of public nature, shall be first laid before the Governor and Council, for their perusal and proposals of amendment, and shall be printed for the consideration of the people, before they are read in General Assembly for the last time of debate and amendment; except temporary acts, which, after being laid before the Governor and Council, may (in the case of sudden necessity) be passed into laws; and no other shall be passed into laws, until the next session of Assembly. And for the more perfect satisfaction of the public, the reasons and motives for making such laws, shall be fully and clearly expressed and set forth in their preambles.

SECTION XV

The style of the laws of this State shall be,—"Be it enacted, and it is hereby enacted, by the Representatives of the Freemen of the State of Vermont, in General Assembly met, and by the Authority of the same."

SECTION XVI

In order that the Freemen of this State might enjoy the benefit of election, as equally as may be, each town within this State, that consists, or may consist, of eighty taxable inhabitants, within one septenary or seven years, next after the establishing this constitution, may hold elections therein, and choose each, two representatives; and each other inhabited town in this State may, in like manner, choose each, one representative, to represent them in General Assembly, during the said septenary or seven years; and after that, each inhabited town may, in like manner, hold such election, and choose each, one representative, forever thereafter.

SECTION XVII

The Supreme Executive Council of this State, shall consist of a Governor, Lieutenant-Governor, and twelve persons, chosen in the following manner, viz. The Freemen of each town, shall, on the day of election for choosing representatives to attend the General Assembly, bring in their votes for Governor, with his name fairly written, to the constable, who shall seal them up, and write on them, votes for the Governor, and deliver them to the representative chosen to attend the General Assembly; and, at the opening of the General Assembly, there shall be a committee appointed out of the Council, and Assembly, who, after being duly sworn to the faithful discharge of their trust, shall proceed to receive, sort, and count, the votes for the Governor, and declare the person who' has the major part of the votes, to be Governor, for the year ensuing. And if there be no choice made, then the Council and General Assembly, by their joint ballot, shall make choice of a Governor.

The Lieutenant Governor and Treasurer, shall be chosen in the manner above directed; and each freeman shall give in twelve votes for twelve councillors, in the same manner; and the twelve highest in nomination shall serve for the ensuing year as Councillors.

The council that shall act in the recess of this Convention, shall supply the place of a council for the next General Assembly, until the new Council be declared chosen. The Council shall meet annually, at the same time and place with the General Assembly; and every member of the Council shall be a Justice of the Peace for the whole State, by virtue of his office.

SECTION XVIII

The Governor, and in his absence, the Lieutenant or Deputy Governor, with the Council—seven of whom shall be a quorum—shall have power to appoint and commissionate all officers (except those who are appointed by the General Assembly), agreeable to this frame of government, and the laws that may be made hereafter; and shall supply every vacancy in any office, occasioned by death, resignation, removal or disqualification, until the office can be filled, in the time and manner directed by law or this constitution. They are to correspond with other States, and transact business with officers of government, civil and military; and to prepare such business as may appear to them necessary to lay before the General Assembly. They shall sit as judges to hear and determine on impeachments, taking to their assistance, for advice only, the justices of the supreme court; and shall have power to grant pardons, and remit fines, in all cases whatsoever, except cases of impeachment, and in cases of treason and murder—shall have power to grant reprieves, but not to pardon, until the end of the next session of the Assembly: but there shall be no remission or mitigation of punishment, on impeachment, except by act of legislation. They are also, to take care that the laws be faithfully executed. They are to expedite the execution of such measures as may be resolved upon by General Assembly; and they may draw upon the Treasurer for such sums as may be appropriated by the House: they may also lay embargoes, or prohibit the exportation of any commodity for any time, not exceeding thirty days, in the recess of the House only: they may grant such licences as shall be directed by law, and shall have power to call together the General Assembly, when necessary, before the day to which they shall stand adjourned. The Governor shall be commander in chief of the forces of the State; but shall not command in person, except advised thereto by the Council, and then, only, as long as they shall approve thereof. The Governor and Council shall have a Secretary, and keep fair books of their proceedings, wherein any Councillor may enter his dissent, with his reasons to support it.

SECTION XIX

All commissions shall be in the name of the freemen of the State of Vermont, sealed with the State seal, signed by the Governor, and in his absence the Lieutenant Governor, and attested by the Secretary; which seal shall be kept by the Council.

SECTION XX

Every officer of State, whether judicial or executive, shall be liable to be impeached by the General Assembly, either when in office, or after his resignation, or removal for mal-administration. All impeachments shall be before the Governor or Lieutenant Governor and Council, who shall hear and determine the same.

SECTION XXI

The supreme court, and the several courts of common pleas of this State shall, besides the powers usually exercised by such courts, have the powers of a court of chancery, so far as relates to perpetuating testimony, obtaining evidence from places not within this State, and the care of persons and estates of those who are non compotes mentis, and such other powers as may be found necessary by future General Assemblies, not inconsistent with this constitution.

SECTION XXII

Trials shall be by jury; and it is recommended to the legislature of this State to provide by law, against every corruption or partiality in the choice, and return, or appointment, of juries.

SECTION XXIII

All counts shall be open, and justice shall be impartially administered, without corruption or unnecessary delay; all their officers shall be paid an adequate, but moderate, compensation for their services; and if any officer shall take greater or other fees than the laws allow him, either directly or indirectly, it shall ever after disqualify him from holding any office in this State.

SECTION XXIV

All prosecutions shall commence in the name and by the authority of the freemen of the State of Vermont, and all indictments shall conclude with these words, "against the peace and dignity of the Same." The style of all process hereafter, in this State, shall be,—The State of Vermont.

SECTION XXV

The person of a debtor, where there is not a strong presumption of fraud, shall not be continued in prison, after delivering up, bona fide, all his estate, real and personal, for the use of his creditors, in such manner as shall be hereafter regulated by law. All prisoners shall be bailable by sufficient securities, unless for capital offences, when the proof is evident or presumption great.

SECTION XXVI

Excessive bail shall not be exacted for bailable offences; and all fines shall be moderate.

SECTION XXVII

That the General Assembly, when legally formed, shall appoint times and places for county elections, and at such times and places, the freemen in each county respectively, shall have the liberty of choosing the judges of inferior court of common pleas, sheriff, justices of the peace, and judges of probate, commissioned by the Governor and council, during good behavior, removable by the General Assembly upon proof of mal-administration.

SECTION XXVIII

That no person, shall be capable of holding any civil office, in this State except he has acquired, and maintains a good moral character.

SECTION XXIX

All elections, whether by the people or in General Assembly, shall be by ballot, free and voluntary; and any elector who shall receive any gift or reward for his vote, in meat, drink, monies or otherwise, shall forfeit his right to elect at that time, and suffer such other penalty as future laws shall direct. And any person who shall, directly or indirectly, give, promise, or bestow, any such rewards to be elected, shall, thereby, be rendered incapable to serve for the ensuing year.

SECTION XXX

All fines, licence money, fees and forfeitures, shall be paid, according to the direction hereafter to be made by the General Assembly.

SECTION XXXI

All deeds and conveyances of land shall be recorded in the town clerk's office, in their respective towns.

SECTION XXXII

The printing presses shall be free to every person who undertakes to examine the proceedings of the legislature, or any part of government.

SECTION XXXIII

As every freeman, to preserve his independence (if without a sufficient estate), ought to have some profession, calling, trade or farm, whereby he may honestly subsist, there can be no necessity for, nor use in, establishing offices of profit, the usual effects of which are dependence and servility, unbecoming freemen, in the possessors or expectants; faction, contention, corruption and disorder among the people. But if any man is called into public service, to the prejudice of his private affairs, he has a right to a reasonable compensation; and whenever an office, through increase of fees, or otherwise, becomes so profitable as to occasion many to apply for it, the profits ought to be lessened by the legislature.

SECTION XXXIV

The future legislature of this State, shall regulate entails, in such manner as to prevent perpetuities.

SECTION XXXV

To deter more effectually from the commission of crimes, by continued visible punishment of long duration, and to make sanguinary punishments less necessary; houses ought to be provided for punishing, by hard labor, those who shall be convicted of crimes not capital; wherein the criminal shall be employed for the benefit of the public, or for reparation of injuries done to private persons; and all persons, at proper times, should be admitted to see the prisoners at their labor.

SECTION XXXVI

Every officer, whether judicial, executive or military, in authority under this State, shall take the following oath or affirmation of allegiance, and general oath of office, before he enter on the execution of his office.

THE OATH OR AFFIRMATION OF ALLEGIANCE

"I .... do solemnly swear by the ever living God (or affirm in presence of Almighty God), that I will be true and faithful to the State of Vermont; and that I will not, directly or indirectly, do any act or thing, prejudicial or injurious, to the constitution or government thereof, as established by Convention."

THE OATH OR AFFIRMATION OF OFFICE

"I .... do solemnly swear by the ever living God (or affirm in presence of Almighty God), that I will faithfully execute the office of .... for the .... of ....; and will do equal right and justice to all men, to the best of my judgment and abilities, according to law."

SECTION XXXVII

No public tax, custom or contribution shall be imposed upon, or paid by, the people of this State, except by a law for that purpose; and before any law be made for raising it, the purpose for which any tax is to be raised ought to appear clear to the legislature to be of more service to the community than the money would be, if not collected; which being well observed, taxes can never be burthens.

SECTION XXXVIII

Every foreigner of good character, who comes to settle in this State, having first taken an oath or affirmation of allegiance to the same, may purchase, or by other just means acquire, hold, and transfer, land or other real estate; and after one years residence, shall be deemed a free denizen of this State; except that he shall not be capable of being elected a representative, until after two years residence.

SECTION XXXIX

That the inhabitants of this State, shall have liberty to hunt and fowl, in seasonable times, on the lands they hold, and on other lands (not enclosed); and, in like manner, to fish in all boatable and other waters, not private property, under proper regulations, to be hereafter made and provided by the General Assembly.

SECTION XL

A school or schools shall be established in each town, by the legislature, for the convenient instruction of youth, with such salaries to the masters, paid by each town, making proper use of school lands in each town, thereby to enable them to instruct youth at low prices. One grammar school in each county, and one university in this State, ought to be established by direction of the General Assembly.

SECTION XLI

Laws for the encouragement of virtue and prevention of vice and immorality, shall be made and constantly kept in force; and provision shall be made for their due execution; and all religious societies and bodies of men, that have or may be hereafter united and incorporated, for the advancement of religion and learning, or for other pious and charitable purposes, shall be encouraged and protected in the enjoyment of the privileges, immunities and estates which they, in justice, ought to enjoy, under such regulations, as the General Assembly of this State shall direct.

SECTION XLII

All field and staff officers, and commissioned officers of the army, and all general officers of the militia, shall be chosen by the General Assembly.

SECTION XLIII

The declaration of rights is hereby declared to be a part of the Constitution of this State, and ought never to be violated on any pretence whatsoever.

SECTION XLIV

In order that the freedom of this Commonwealth may be preserved inviolate, forever, there shall be chosen, by ballot, by the freemen of this State, on the last Wednesday in March, in the year one thousand seven hundred and eighty-five, and on the last Wednesday in March, in every seven years thereafter, thirteen persons, who shall be chosen in the same manner the council is chosen—except they shall not be out of the Council or General Assembly—to be called the Council of Censors; who shall meet together, on the first Wednesday of June next ensuing their election; the majority of whom shall be a quorum in every case, except as to calling a Convention, in which two thirds of the whole number elected shall agree; and whose duty it shall be to enquire whether the legislative and executive branches of government have performed their duty as guardians of the people; or assumed to themselves, or exercised, other or greater powers, than they are entitled to by the constitution. They are also to enquire whether the public taxes have been justly laid and collected, in all parts of this Commonwealth—in what manner the public monies have been disposed of, and whether the laws have been duly executed. For these purposes they shall have power to public censures—to order impeachments, and to recommend to the legislature the repealing such laws as appear to them to have been enacted contrary to the principles of the constitution. These powers they shall continue to have, for and during the space of one year from the day of their election, and no longer. The said Council of Censors will also have power to call a Convention, to meet within two years after their sitting, if there appears to them an absolute necessity of amending any article of this constitution which may be defective—explaining such as may be thought not clearly expressed, and of adding such as are necessary for the preservation of the rights and happiness of the people; but the articles to be amended, and the amendments proposed, and such articles as are proposed to be added or abolished, shall be promulgated at least six months before the day appointed for the election of such convention, for the previous consideration of the people, that they may have an opportunity of instructing their delegates on the subject.

Appendix C

LEADING EVENTS IN THE HISTORY OF VERMONT

Originally prepared by
H. J. CONANT, RETIRED STATE LIBRARIAN
with subsequent additions.

1609 July 4. Lake Champlain discovered by Samuel de Champlain.
1664 Charter of King Charles II to Duke of York.
1666 Fort St. Anne built by the French on Isle La Motte.
Expedition of the French against the Mohawk villages.
1690 Expedition of the French against Schenectady, N. Y.
Expedition of the English against Montreal.
Fort at Chimney Point built by the English.
First settlement at Vernon.
1704 Expedition of the French against Deerfield, Mass.
1724 Fort Dummer built by colonists from Massachusetts.
1730 French Settlement at Chimney Point.
1737 Ethan Allen born.
1738 Sartwell's fort built at Vernon.
1741 Southern boundary line of the State run between New Hampshire and Mass.
1749 January. Bennington chartered by New Hampshire.
1751 Ira Allen born.
1752 Ferries established across the Connecticut River at Dummerston.
1753 Settlements at Bellows Falls and Springfield.
1759 Crown Point military road built across the State.
Rogers Expedition against St. Francis Indians.
1761 Settlement at Bennington and five other towns.
1764 Jurisdiction of New York sustained and Eastern boundary of the State fixed
by decree of King in Council.
October. Green Mountain Boys organized.
1765 First Convention of settlers held at Bennington relative to jurisdiction controversy.
1768 Cumberland County, first county within limits of State, established by New
York.
1769 First open resistance offered to New York officers attempting to dispossess
settlers under N. H. grants.
1775 March 14. Westminster Massacre.
May 10. Ticonderoga captured by Green Mountain Boys under Ethan Allen.
Expedition into Canada and capture of Ethan Allen.
1776 Naval battle on Lake Champlain and defeat of Americans under Arnold.
Building of Hazen road commenced.
1777 Jan. 15. Westminster convention. Vermont declared to be an independent State
under name of "New Connecticut."
June 4. Name of State changed to Vermont.
July 2-8. State Constitution adopted at Windsor.
Burgoyne Campaign.
July 7. Battle of Hubbardton.
Aug. 16. Battle of Bennington.
1778 March 3. First election under the Constitution.
Thomas Chittenden elected Governor.
Mar. 12. First session of the Legislature.
May. Ethan Allen released and returned to Vermont.
1780 Oct. 16. Burning of Royalton.
1781 Feb. 12. First newspaper printed.
1781-3 Haldimand negotiations.
1785 Grant of town of Wheelock to Dartmouth College.
First marble quarry opened.
1786 Constitution was re-drafted by council of censors.
1789 Ethan Allen died. Age 52 years.
1790 Difficulties with New York adjusted and western boundary determined.

LEADING EVENTS IN THE HISTORY OF VERMONT

1791   Jan. 10. Vermont adopted U. S. Constitution.
      March 4. Vermont admitted to Union.
      Library established in Brookfield.
      Steamboat operated on Lake Morey by Samuel Morey.
      University of Vermont chartered.
1793   Copper ore discovered in Strafford.
      Nathaniel Chipman published a volume of law reports—the third to be printed
         in the U. S.
      Convention of 1793 certified the Constitution of 1793 at Windsor.
1800   Middlebury College chartered.
      Academy for women opened in Middlebury.
1803   State flag established.
1805   Montpelier chosen as state capital.
1806   First State bank established.
1807   State Prison established; built at Windsor in 1809.
1808   Legislature held at Montpelier for the first time.
      First fire insurance society chartered.
1812   War with Great Britain.
1813   State Medical Society incorporated.
1814   Ira Allen died. Age 62 years.
      Sept. 11. MacDonough won naval battle of Plattsburgh.
      Jas. Wilson of Bradford manufactured a school geographical globe.
1816   "The famine year" of crop failures.
      Mrs. Emma Willard of Middlebury wrote "Plan for the Improvement of
         Female Education."
1817   Pres. Monroe visited the State.
      Legislature appointed a special committee to study the Temperance question.
      First private bank chartered.
1819   Norwich University chartered.
      Phineas Bailey of Chelsea published a system of shorthand.
1823   Champlain canal opened.
      First normal school in America opened at Concord.
1825   General Lafayette visited the State.
      State Library established.
1827   State Board of Commissioners for common schools organized.
1828   Presidential electors first chosen by freemen.
1830   Serious floods.
      Mormonism founded by Joseph Smith.
1831   State Bank Commissioner established.
1834   Electric motor invented by Thomas Davenport of Brandon.
1836   Brattleboro retreat opened.
      State Senate established; executive council abolished.
1838   Second State House erected.
1848   First railroad train operated in Vermont; also first telegraph line.
1850   State Teachers Association organized. County officers first chosen by freemen.
1852   Manufacture and sale of intoxicating liquor as a beverage, prohibited by law.
      State Board of Insurance Commissioners organized.
1855   Office of Railroad Commissioner established.
1857   January 6. State House destroyed by fire.
1861   April 23. Extra session of legislature held on account of Civil War. First call
         for troops.
1861-65   Civil War:

Number of Vermont men in service	34,238
Number of deaths (Killed in action—1,071)	5,128
Number of wounded	4,360
Amount expended by Vermont, including bounties by towns—$9,323,407.	

1862   Morrill land grant college bill passed Congress.
1864   Oct. 19. St. Albans raided by Confederate guerillas.
1870   Biennial sessions of Legislature began.
      Fenians attempt invasion of Canada.
      Town authorized to abolish school district system.
1872   Counties became self-taxing bodies.

LEADING EVENTS IN THE HISTORY OF VERMONT

1876   Practice of medicine restricted to licensed physicians.
1877   President Rutherford B. Hayes was a guest of Vermont for the Centennial Anniversary of the Independence of the State of Vermont, and the Battle of Bennington. Mr. Hayes' parents were born in Vermont.
1878   Vermont Bar Association organized.
1881   Chester A. Arthur, native of Fairfield, became President.
1885   First electric lights in Vermont.
1886   State Board of Health organized.
1887   President Cleveland visited Vermont.
1891   Bennington Monument dedicated.
       Pres. Harrison visited the State.
1894   Red Clover made the State Flower.
1897   Pres. McKinley visited the State.
1898   Office of State Highway Commissioner established.
1899   Admirals Dewey and Clark welcomed to Vermont.
1902   Pres. Roosevelt visited the State.
       License local-option law passed.
       Operation of motor vehicles restricted by law.
1905   Dedication of Ethan Allen Memorial Tower.
       Centennial celebration of Montpelier as Capital.
1909   President Taft visited the State. Tercentary celebration of discovery of Lake Champlain.
1913   Constitution revised. Also amended changing date of state elections to November. Workmen compensation legislation authorized.
1917   State appropriates one million dollars for war purposes.
       World War 1:

Number of Vermont men in service	16,013
Number of deaths (Killed in action—119)	642
Number of wounded	886

1918   State Library and Supreme Court Building completed.
1919   Prohibition amendment adopted by Vermont.
1921   Woman Suffrage amendment adopted by Vermont.
1923   Calvin Coolidge, native of Plymouth, became President.
       Gasoline tax adopted.
       Operation of airplanes regulated by law.
1925   Intangible tax adopted.
1927   November 3. Flood disaster.
       Legislature appropriated eight and one-half million dollars for reconstruction.
1931   State Income Tax adopted.
       Federal Aid system of highways managed and controlled by the state.
1933   Twenty-first article of Amendment to U. S. Constitution ratified.
       Banking crisis and emergency legislation.
1934   Sale of intoxicating liquor legalized.
       Air mail and passenger service on regular schedules.
1935   Old Age Assistance law passed.
1936   President Roosevelt visited flood control projects in Vermont.
       Unemployment compensation insurance law passed.
1937   Regional library service established by the state.
1938   Sept. 21. Tropical hurricane does over 12 million dollars damage and causes death of five persons in Vermont.
1939   Sept. 1. Second World War begins by Germany attacking Poland.
1940   United States Selective Service and Training Act adopted.
       Feb. 24. 172nd Inf. and other elements of 43rd Div. ordered into active federal duty.
1941   State Guard organized.
       Sept. 10. Special Session of General Assembly.
       Vermont Council of Safety established.
       Sept. 11. "Armed Conflict" begins as basis for Vermont war bonus.
       Dec. 7. Japan attacks Pearl Harbor.
1942   Nov. 7. Landing operations in North Africa by U. S. forces.
1943   Feb. 23. War Powers Act enacted creating a War Council.

Appendices

LEADING EVENTS IN THE HISTORY OF VERMONT

1944　Mar. 15-18. Special session of the legislature passed Soldiers Voting Act.
　　　June 6. Invasion of Normandy by Allied Forces.
　　　Oct. 9. Dumbarton Oaks Conference Proposals for International Organization
　　　　　made public.
1945　May 8. Final surrender of Germany.
　　　June 26. United Nations Charter signed by 50 nations.
　　　July 16. First atom bomb exploded.
　　　Sept. 2. Japan surrenders.
　　　World War II:
　　　　　Number of Vermont men in service　　　　　　　　　　49,942
　　　　　Number of deaths　　　　　　　　　　　　　　　　　1,233
　　　　　Number of wounded　　　　　　　　　　　　　　　　3,870
1946　Dwight D. Eisenhower delivered Commencement Address at Norwich Uni-
　　　　versity.
　　　June 5. Senator Austin appointed U. S. delegate to the United Nations Security
　　　　Council.
　　　Sept. 26. Special session of the General Assembly.
　　　State magazine *Vermont Life* published.
1947　State Police created.
　　　Administrative reorganization.
　　　Miss Helen E. Burbank appointed first woman Secretary of State.
1948　New State Office Building, construction started.
1949　"Merci Train" arrived from France.
　　　Sept. 16. New State Office Building dedicated.
1950　Jan. 16. Governor Gibson resigned to accept appointment as Federal District
　　　　Judge for Vermont; Lieut.-Gov. Harold J. Arthur took oath as Governor.
　　　Sept. 5. National Guard of Vermont (elements of 43rd Inf. Div.) ordered into
　　　　federal service. (Alerted Aug. 1, while at Pine Camp, N. Y.)
　　　Nov. 25, 26. Land hurricane does several million dollars damage to property
　　　　in Vermont.
1951　Feb. 1. 134th Fighter Squadron and Weather Station, Vermont Air National
　　　　Guard, ordered into active federal service and stationed at Burlington Air-
　　　　port and Forth Ethan Allen.
1952　*Vermont: A History of the Green Mountain State* by Edmund Fuller pub-
　　　　lished by Education Department.
1953　Jan. 7. Consuelo Northrop Bailey elected first woman Speaker of House of
　　　　Representatives.
　　　Jan. 20. Warren R. Austin retires as U. S. Ambassador to the United Nations.
　　　$7,300,000.00 bond issue for state-aid for construction of school buildings.
1954　Mrs. Consuelo Northrop Bailey elected Lieutenant-Governor.
　　　First television broadcasting station in State erected on Mt. Mansfield.
　　　Vermont Mutual Fire Insurance Company's building bought by the State for
　　　　office space; and Tax Department located in this building in Jan. 1955.
1955　State pay for residents in U. S. military service, 1950-1955, terminated January
　　　　31, 1955. Total state pay was one million dollars.
　　　Poliomyelitis vaccine perfected by Dr. Salk and administered to all children
　　　　at state expense.
　　　President Eisenhower visited Vermont, attending Rutland Fair and staying at
　　　　Mountain Top Inn.
1956　Federal Social Security Act extended to state employees.
1957　$26,000,000.00 bond issue authorized by 1957 Legislature for purpose of high-
　　　　way construction.
　　　100,000 kilowatts of St. Lawrence River Power reserved for use of Vermont,
　　　　and power transmission contract between State of Vermont and Vermont
　　　　Electric Power Co. signed.
　　　President Coolidge Homestead in Plymouth given to State of Vermont.
　　　National Life Insurance building purchased by State of Vermont at a cost of
　　　　$850,000.
1958　William H. Meyer elected as Vermont's Representative to Congress; first
　　　　Democrat so elected in over 100 years.
　　　First re-count called in gubernatorial contest, resulting in a plurality of 719
　　　　votes for Robert T. Stafford.

LEADING EVENTS IN THE HISTORY OF VERMONT

1959 First annotated statutes in Vermont history enacted into positive statute law.
      Celebration of Vermont's "Year of History," centered around the 350th Anniversary of the discovery of Lake Champlain.
      Commemoration of the 100th anniversary of the birth of John Dewey, philosopher and educator, with ceremonies at his birthplace in Burlington, at U. V. M. and at Goddard College.

1960 Adjourned session of Legislature convened to consider report of the Commission to Study State Government and adopted its major proposals.
      Department of Administration established, including divisions of budget and management, finance, personnel, public records, purchasing, and state buildings.
      Administrative departments re-organized and new ones created; division of registration, licensing and secretarial service established in the office of the Secretary of State.
      Pari-mutuel race track betting authorized by statewide referendum.

1961 General Assembly convenes for its longest session to date; January 4 to August 1, inclusive.
      Vermont State Colleges established to include the state teachers colleges and the Vermont Agricultural and Technical Institute.

1962 Philip H. Hoff of Burlington elected first Democratic governor of Vermont in 108 years.

1963 Historic lawsuit filed in U.S. District Court at Burlington designed to force reapportionment of Senate and House of Representatives of General Assembly.

1964 Democratic Party carried State in Presidential elections for first time in history of Vermont.

1966 First session of reapportioned General Assembly and 175th anniversary year of date Vermont became fourteenth state, March 4, 1791.

1968 Governor Hoff, the first Democratic governor to break from President Johnson's camp, gave his support to Robert Kennedy.

1969 A sales tax (three percent) was adopted.

1970 The executive branch of government was reorganized, and a cabinet structure adopted.
      Far reaching environmental and water pollution control measures adopted.
      Green-up Day held throughout the state at the call of Governor Davis.
      The 1970 Census revealed a population increase from 389,881 in 1960, to 444,732 in 1970, a 14% increase.
      A Bicentennial Commission was established.

1971 Age of majority changed from 21 to 18.

1972 Bottle deposit law passed.

1973 Property tax relief program instituted.

1974 Patrick Leahy elected the first Democratic U.S. Senator since the founding of the Republican Party.

1976 Presidential primary re-established in Vermont.

1981 Juvenile criminal law statutes revised.

1982 Governor Snelling, re-elected for a fourth term - the longest tenure for any governor since 1820.

1984 Contract signed with Hydro-Quebec relating to Canadian power.
      Madeleine Kunin elected the first woman governor in Vermont.

1987 Solid Waste Law adopted.

1988 Passage of Act 200 - Local, Regional and State Planning.

1991 Bicentennial Year of Vermont's ratification of the U.S. Constitution and Vermont's admission to the Union.

Appendix D

During the Vermont Republic, politics were largely personal. Thomas Chittenden was governor during these years and after the admission of Vermont into the Union and the emergence of political parties, he continued to be elected governor but his political affiliation has never been clearly defined. In view of the fact that during these later years he was opposed by Isaac Tichenor, a Federalist, it might be argued that he leaned to the views of the Jeffersonian Republicans or Democratic-Republicans. Moses Robinson, who was governor in 1789, became, when a member of the United States Senate, a strong Jeffersonian; Paul Brigham, who became acting governor after Chittenden's death in 1797, started out a Federalist but ended up a Jeffersonian.

Isaac Tichenor (1797-1807, 1808-1809) was a Federalist as was Martin Chittenden (1813-1815). From 1818 to 1828 there was virtually no opposition to the Jeffersonians, the Federalists having disintegrated.

With the emergence of Andrew Jackson as a national figure the old Jeffersonian Party split into the National Republicans (later the Whigs) and the Jacksonians or Democrats. Governor Samuel C. Crafts (1828-1831) was identified with the National Republicans.

William A. Palmer (1831-1835), a member of the Anti-Masonic Party, was elected three times by the legislature after failing to obtain a majority of the popular vote (exception, 1833). Silas H. Jennison (1835-1836), who as lieutenant-governor became governor after the legislature failed to choose a governor from among the minority candidates, received the support of both the Whigs and the Anti-Masons.

From 1836 to 1855 the governors with one exception were members of the Whig Party. The exception was Governor John S. Robinson (1853-1854) who was a Democrat elected by the legislature as a result of the fact that the Whig candidate failed to obtain a majority of the votes over his Democratic and Free Soil Democratic opponents. However, the votes cast for anti-slavery parties often threw the election into the legislature. From 1855 until 1963 all governors were Republicans and since then the office has alternated between parties.

The following governors of Vermont have been elected by the legislature due to the failure of any candidate to receive a majority of the popular vote. The legislative elections were held in the year indicated:

Moses Robinson (1789)
Isaac Tichenor (1797)
Martin Chittenden (1813, 1814)
Samuel C. Crafts (1830)
William A. Palmer (1831, 1832, 1834)
Silas H. Jenison (1835)
Charles Paine (1841)
John Mattocks (1843)
William Slade (1845)
Horace Eaton (1846, 1847)
Carlos Coolidge (1848, 1849)
Erastus Fairbanks (1852)
John S. Robinson (1853)
John G. McCullough (1902)
Allen M. Fletcher (1912)

GOVERNORS [1]

Thomas Chittenden	1778-1789
Moses Robinson	1789-1790
Thomas Chittenden [2]	1790-1797
Paul Brigham [3]	1797
Isaac Tichenor	1797-1807
Israel Smith	1807-1808
Isaac Tichenor	1808-1809
Jonas Galusha	1809-1813
Martin Chittenden	1813-1815
Jonas Galusha	1815-1820
Richard Skinner	1820-1823
Cornelius P. Van Ness	1823-1826
Ezra Butler	1826-1828
Samuel C. Crafts	1828-1831
William A. Palmer	1831-1835
Silas H. Jenison [4]	1835-1836
Silas H. Jenison	1836-1841
Charles Paine	1841-1843
John Mattocks	1843-1844
William Slade	1844-1846

Horace Eaton	1846-1848
Carlos Coolidge	1848-1850
Charles K. Williams	1850-1852
Erastus Fairbanks	1852-1853
John S: Robinson	1853-1854
Stephen Royce	1854-1856
Ryland Fletcher	1856-1858
Hiland Hall	1858-1860
Erastus Fairbanks	1860-1861
Frederick Holbrook	1861-1863
J. Gregory Smith	1863-1865
Paul Dillingham	1865-1867
John B. Page	1867-1869
Peter T. Washburn [5]	1869-1870
George W. Hendee [6]	1870
John W. Stewart	1870-1872
Julius Converse	1872-1874
Asahel Peck	1874-1876
Horace Fairbanks	1876-1878
Redfield Proctor	1878-1880
Roswell Farnham	1880-1882
John L. Barstow	1882-1884
Samuel E. Pingree	1884-1886
Ebenezer J. Ormsbee	1886-1888
William P. Dillingham	1888-1890
Carroll S. Page	1890-1892
Levi K. Fuller	1892-1894
Urban A. Woodbury	1894-1896
Josiah Grout	1896-1898
Edward C. Smith	1898-1900
William W. Stickney	1900-1902
John G. McCullough	1902-1904
Charles J. Bell	1904-1906
Fletcher D. Proctor	1906-1908
George H. Prouty	1908-1910
John A. Mead	1910-1912
Allen M. Fletcher	1912-1915
Charles W. Gates	1915-1917
Horace F. Graham	1917-1919
Percival W. Clement	1919-1921
James Hartness	1921-1923
Redfield Proctor	1923-1925

Franklin S. Billings	1925-1927
John E. Weeks	1927-1931
Stanley C. Wilson	1931-1935
Charles M. Smith	1935-1937
George D. Aiken	1937-1941
William H. Wills	1941-1945
Mortimer R. Proctor	1945-1947
Ernest W. Gibson [7]	1947-1950
Harold J. Arthur [8]	1950-1951
Lee E. Emerson	1951-1955
Joseph B. Johnson	1955-1959
Robert T. Stafford	1959-1961
F. Ray Keyser, Jr.	1961-1963
Philip H. Hoff	1963-1969
Deane C. Davis	1969-1973
Thomas P. Salmon	1973-1977
Richard A. Snelling	1977-1985
Madeleine Kunin	1985-1991
Richard Snelling	1991
Howard Dean [9]	1991-

---

[1] The Governor's term was for one year from 1778 to 1870, and has been two years from 1870 to the present. Until after 1912, general elections were held in September and Governors were inaugurated in October. After 1912, Governors were elected in November and inaugurated in January.

[2] Died Aug. 25, 1797.

[3] Lieutenant-Governor; acting Governor on the death of Governor Chittenden. Served Aug. 25 to Oct. 16, 1797.

[4] Lieutenant-Governor; Governor by reason of no election of Governor by the people.

[5] Died in office, Feb. 7, 1870.

[6] Lieutenant-Governor; Governor by reason of the death of Governor Washburn.

[7] Resigned and appointed U.S. District Judge by President Truman, Jan. 16, 1950.

[8] Became Governor when Governor Gibson resigned, Jan. 15, 1950.

[9] Became Governor by reason of the death of Governor Snelling, August 13, 1991.

Appendix E

GOVERNORS, 1870-1985

Name	Dates Elected	Age	Birth Place	Residence	MT Side	Principal Occupation	Pre-Gubernatorial		Lt. Gov.
							House #	Senate #	
Stewart, John W.	1870	45	Middlebury	Middlebury	W	Lawyer	6/3	2/0	no
Converse, Julius	1872	74	Connecticut	Woodstock	E	Lawyer	6/0	4/0	yes
Peck, Asahel	1874	73	Massachusetts	Jericho	W	Lawyer	0/0	1/0	no
Fairbanks, Horace	1876	58	Barnet	St. Johnsbury	E	Fairbanks Scale	0/0	1/0	no
Proctor, Redfield	1878	47	Cavendish	Rutland	W	Vermont Marble	2/0	1/1	yes*
Farnham, Roswell	1880	53	Massachusetts	Bradford	E	Lawyer	0/0	2/0	no
Barstow, John	1882	50	Shelburne	Shelburne	W	Farmer / Politician	2/0	2/0	yes*
Pingree, Samuel	1884	52	New Hampshire	Hartford	E	Lawyer	0/0	0/0	yes*
Ormsbee, Ebenezer	1886	52	Shoreham	Brandon	W	Lawyer	1/0	1/0	yes*
Dillingham, William	1888	45	Waterbury	Waterbury	E	Lawyer	2/0	2/0	no
Page, Carroll	1890	47	Westfield	Hyde Park	W	Calfskin Dealer	2/0	1/0	no
Fuller, Levi	1892	51	New Hampshire	Brattleboro	E	Estey Organ	0/0	1/0	yes
Woodbury, Urban	1894	56	New Hampshire	Burlington	W	Lumber / Hotel	0/0	0/0	yes
Grout, Josiah	1896	55	Quebec	Derby	E	Lawyer	5/2	1/0	no
Smith, Edward	1898	44	St. Albans	St. Albans	W	Central Vt. Railroad	1/0	0/0	no
Stickney, William	1900	47	Plymouth	Ludlow	E	Lawyer	2/2	0/0	no
McCullough, John	1902	67	Delaware	Bennington	W	Bennington-Rutland	0/0	1/1	no

GOVERNORS, 1870-1985

Name	Dates Elected	Age	Birth Place	Residence	MT Side	Principal Occupation	Pre-Gubernatorial		
							House #	Senate #	Lt. Gov.
Bell, Charles	1904	59	Walden	Walden	E	Railroad Farmer	1/0	1/0	no
Proctor, Fletcher	1906	46	Cavendish	Proctor	W	Vermont Marble	3/1	1/0	no
Prouty, George	1908	46	Newport	Newport	E	Lumber	1/0	1/1	yes*
Mead, John	1910	69	Fair Haven	Rutland	W	Howe Scale	1/0	1/0	yes*
Fletcher, Allen	1912	59	Indiana	Cavendish	E	Banking	4/0	1/0	no
Gates, Charles =	1914	59	Franklin	Franklin	W	State Highway	1/0	1/0	no
Graham, Horace	1916	55	New York	Craftsbury	E	Lawyer/State Auditor	2/0	0/0	no
Clement, Percival	1918	73	Rutland	Rutland	W	Railroad/Rutland Herald	1/0	1/0	no
Hartness, James	1920	60	New York	Springfield	E	Machine Tool	0/0	0/0	no
Proctor, Redfield	1922	44	Proctor	Proctor	W	Vermont Marble	2/0	1/0	no
Billings, Franklin S.	1924	63	Massachusetts	Woodstock	E	Farmer	3/1	0/0	yes*
Weeks, John E.	1926 1928	73	Salisbury	Middlebury	W	Farmer/Politician	3/1	1/0	no
Wilson, Stanley C.	1930 1932	52	Orange	Chelsea	E	Lawyer	3/1	1/0	yes*
Smith, Charles M.	1934	67	West Rutland	Rutland	W	Banking	1/0	2/0	yes*
Aiken, George D.	1936 1938	45	Dummerston	Putney	E	Horticulturist	2/1	0/0	yes*
Wills, William H.	1940 1942	59	Illinois	Bennington	W	Insurance	1/0	2/2	yes*
Proctor, Mortimer R.	1944	56	Proctor	Proctor	W	Vermont Marble	3/1	1/1	yes*

GOVERNORS, 1870-1985

Name	Dates Elected	Age	Birth Place	Residence	MT Side	Principal Occupation	Pre-Gubernatorial House #	Senate #	Lt. Gov.
Gibson Jr., Ernest W.	1946 1948	46	Brattleboro	Brattleboro	E	Lawyer	0/0	0/0	no
Arthur, Harold J.	+	46	*New York*	Brandon	W	Lawyer	0/0	0/0	yes*
Emerson, Lee E.	1950 1952	53	Hardwick	Barton	E	Lawyer	2/1	1/1	yes
Johnson, Joseph B.	1954 1956	62	*Sweden*	Springfield	E	Machine Tool	1/0	2/0	yes*
Stafford, Robert T.	1958	46	Rutland	Rutland	W	Lawyer	0/0	0/0	yes*
Keyser Jr., F. Ray	1960	34	Chelsea	Chelsea	E	Lawyer	3/1	0/0	no
Hoff, Philip H.	1962 1964 1966	39	*Massachusetts*	Burlington	W	Lawyer	1/0	0/0	no
Davis, Deane C.	1968 1970	69	East Barre	Barre	E	Lawyer	0/0	0/0	no
Salmon, Thomas P.	1972 1974	41	*Ohio*	Bellows Falls	E	Lawyer	4/0	0/0	no
Snelling, Richard A.	1976 1978 1980 1982	49	*Pennsylvania*	Shelburne	W	Manufacturer	3/0	0/0	no
Kunin, Madeleine	1984 1986 1988	52	*Switzerland*	Burlington	W	Journalist	3/0	0/0	yes
Richard Snelling	1990	63	*Pennsylvania*	Shelburne	W	Manufacturer	3/0	0/0	no

\# In both the House and Senate columns the first number denotes terms served; the second figure denotes terms served as Speaker or president pro tem. Stewart served an additional term as Speaker after having been governor.

* Denotes lieutenant governors who acceded directly to the governorship.

= Vermont state elections now held in November and governor begins term in following January.

+ Harold J. Arthur assumed office when Ernest W. Gibson Jr. resigned on January 15, 1950 to become Vermont's U.S. District Judge.

Names in *italics* denote Democratic affiliation.

Appendix F

UNITED STATES REPRESENTATIVES

DATE[1]	DISTRICT	REPRESENTATIVE	HOME TOWN
1791	2 Districts	Nathaniel Niles	West Fairlee
		Israel Smith	Rutland
1792	2 Districts	Nathaniel Niles	West Fairlee
		Israel Smith	Rutland
1794	2 Districts	Daniel Buck	Norwich
		Israel Smith	Rutland
1796	2 Districts	Lewis R. Morris	Springfield
		Matthew Lyon	Fair Haven
1798	2 Districts	Lewis R. Morris	Springfield
		Matthew Lyon	Fair Haven
1800	2 Districts	Lewis R. Morris	Springfield
		Israel Smith	Rutland
1802	4 Districts	William Chamberlain	Peacham
		Martin Chittenden	Jericho
		James Elliot	Brattleboro
		Gideon Olin	Shaftsbury
1804	4 Districts	James Fisk	Barre
		Martin Chittenden	Jericho
		James Elliot	Brattleboro
		Gideon Olin	Shaftsbury
1806	4 Districts	James Fisk	Barre
		Martin Chittenden	Jericho
		James Elliot	Brattleboro
		James Witherell[2]	Fair Haven
1808	4 Districts	William Chamberlain	Peacham
		Martin Chittenden	Jericho
		Jonathan H. Hubbard	Windsor
		Samuel Shaw	Castleton
1810	4 Districts	James Fisk	Barre
		Martin Chittenden	Jericho
		William Strong	Hartford
		Samuel Shaw	Castleton
1812	6 at Large	William Bradley	Westminster
		Ezra Butler	Waterbury
		James Fisk	Barre
		Charles Rich	Shoreham
		Richard Skinner	Manchester
		William Strong	Hartford

Appendices

DATE[1]	DISTRICT	REPRESENTATIVE	HOME TOWN
1814	6 at Large	Daniel Chipman	Middlebury
		Luther Jewett	St. Johnsbury
		Chauncey Langdon	Castleton
		Asa Lyon	Grand Isle
		Charles Marsh	Woodstock
		John Noyes	Brattleboro
1816	6 at Large	Heman Allen	Colchester
		Samuel C. Crafts	Craftsbury
		William Hunter	Windsor
		Orsamus C. Merrill	Bennington
		Charles Rich	Shoreham
		Mark Richards	Westminster
1818	6 Districts	Orsamus C. Merrill[3]	Bennington
		Mark Richards	Westminster
		Charles Rich	Shoreham
		William Strong	Hartford
		Ezra Meech	Shelburne
		Samuel C. Crafts	Craftsbury
1820	6 Districts	Rollin C. Mallary	Poultney
		Phineas White	Putney
		Charles Rich	Shoreham
		Elias Keyes	Stockbridge
		John Mattocks	Peacham
		Samuel C. Crafts	Craftsbury
1822	5 Districts	William C. Bradley	Westminster
		Rollin C. Mallary	Poultney
		Charles Rich[4]	Shoreham
		Samuel C. Crafts	Craftsbury
		D. Azro A. Buck	Chelsea
1824	5 Districts	William C. Bradley	Westminster
		Rollin C. Mallary	Poultney
		George E. Wales	Hartford
		Ezra Meech	Shelburne
		John Mattocks	Peacham
1826	5 Districts	Jonathan Hunt	Brattleboro
		Rollin C. Mallary	Poultney
		George E. Wales	Hartford
		Benjamin Swift	St. Albans
		D. Azro A. Buck	Chelsea
1828	5 Districts	Jonathan Hunt	Brattleboro
		Rollin C. Mallary	Poultney
		Horace Everett	Windsor
		Benjamin Swift	St. Albans
		William Cahoon	Lyndon

DATE [1]	DISTRICT	REPRESENTATIVE	HOME TOWN
1830	5 Districts	Jonathan Hunt [5]	Brattleboro
		Rollin C. Mallary [6]	Poultney
		Horace Everett	Windsor
		Heman Allen	Burlington
		William Cahoon [7]	Lyndon
1832	5 Districts	Hiland Hall	Bennington
	(redefined)	William Slade	Middlebury
		Horace Everett	Windsor
		Heman Allen	Burlington
		Benjamin F. Deming [8]	Danville
1834	5 Districts	Hiland Hall	Bennington
		William Slade	Middlebury
		Horace Everett	Windsor
		Heman Allen	Burlington
		Henry F. Janes	Waterbury
1836	5 Districts	Hiland Hall	Bennington
		William Slade	Middlebury
		Horace Everett	Windsor
		Heman Allen	Burlington
		Isaac Fletcher	Lyndon
1838	5 Districts	Hiland Hall	Bennington
		William Slade	Middlebury
		Horace Everett	Windsor
		John Smith	St. Albans
		Isaac Fletcher	Lyndon
1840	5 Districts	Hiland Hall	Bennington
		William Slade	Middlebury
		Horace Everett	Windsor
		Augustus Young	Craftsbury
		John Mattocks	Peacham
1842	4 Districts	Solomon Foot	Rutland
		Jacob Collamer	Woodstock
		George P. Marsh	Burlington
		Paul Dillingham	Waterbury
1844	4 Districts	Solomon Foot	Rutland
		Jacob Collamer	Woodstock
		George P. Marsh	Burlington
		Paul Dillingham	Waterbury
1846	4 Districts	William Henry	Rockingham
		Jacob Collamer	Woodstock
		George P. Marsh	Burlington
		Lucius B. Peck	Montpelier
1848	4 Districts	William Henry	Rockingham
		William Hebard	Chelsea
		George P. Marsh [9]	Burlington
		Lucius B. Peck	Montpelier

Appendices

DATE[1]	DISTRICT	REPRESENTATIVE	HOME TOWN
1850	4 Districts	Ahiman L. Miner	Manchester
		William Hebard	Chelsea
		James Meacham	Middlebury
		Thomas Bartlett, Jr.	Lyndon
1852	3 Districts	James Meacham	Middlebury
		Andrew Tracy	Woodstock
		Alvah Sabin	Georgia
1854	3 Districts	James Meacham[10]	Middlebury
		Justin S. Morrill	Strafford
		Alvah Sabin	Georgia
1856	3 Districts	Eliakim P. Walton	Montpelier
		Justin S. Morrill	Strafford
		Homer E. Royce	St. Albans
1858	3 Districts	Eliakim P. Walton	Montpelier
		Justin S. Morrill	Strafford
		Homer E. Royce	St. Albans
1860	3 Districts	Eliakim P. Walton	Montpelier
		Justin S. Morrill	Strafford
		Portus Baxter	Derby
1862	3 Districts	Frederick E. Woodbridge	Vergennes
		Justin S. Morrill	Strafford
		Portus Baxter	Derby
1864	3 Districts	Frederick E. Woodbridge	Vergennes
		Justin S. Morrill	Strafford
		Portus Baxter	Derby
1866	3 Districts	Frederick E. Woodbridge	Vergennes
		Luke P. Poland	St. Johnsbury
		Worthington C. Smith	St. Albans
1868	3 Districts	Charles W. Willard	Montpelier
		Luke P. Poland	St. Johnsbury
		Worthington C. Smith	St. Albans
1870	3 Districts	Charles W. Willard	Montpelier
		Luke P. Poland	St. Johnsbury
		Worthington C. Smith	St. Albans
1872	3 Districts	Charles W. Willard	Montpelier
		Luke P. Poland	St. Johnsbury
		George W. Hendee	Morristown
1874	3 Districts	Charles H. Joyce	Rutland
		Dudley C. Dennison	Royalton
		George W. Hendee	Morristown
1876	3 Districts	Charles H. Joyce	Rutland
		Dudley C. Dennison	Royalton
		George W. Hendee	Morristown

DATE[1]	DISTRICT	REPRESENTATIVE	HOME TOWN
1878	3 Districts	Charles H. Joyce James M. Tyler Bradley Barlow	Rutland Brattleboro St. Albans
1880	3 Districts	Charles H. Joyce James M. Tyler William W. Grout	Rutland Brattleboro Barton
1882	2 Districts	John W. Stewart Luke P. Poland	Middlebury St. Johnsbury
1884	2 Districts	John W. Stewart William W. Grout	Middlebury Barton
1886	2 Districts	John W. Stewart William W. Grout	Middlebury Barton
1888	2 Districts	John W. Stewart William W. Grout	Middlebury Barton
1890	2 Districts	H. Henry Powers William W. Grout	Morristown Barton
1892	2 Districts	H. Henry Powers William W. Grout	Morristown Barton
1894	2 Districts	H. Henry Powers William W. Grout	Morristown Barton
1896	2 Districts	H. Henry Powers William W. Grout	Morristown Barton
1898	2 Districts	H. Henry Powers William W. Grout	Morristown Barton
1900	2 Districts	David J. Foster Kittredge Haskins	Burlington Brattleboro
1902	2 Districts	David J. Foster Kittredge Haskins	Burlington Brattleboro
1904	2 Districts	David J. Foster Kittredge Haskins	Burlington Brattleboro
1906	2 Districts	David J. Foster Kittredge Haskins	Burlington Brattleboro
1908	2 Districts	David J. Foster Frank Plumley	Burlington Northfield
1910	2 Districts	David J. Foster[11] Frank Plumley	Burlington Northfield
1912	2 Districts	Frank L. Greene Frank Plumley	St. Albans Northfield
1914	2 Districts	Frank L. Greene Porter H. Dale	St. Albans Island Pond
1916	2 Districts	Frank L. Greene Porter H. Dale	St. Albans Island Pond

Appendices

DATE[1]	DISTRICT	REPRESENTATIVE	HOME TOWN
1918	2 Districts	Frank L. Greene	St. Albans
		Porter H. Dale	Island Pond
1920	2 Districts	Frank L. Greene	St. Albans
		Porter H. Dale	Island Pond
1922	2 Districts	Frederick Fleetwood	Morrisville
		Porter H. Dale[12]	Island Pond
1924	2 Districts	Elbert S. Brigham	St. Albans
		Ernest W. Gibson, Sr.	Brattleboro
1926	2 Districts	Elbert S. Brigham	St. Albans
		Ernest W. Gibson, Sr.	Brattleboro
1928	2 Districts	Elbert S. Brigham	St. Albans
		Ernest W. Gibson, Sr.	Brattleboro
1930	2 Districts	John E. Weeks	Middlebury
		Ernest W. Gibson, Sr.	Brattleboro
1932	1 District	Ernest W. Gibson, Sr.[13]	Brattleboro
1934-1950		Charles A. Plumley	Northfield
1950-1958		Winston L. Prouty	Newport City
1958-1960		William H. Meyer	West Rupert
1960-1971		Robert T. Stafford[14]	Rutland
1971-1974		Richard Mallary[14]	Fairlee
1974-1988		James M. Jeffords	Rutland
1988-1990		Peter P. Smith	Middlesex
1990-		Bernard Sanders	Burlington

[1] Year of election.
[2] Resigned in 1808; replaced by Samuel Shaw, Castleton.
[3] Seat contested and awarded Jan. 13, 1820 to Rollin C. Mallary, Poultney.
[4] Died in 1824; seat filled by Henry Olin, Leicester.
[5] Died May 14, 1832; replaced by Hiland Hall, Bennington.
[6] Died April 15, 1831; replaced by William Slade, Middlebury.
[7] Died May 30, 1833; replaced by Benjamin F. Deming, Danville.
[8] Died July 11, 1834; replaced by Henry F. Janes, Waterbury.
[9] Appointed U.S. Minister to Turkey; replaced by James Meacham, Middlebury.
[10] Died Aug. 23, 1856; replaced by George T. Hodges, Rutland.
[11] Died March 21, 1912; replaced by Frank L. Greene, St. Albans.
[12] Resigned to become U.S. Senator; replaced by Ernest W. Gibson, Sr., Brattleboro.
[13] Elected U.S. Senator in 1934; replaced by Charles A. Plumley, Northfield.
[14] Appointed U.S. Senator upon death of Winston Prouty, Oct. 25, 1971; replaced by Richard Mallary, Fairlee.

Appendix G

UNITED STATES SENATORS
(SINCE 1791)

CLASS* 1 (West)	CLASS 3 (East)
1791-1797	**1791-1795**
Moses R. Robinson [1]	Stephen R. Bradley
Isaac Tichenor [1]	
1797-1803	**1795-1801**
Nathaniel Chipman [1]	Elijah Paine
1803-1809	**1801-1807**
Israel Smith [3]	Elijah Paine [2]
Jonathan Robinson [3]	Stephen R. Bradley [2]
1809-1815	**1807-1813**
Jonathan Robinson	Stephen R. Bradley
1815-1821	**1813-1819**
Isaac Tichenor	Dudley Chase [4]
	James Fish [4, 5]
	William A. Palmer [5]
1821-1827	**1819-1825**
Horatio Seymour	William A. Palmer
1827-1833	**1825-1831**
Horatio Seymour	Dudley Chase
1833-1839	**1831-1837**
Benjamin Swift	Samuel Prentiss
1839-1845	**1837-1843**
Samuel S. Phelps	Samuel Prentiss [6]
	Samuel C. Crafts [6]
1845-1851	**1843-1849**
Samuel S. Phelps	William Upham

---

*For a discussion of Senate Class see Clark H. Bensen, "The Luck of the Draw: The Classification of Senators from Vermont, *Vermont History*, Vol. 49, No. 3 (Summer 1981), 169-171.

CLASS* 1 (West)	CLASS 3 (East)
1851-1857 Solomon Foot	1849-1855 William Upham [7] Samuel S. Phelps [7] Lawrence Brainerd [7]
1857-1863 Solomon Foot	1855-1861 Jacob Collamer
1863-1869 Solomon Foot [9] George F. Edmunds [9]	1861-1867 Jacob Collamer [8] Luke P. Poland [8]
1869-1875 George F. Edmunds	1867-1873 Justin S. Morrill
1875-1881 George F. Edmunds	1873-1879 Justin S. Morrill
1881-1887 George F. Edmunds	1879-1885 Justin S. Morrill
1887-1893 George F. Edmunds [10] Redfield Proctor [10]	1885-1891 Justin S. Morrill
1893-1899 Redfield Proctor	1891-1897 Justin S. Morrill
1899-1905 Redfield Proctor	1897-1903 Justin S. Morrill [11] Jonathan Ross [11] William P. Dillingham [11]
1905-1911 Redfield Proctor [12] John W. Stewart [12] Carroll S. Page [12]	1903-1909 William P. Dillingham
1911-1917 Carroll S. Page [13]	1909-1915 William P. Dillingham
1917-1923 Carroll S. Page	1915-1921 William P. Dillingham [13]
1923-1929 Frank L. Greene	1921-1927 William P. Dillingham [14] Porter H. Dale [14]

CLASS* 1 (West)	CLASS 3 (East)
1929-1935 Frank L. Greene[15] Frank C. Partridge[15] Warren R. Austin[15]	1927-1933 Porter H. Dale
1935-1941 Warren R. Austin	1933-1939 Porter H. Dale[16] Ernest W. Gibson[16]
1941-1947 Warren R. Austin	1939-1945 Ernest W. Gibson[17] Ernest W. Gibson, Jr.[17] George D. Aiken[17]
1947-1953 Ralph E. Flanders	1945-1951 George D. Aiken
1953-1959 Ralph E. Flanders	1951-1957 George D. Aiken
1959-1965 Winston L. Prouty	1957-1963 George D. Aiken
1965-1971 Winston L. Prouty	1963-1969 George D. Aiken
1971-1977 Winston L. Prouty[18] Robert T. Stafford[18]	1969-1975 George D. Aiken
1977-1989 Robert T. Stafford	1975-1981 Patrick J. Leahy
1989- James M. Jeffords	1981-1989 Patrick J. Leahy
	1989- Patrick J. Leahy

[1] Robinson resigned on Oct. 15, 1796. Tichenor was elected on Oct. 18, 1796 for the balance of the term, but resigned in 1797 to become Governor of Vermont; Chipman was elected to fill vacancy.

[2] Paine resigned to become U.S. District Judge for District of Vermont; Bradley elected in 1801 to fill vacancy.

[3] Smith resigned to become Governor in 1807; Robinson elected Oct. 10, 1807.

[4] Chase resigned in 1817 to become Chief Judge of Vermont Supreme Court; Fish elected Nov. 4, 1817.

Appendices

[5] Fish resigned Jan. 29, 1818 to be Collector of Customs for Vermont; Palmer elected Oct. 20, 1818 for balance of term.

[6] Prentiss resigned Apr. 11, 1842 to become U.S. Judge for District of Vermont; Crafts appointed pending an election, and elected Oct. 26, 1842 for balance of term.

[7] Upham died Jan. 14, 1853; Phelps appointed on a temporary basis. After 22 ineffectual ballotings the legislature could not elect, and resolved to wait until following session to fill vacancy; Brainerd elected Oct. 14, 1854.

[8] Collamer died Nov. 9, 1865; Poland appointed Nov. 21, 1865 and elected Oct. 23, 1866 for balance of term.

[9] Foot died Mar. 28, 1866; Edmunds appointed Apr. 5, 1866 and elected Oct. 23, 1866 for balance of term.

[10] Edmunds resigned in Nov., 1891 to change climate for health reasons; Proctor appointed pending an election, and elected Oct. 18, 1892 for balance of term.

[11] Morrill died Dec. 28, 1898; Ross appointed Jan. 16, 1899 pending an election; Dillingham elected Oct. 18, 1900 for balance of term.

[12] Proctor died Mar. 4, 1908; Stewart appointed Mar. 24, 1908 pending an election; Page elected Oct. 20, 1908 for balance of term.

[13] Last Senate election by the legislature; first popularly elected Senator.

[14] Dillingham died July 12, 1923; Dale elected Nov. 6, 1923.

[15] Greene died Dec. 17, 1930; Partridge appointed pending an election; Austin elected Mar. 31, 1931 for balance of term.

[16] Dale died Oct. 6, 1933; Gibson elected Jan. 16, 1934.

[17] Gibson died June 20, 1940. Gibson Jr. appointed pending an election. Aiken elected Nov. 5, 1940.

[18] Prouty died Sept. 10, 1971 and Stafford was appointed Sept. 16, 1971. He was elected Jan. 7, 1972 to fill the unexpired term.

Editor's Note: From the establishment of the Republican Party until the election of Patrick Leahy in 1974, all U.S. Senators elected from Vermont were of the Republican Party. Leahy was the first Vermonter from the west to be elected to a Class 3 Senate seat.

Appendix H

GEORGE WASHINGTON TO
CONGRESSMAN JOSEPH JONES, 1783 (Abridged)

This letter was provoked by "an indecent and tart" remonstrance sent to Congress by Governor Thomas Chittenden protesting Congress' refusal to seat delegates from Vermont. David Kelley from Montpelier raised $13,000 to buy this letter for Vermont at a New York auction in December of 1984.

NEWBURGH, 11 February, 1783.

Dear Sir:—I am about to write you a letter on a subject equally important and delicate, which may be extensive in its consequences and serious in its nature.

The printed remonstrance of Mr. Chittenden and his council, addressed to the President of Congress and founded upon the resolves of the 5th of December last, contains a favorable recital in their own behalf of what I suppose to be facts; but, if my memory serves me, it is an uncandid performance, inasmuch as it keeps out of view an important transaction of theirs which was consequent on those resolves. Be this as it may, matters seem to be approaching too fast to a disagreeable issue for the quiet of my mind. . . .

Affairs being thus situated, permit me to ask how far and by what means coercion is to be extended. The army, I presume, will be the answer to the latter. Circumstances, (for there can be no determination after blood is once drawn) alone can prescribe bounds to the former. It has been said, but of this you can judge better than I, that the delegates of the New England States in Congress, or a majority of them, are willing to admit these people into the Federal Union as an independent and sovereign State. Be this as it may, two things I am sure of, namely, that they have a powerful interest in those States, and pursued very politic measures to strengthen and increase it long before I had any knowledge of the matter, and before the tendency of it was seen into or suspected, by granting upon very advantageous terms large tracts of land; in which, I am sorry to find, the army in some degree have participated.

Let me next ask, by whom is this district of country principally settled? And of whom is your present army . . . comprised? The answers are evident,—New England men. It has been the opinion of some that the appearance of force would awe these people into submission. If the General Assembly ratify and confirm what Mr. Chittenden and his council have done, I shall be of a very different sentiment; and, moreover, that it is not a trifling force that will subdue them, even supposing they derive no aid from the enemy in Canada; and that it would be a very arduous task indeed, if they should, to say nothing of a diversion, which may and doubtless would be made in their favor from New York, if the war with Great Britain should continue.

The country is very mountainous, full of defiles, and extremely strong. The inhabitants, for the most part, are a hardy race, composed of that kind of people who are best calculated for soldiers; in truth, who *are* soldiers; for many, many hundreds of them are deserters from this army, who, having acquired property there, would be desperate in the defense of it, well knowing that they were fighting with halters about their necks. . . .

With great regard, I am, GEORGE WASHINGTON.

Appendix I

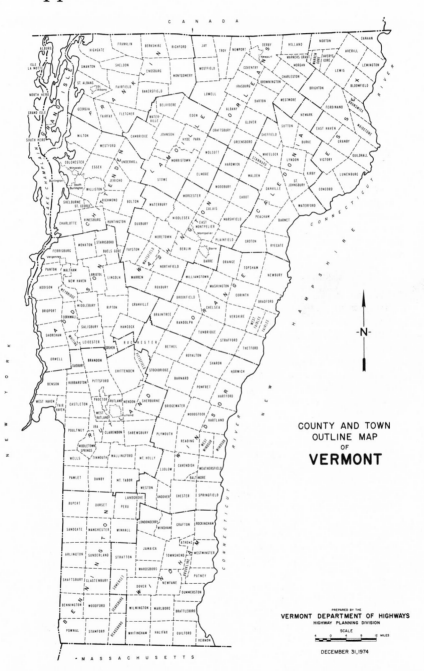

COUNTY AND TOWN
OUTLINE MAP
OF
VERMONT

PREPARED BY THE
VERMONT DEPARTMENT OF HIGHWAYS
HIGHWAY PLANNING DIVISION
SCALE
4   0   4   8   12 MILES

DECEMBER 31, 1974

Selected Annotated Bibliography

J. Kevin Graffagnino
Curator, Wilbur Collection
University of Vermont

T HIS IS A BASIC LIST of two dozen standard or particularly useful books on Vermont history. Some are long out-of-print, while others have appeared quite recently, but the majority are available at the larger public and college libraries.

As anyone familiar with Green Mountain history can attest, substantial eras and aspects of the state's development have traditionally failed to attract their share of attention from either professional or amateur historians. The last 10 or 15 years have witnessed a new wave of publishing on hitherto unexamined areas, but large gaps remain in our understanding of Vermont's heritage. The annotations on this list may help to point out some of the more striking strengths and weaknesses evident in the published record of the state's past.

With the exception of *Vermont History*, the Vermont Historical Society's quarterly journal, this list includes only book-length studies dealing with statewide topics. For an invaluable guide to the thousands of pamphlets, articles and monographs on state, county and town history, as well as to the many other useful books on Vermont's past, researchers should turn to T. D. Seymour Bassett's *Vermont: A Bibliography of Its History*, the first title on this list.

Bassett, T.D. Seymour. VERMONT: A BIBLIOGRAPHY OF ITS HISTORY. Boston: G. K. Hall & Co., 1981. An essential reference work for any research on Vermont's history. Lists more than 6400 titles on town, county and state history, with an excellent index.

Benedict, George G. VERMONT IN THE CIVIL WAR. Burlington: Free Press Association, 1886-88. Two volumes. Although published nearly a century ago, Benedict's work remains the most detailed account of Vermont's participation in the war. Concentrates largely on the state's military contributions to the Union cause.

Biddle, Arthur W. & Eschholz, Paul A., eds. THE LITERATURE OF VERMONT: A SAMPLER. Hanover: University Press of New England, 1973. Contains excerpts from a variety of Vermont prose, poetry and fiction, with a useful introductory essay on the state's literary history.

Bryan, Frank M. YANKEE POLITICS IN RURAL VERMONT. Hanover: University Press of New England, 1974. A perceptive analysis of politics in contemporary Vermont, with some good historical background.

Crockett, Walter H. VERMONT: THE GREEN MOUNTAIN STATE. New York: Century History Co., 1921-23. Five volumes. Slow-paced and outdated, but still the most detailed history of Vermont through 1920.

Fuller, Edmund. VERMONT: A HISTORY OF THE GREEN MOUNTAIN STATE. Montpelier: State Board of Education, 1952. Elementary and long out-of-date, but still used as a text in many Vermont schools.

Graffagnino, J. Kevin. THE SHAPING OF VERMONT: FROM THE WILDERNESS TO THE CENTENNIAL 1749-1877. Rutland: Vermont Heritage Press and the Bennington Museum, 1983. An attempt to look at Vermont's early history through the state's 18th and 19th-century cartographic heritage.

Hall, Benjamin H. HISTORY OF EASTERN VERMONT. New York: D. Appleton & Co., 1858. A valuable study of early Vermont east of the Green Mountains, with a biography chapter and useful appendices.

Hall, Hiland. THE HISTORY OF VERMONT, FROM ITS DISCOVERY TO ITS ADMISSION INTO THE UNION IN 1791. Albany: J. Munsell, 1868. Detailed and influential study, although modern revisionist historians have questioned Hall's conclusions about early Vermont.

Haviland, William A. & Power, Marjory W. THE ORIGINAL VER-
MONTERS: NATIVE INHABITANTS, PAST AND PRESENT.
Hanover: University Press of New England, 1981. A detailed
scholarly study of Vermont's Indian cultures.

Hemenway, Abby M., ed. THE VERMONT HISTORICAL GAZET-
TEER. Various locations and printers, 1867-91. Five volumes, plus
one index volume. Arranged by county and town, contains a wealth
of information on local Vermont history through the Civil War.

Jellison, Charles A. ETHAN ALLEN: FRONTIER REBEL. Syracuse:
Syracuse University Press, 1969. A fine biography of Allen, with
much valuable background on 18th-century Vermont.

Jones, Matt B. VERMONT IN THE MAKING 1750-1777. Cambridge: Harvard University Press, 1939. Scholarly, detailed history
of Vermont's turbulent pre-Revolution period.

Judd, Richard M. THE NEW DEAL IN VERMONT: ITS IMPACT
AND AFTERMATH. New York: Garland Publishing, Inc., 1979.
Scholarly history, valuable for the study of 20th-century Vermont.

Ludlum, David M. SOCIAL FERMENT IN VERMONT 1791-1850.
New York: Columbia University Press, 1939. Important study of
various social issues and reform movements in antebellum Vermont.

Morrissey, Charles T. VERMONT: A BICENTENNIAL HISTORY.
New York: W. W. Norton & Co., 1981. Interesting mixture of
history and personal observation, centered on Vermont's heritage.

Muller, H. Nicholas, III & Duffy, John J. AN ANXIOUS
DEMOCRACY: ASPECTS OF THE 1830's. Westport, Ct.: Green-
wood Press, 1982. Scholarly look at several examples of social ferment in Vermont during the 1830's.

Muller, H. Nicholas, III & Hand, Samuel B., eds. IN A STATE OF
NATURE: READINGS IN VERMONT HISTORY. Mont-
pelier: Vermont Historical Society, 1982. Valuable compilation of
the best recent scholarship in Vermont history, with useful editorial
essays and notes. An essential volume for anyone starting on the
study of Vermont's past.

Selected Annotated Bibliography

Newton, Earle W. THE VERMONT STORY: A HISTORY OF THE PEOPLE OF THE GREEN MOUNTAIN STATE 1749-1949. Montpelier: Vermont Historical Society, 1949. Somewhat out-of-date, but still an essentially sound and readable survey.

Stilwell, Lewis D. MIGRATION FROM VERMONT. Montpelier: Vermont Historical Society, 1948. Scholarly study of early emigration from Vermont and its causes.

Swift, Esther M. VERMONT PLACE-NAMES: FOOTPRINTS OF HISTORY. Brattleboro: Stephen Greene Press, 1977. Interesting and useful compilation of material on Vermont local history.

Van de Water, Frederic F. THE RELUCTANT REPUBLIC: VERMONT 1724-1791. New York: The John Day Co., 1941. An enjoyable overview, probably the most readable traditional interpretation of early Vermont.

Vermont History. The quarterly journal of the Vermont Historical Society. *Vermont History* and its predecessors, dating back to 1930, contain an invaluable variety of scholarly articles on Vermont's past. Indexed.

Williamson, Chilton. VERMONT IN QUANDARY 1763-1825. Montpelier: Vermont Historical Society, 1949. Important revisionist study of early Vermont, centering on west-side political and economic issues.

Index

Index